P9-CKO-611

DATE DUE

OC 18 99			

DEMCO 38-296

CD-ROM in Libraries

CD-ROM in Libraries:
Management Issues

Edited by

Terry Hanson and Joan Day

BOWKER
SAUR

London · Melbourne · Munich · New Jersey

British Library Cataloguing in Publication Data

CD-ROM in Libraries: Management Issues
    I. Hanson, Terry II. Day, Joan M.
    025.04
    ISBN 1-85739-086-5

Library of Congress Cataloging-in-Publication Data

CD-ROM in libraries: management issues / Terry Hanson and Joan Day.
    p.cm
    Includes bibliographical references (p.) and index.
    ISBN 1-85739-086-5 (alk.paper) : £35.00
    I. Hanson, Terry. II. Day, Joan M.
Z678.93.07C3   93-34161
025.1--dc20   CIP

Published by Bowker-Saur, Maypole House, Maypole Road,
East Grinstead, West Sussex RH19 1HH
Tel: +44(0)342 330100 Fax: +44(0)342 330191
e-mail: lis@bowker-saur.co.uk
Bowker-Saur is a division of REED REFERENCE PUBLISHING

Reprinted 1994

ISBN 1-85739-086-5

Cover design by John Cole
Typesetting by Castlefield Press Ltd, Kettering, Northants
Printed on acid-free paper
Printed and bound in Great Britain by Bookcraft (Bath) Ltd

About the contributors

Christine Abbott
Currently Head of Management Services at Aston University Library and Information Services. After a short time in the Library of the University of East Anglia, Christine joined the British Council, where she held a number of information posts in the UK and overseas. In 1988 she was appointed to a research officer post at Aston University, and in 1990 joined the senior management team. Her principal professional interests are management information and performance indicators, on which she has written and spoken extensively.

Phil Bradley
Worked for over six years for the British Council, and is living proof that you can travel the world on a degree in librarianship. He has worked for Silver Platter for five years, initially establishing their Technical Support department before moving on to set up their Training Section. He is currently on the management committee of the UK Online User Group and regularly writes articles on different aspects of CD-ROM technology for a number of different journals.

Peter Chapman
Currently Chief Librarian of The Scotsman, he was Head Librarian of The Northern Echo until August 1992. At The Northern Echo he

introduced an in-house full-text database of the newspaper and developed *The Northern Echo on CD-ROM*. He worked closely with Information North in exploiting CD-ROM as an information medium within the North-East of England.

Geoffrey Cleave

Has degrees from Southampton, Open and Warwick Universities. Since 1978 he has been Economics and Business Studies Librarian at the University of Warwick. He manages the collection of working papers in economics and management at Warwick. From 1990–1992 he was President of the European Business Schools Librarians Group, on whose behalf he edits the *SCIMP/SCAMP Thesaurus of Management Terms*.

John Cox

Is Head of Information Services at the Wellcome Foundation, London. From 1989 until mid 1993 he was Head of Information Services at the Royal Free Hospital School of Medicine, London. Prior to that he was Engineering Information Specialist at Aston University. He is a member of the management committee of the UK Online User Group and is author of *Keyguide to Information Sources in Online and CD-ROM Database Searching* and a number of articles on CD-ROM, bibliographic software and electronic current awareness services.

Joan Day

After a career in academic libraries, joined the Department of Information and Library Management at the University of Northumbria at Newcastle, (formerly Newcastle Polytechnic), with particular responsibility for education and training in online information services, including CD-ROM; she is now Head of Department. She was a recent Chair of UKOLUG – the UK national user group for online and CD-ROM affairs. She runs regular workshops on managing CD-ROM services generally, and training staff and end-users in particular.

Laurence Fouweather
Is a graduate engineer and worked in industry before moving into academic computing. He has previously occupied senior posts at the London School of Economics and Oxford University and was appointed Information Technology Manager at Templeton College, Oxford in 1989.

Feona Hamilton
Formerly Manager of Information and Corporate Communications at Bain & Co., the management consultants, she is now Commissioning Editor with Mansell Publishing. Previously she spent six years as a self-employed consultant, writer and lecturer in information management. Earlier posts include Information, Research and Consultancy Group Manager at Aslib, the Association for Information Management, and Press and Information Officer at the Library Association.

Terry Hanson
Is Sub-Librarian, Electronic Information Services at the University of Portsmouth. He is also the Social Sciences Subject Librarian and responsible for official publications. Has also worked at Liverpool Polytechnic (1978–1980) and on exchange at the University of Connecticut (1987–1988). He is on the management committee of the UK Online User Group and is Chairman of the UK Pro-Cite User Group. He has published widely on CD-ROM, bibliographic software, European Community information, etc.

Heather Kirby
Is Head of the Reference and Information Service of Croydon Libraries, and has been involved in the planning and preparation for the new central library. She is particularly interested in the use of information technology within the Reference Service, where she established a CD-ROM network which is expanding rapidly.

Carol Lefebvre
Is the Information Specialist at the Cochrane Centre, part of the National Health Service Research and Development Programme, based in Oxford. From January 1986 to November 1992, she was the

Information Services Librarian at the Cairns Library, Oxford, where she was responsible for online and CD-ROM services, including staff and end-user training. She has lectured on the subject of CD-ROM training for various organizations including the British Council, the Medical Health and Welfare Libraries Group of the Library Association and UKOLUG, of which she was Chairman from 1992–1993.

Mike Lewis
Has worked as a professional librarian at the University of Sussex Library since 1975. Since 1986 he has been involved in new technology developments within the Library, firstly as a member of the Research Support Group, and since 1988, Information Services. Within Information Services he has been part of a team managing CD-ROMs, which since early 1991 have been networked. His special interests include CD-ROM management, user education, and document delivery.

Christopher Marks
Has worked in a variety of Libraries in the UK, Trinidad and Nigeria. He joined Staffordshire University in 1984 where he is currently the Central Services Librarian. He has published various articles on Automation and Management in Libraries.

Kath O'Donovan
Is Library Network Manager at the Library of the University of Sheffield. From 1977 to 1993 she worked in the Library of the University of Newcastle upon Tyne, as Engineering Librarian, Medical Librarian, and finally as Sub-Librarian: IT and Liaison. She has also worked in special libraries.

David Perrow
Is Information Manager and Librarian at Templeton College, Oxford. Following an undergraduate degree at Cambridge, he took an MA in Librarianship at Sheffield University, and then worked as Assistant Librarian in Economics and Management in Sheffield for 10 years before moving to Oxford in 1988.

Michele Shoebridge

Is Sub-Librarian, Administration and Systems at the University of Birmingham. She has had considerable experience with library housekeeping systems, PC networking and CD-ROM technology. Before moving into the systems area she was Librarian at the Sports Documentation Centre and recently edited *Information sources in sport and leisure*.

Eileen Elliott de Saez

Is Senior Lecturer in the Department of Information and Library Management at the University of Northumbria. A qualified librarian and teacher, she then qualified in marketing and market research as her career moved from academic librarianship to industrial information and development work to higher education. She is the author of *Marketing for libraries and information services*.

Nick Smith

Is Head of Information Services in the Library and Information Services at Aston University. He previously held posts at University College, Cardiff, first as Library Information Officer and then as Site Librarian in the Science Library. Nick graduated from Southampton University with a degree in physics and subsequently went on to complete a PhD in theoretical physics at the same institution, followed by an MSc in Information Studies at Sheffield University. His main professional interests are in the management of electronic information services and in the transfer of information management skills.

Morag Watson

Joined the University of Birmingham Library in 1990 as Deputy Systems Librarian after completing her Diploma in Librarianship at the University of Central England. She is now Assistant Librarian, Systems: PC Networks, in the Library and is responsible for all PC based networks and stand alone PCs. One of her main areas of expertise is in networking of databases on CD-ROM to both local and wide area networks.

Contents

General case studies

CHAPTER ONE

Introduction

Terry Hanson and Joan Day

CD-ROM is now a well established technology in libraries of all kinds where it is has found a role as an alternative to printed indexing and abstracting journals, to microfilmed newspaper archives, to encyclopedias and for an increasing variety of other applications. It is clearly a very versatile technology and one which most library managers have welcomed enthusiastically.

As a relatively mature technology, if less than a decade can be considered such, librarians have had time to consider the many management questions that CD-ROM has raised and to experiment until satisfactory arrangements are implemented. Similarly, the literature on CD-ROM in libraries is now very considerable and librarians can normally find written accounts of management issues and plenty of individual case studies to assist the local decision-making process.

The purpose of this book has been to present in a more systematic manner the collective experience of the pioneer managers of CD-ROM in libraries. Rather than gather together a collection of previously published material as a set of loosely related 'readings', we agreed on a structure which we felt would be useful to both library managers and students. Chapters were then commissioned from known writers and practitioners who were asked to write on specific themes within the detailed framework agreed for the volume as a whole. In this way, variety of experience is contained within a thematic structure, while encouraging reflection and comparison.

Structure

The book contains a mixture of overviews and case studies. The purpose of the overview chapters is to present a general theoretical treatment of the topic, identifying the main issues, trends and developments in recent years so as to allow the reader to gain the perspective with which then to examine the accompanying case studies. In addition to the case studies attached to the overviews there are three general management case studies from different types of library which cover most of the section headings from throughout the book.

There is inevitably a degree of overlap between the sections and between individual papers. This is a consequence of the structure we have chosen but we feel that the reader will benefit from a topic being considered by different writers from different perspectives. Thus, for example, CD-ROM networking is touched on in several chapters as are the questions of training, technical support, etc. Nevertheless, the chapters and related case studies do largely stand alone, so that the reader looking for information on a specific topic can do so.

The order of the chapters is meant to be logical, beginning with a consideration of the current state of the market and ending with a look to the future and whether CD-ROM will be a major player in the information strategy of the average library. In between we begin with an overview of management issues relating to all libraries and then follow a path through acquisition to diferent aspects of exploitation. As well as the 'traditional' aspects of managing CD-ROM we have also included papers on the use of CD-ROM for full-text article storage and retrieval and on the use of CD-ROM for local inhouse purposes.

Library focus

In the early stages of planning this volume we intended that there should be a balance of representation of the standard three types of library: academic, public and special. To this end we commissioned case studies from appropriate sources. However it quickly became obvious to us that the academic library world was by far the most active in terms of its exploitation of CD-ROM technology, followed by special libraries. We decided therefore, for very positive reasons, that this fact had to be reflected in the book; indeed it would have been impossible not to do so. Thus it is primarily in the academic and research situation that issues are explored, but in such a way that managers in all types of library or information unit can anticipate the extent to which the problems and solutions might apply to them.

Geographic focus

The geographic focus of the book, in as far as it has one, is the United Kingdom but the issues raised and the management problems described are universal. The UK academic library situation may not be a perfect representation of the world of CD-ROM and libraries but we think it is a good representation. The most obvious areas of difference in the developed world are those of institution and library size, and acquisition and distribution arrangements. Thus a typical American university with 20–30 000 students will have magnitude problems with which a small British university would be unfamiliar but the issues are still the same. However, we must acknowledge that, even though the issues are universal, there is a range of problems associated with magnitude that could only be properly explored in a similar volume to this devoted to the theme.

Management focus

The principal function of the book is to concentrate on management issues of CD-ROM in libraries and not on the technological aspects. Our aim is to assist the library decision-maker in particular rather than the technical support staff. Whatever technical detail is included is provided in order to assist the management and decision-making process.

Bibliography

Finally, the bibliography at the end of the book is substantially more than the sum of references from the individual chapters. The items have been selected from recent writings from a great variety of sources and together they will provide the reader with a comprehensive collection of recent references on the main topics covered in the book.

CHAPTER TWO

The CD-ROM market

John Cox

The CD-ROM medium and its origins

CD-ROM is one of a family of compact disc formats. The best known is Compact Disc-Digital Audio (CD-DA), commonly called CD, which was jointly developed by the Sony and Philips companies and announced in 1980. This format has enjoyed spectacular success in the home audio market and has replaced the vinyl record in many music collections due to the higher fidelity of its recordings and its greater portability and durability. A standard for the CD-ROM format was announced by Sony and Philips in 1983. It represented a logical extension of compact disc technology since a CD could store any type of computer-processible data. The development of a format for text storage therefore followed naturally from the success of the audio CD.

A CD-ROM disc is identical in appearance to an audio CD, being 12 centimetres in diameter with a thickness of 1.2 millimetres. It is produced through similar processes, and plants designed for audio CD production can be adapted for mastering and replication of CD-ROMs (Hendley, 1988). The main difference is that additional error detection and correction features are required for accurate retrieval and representation of data on a computer screen. Data are recorded as a series of pits burned onto the disc by a laser beam in the mastering process. The technology of CD-ROM production is described elsewhere (Buddine and Young, 1987; Hendley, 1988;

Saffady, 1992). Despite its small size a CD-ROM disc can store vast amounts of data, equivalent to around 250 000 A4 pages of text. A total of more than 600 megabytes of storage space is available, although error correction coding requirements mean that the amount of data stored is actually limited to around 540 megabytes.

The audio CD legacy is also evident in the hardware required for reading data from a CD-ROM disc. A CD-ROM player or drive offers an extra layer of error detection and correction but is in most other respects similar to a CD player and recent models offer audio output and CD-DA compatibility. The disc uses the same rotation technique, Constant Linear Velocity (CLV), as the audio CD. This means that it rotates faster when reading the shorter inside tracks of the disc but takes longer to access data stored towards the outside edge. As a result average access times are slower than for other storage media, notably magnetic disks.

Evolution of the CD-ROM market

The mass storage capabilities of CD-ROM accounted most clearly for its initial appeal to the library market. Staff in many libraries had for more than 10 years previously been using telecommunications networks to access large quantities of computer-readable bibliographic data stored in remote online databases, primarily for subject searching on behalf of readers, local catalogue compilation or book ordering. The prospect of publication of such databases on CD-ROM, at fixed annual charges and without the need to rely upon telecommunications networks for access, was obviously attractive. This was true in particular for those online databases which indexed the literature of individual subject areas such as business, medicine and technology. Although offering powerful retrieval facilities and containing much information of value to library users, these databases were only used selectively since charges were levied for every use according to a combination of the length of time for which the user was connected to them and the data retrieved from them. Actual users of online databases tended mainly to be librarians or information scientists whose training enabled them to run searches on behalf of clients with information needs and to minimize search costs. Their skills were also needed to negotiate the varied and, to the lay person, somewhat arcane command languages used by online databases. CD-ROM held out the possibility of greatly improving conditions of access to the information contained in these databases by making them available locally rather than remotely, offering unlimited access at a guaranteed cost and encouraging library users to conduct their own searches through simpler retrieval interfaces with liberal use of menus and help screens.

Despite its appeal, CD-ROM was not an instant success. The market for CD-ROM products was slow to take off for a number of reasons. One of these was logistical. Turnaround times for mastering and replication of discs were unacceptably long in the early days due to a shortage of companies providing such services and competition with audio CD production. The Information Access Company, for instance, experienced a 10 week delay (Herther, 1985). Publishers of successful online or printed products were also (and to some extent still are (Arnold, 1992)) concerned about the possibility that CD-ROM could seriously threaten revenues from these products. As a result publishers tended to experiment carefully with CD-ROM by making only part of their online or printed data available through this medium and by charging high subscription fees (Pooley, 1990). The spirit of adventure was further compromized by a slump in computer sales in the mid-1980s which meant that companies were unwilling to take the lead by investing heavily in CD-ROM (Herther, 1985). Libraries were also deterred at this early stage by the high subscription charges and equipment costs involved. Microcomputers, CD-ROM drives and printers were all relatively expensive at this stage compared to today. This was especially true of CD-ROM drives whose initial cost was close to £1000, representing a significant call on any library budget. There was also some feeling that, although CD-ROM was an exciting development, it could be rendered obsolete very quickly by some new technology due to the prevailing pace of innovation in the area of data storage (Dreiss and Bashir, 1990).

Another publishing problem needed to be resolved, namely the lack of an established standard for placing data on CD-ROM discs. Although the Yellow Book standard announced by Sony and Philips in 1985 established the physical format of the disc, including its organization into tracks and sectors and its error correction requirements, there was a need for a standard to regulate directory structure and file management facilities (Saffady, 1992). While CD-ROM offered mass storage capabilities, its slower access times meant that complex hierarchical directory structures needed to be avoided. A different arrangement from that used for magnetic disks was required but, in the absence of any standard, companies used a range of proprietary, and not always compatible, file management procedures. This situation certainly inhibited market growth since there was no guarantee that a CD-ROM drive capable of reading one disc would be able to read a disc from a different publisher. The problem was addressed in late 1985 by a group of experts from different sectors of the CD-ROM industry. This group established the High Sierra standard in mid-1986. The High Sierra standard was adopted by most publishers from this point onwards and formed the basis of the international standard ISO 9660 which was approved in 1988 and has since become accepted throughout the industry.

It is not surprising, given the uncertainties surrounding its early years, that only modest progress should be reflected in a report of publishing activity issued towards the end of 1988 (Nicholls, 1988). A total of around 200 commercially available products was projected and the average price of known products was $1273. The library market was dominant and was targeted by cataloguing and acquisitions support tools such as *Bibliofile* and *Books in Print*, or reference material such as the *Oxford English Dictionary*. Indexing and abstracting databases on CD-ROM were also beginning to have an impact. A similar survey in early 1993 (Nicholls and Sutherland, 1993) was able to report a vastly different situation, however, since 3216 unique CD-ROM titles were available, representing a wide range of subjects and categories of information, with an average price of $453. A further survey by the US company InfoTech, reported in *Byte*, suggests that the number of titles in print stands at about 5000 but this includes inhouse products. The same survey also reports that the installed base of CD-ROM drives is over five million (Udell, 1993). The CD-ROM market has come of age.

This transformation was wrought by a number of factors. Improvements in the economic situation in the late 1980s gave publishers more scope for investment in CD-ROM and for reducing the cost of their products. Publishing confidence was also increased by the establishment of the ISO 9660 standard for recording data on CD-ROM discs. The disc production process became much faster as more companies entered the industry to provide mastering and replication services and turnaround times of a few days became the norm (Capers, 1991). Other real sources of encouragement for publishers and users were the reductions in the costs of replication, estimated to have fallen from $12 to $3 per disc between 1987 and 1990, and of CD-ROM drives from $1500 to $600 in the same period (Dreiss and Bashir, 1990). Falling prices of discs, drives and also of microcomputers and printers in recent years have made it much easier for libraries to take the plunge with CD-ROM. The library literature has been littered with reports of successful implementations and high user demand, thus encouraging wider take-up. Publishers have come to see CD-ROM as a generator of revenue in its own right and have placed a wide range of products on the market.

CD-ROM products

As mentioned earlier, 3216 commercially available CD-ROM products were identified from two directories published in 1992 (Nicholls and Sutherland, 1993). In fact this total was surpassed by the 3597 products listed in the 1993 edition of TFPL Publishing's *The CD-ROM directory* (Finlay and Mitchell, 1992). This directory has proved a good barometer of CD-ROM market growth (Figure 1). Whatever the actual number of CD-ROM titles there is no doubting their variety in terms of subject coverage and types of information. There can be few subject areas without at least one CD-ROM title. In general terms the series of annual surveys conducted since 1988 in the journals *CD-ROM Professional* (formerly *Laserdisk Professional*) and *Database* (Nicholls, 1988; Nicholls, 1989; Nicholls and Van Den Elshout, 1990; Nicholls, 1991; Nicholls and Sutherland, 1992; Nicholls and Sutherland, 1993) shows that science and technology, including medicine, and business have been strongly represented throughout, while arts and humanities titles have increased their share of the total to a respectable eight per cent after a slow

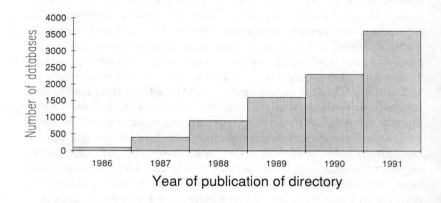

Year of publication of directory

Figure 1 Growth of CD-ROM Databases

beginning. Although CD-ROM has been used as a distribution medium for such diverse applications as instruction manuals, computer software and clip-art for desktop publishing, in terms of the library market the main information categories are: bibliographic support tools; indexing and abstracting services; full-text; reference; and multimedia.

Bibliographic support tools were among the first CD-ROM products to succeed in the library market and their popularity has endured. This is not surprising since they facilitate the traditional library processes of cataloguing, acquisition and collection development especially, and are also helpful in general bibliographic checking for inter-library loan requests or reference verification queries raised by library users. MARC records for use in local catalogue compilation have been distributed on a number of CD-ROM products, offering a cheaper alternative to membership of a cataloguing consortium particularly for smaller libraries. The British Library and Library of Congress offer retrospective and current MARC records through the BNB on CD-ROM (*British*

National Bibliography) and CDMARC bibliographic products respectively. The German, French and Spanish national bibliographies are also on CD-ROM and, like the BNB, allow menus and help messages to be displayed in a number of languages. The work of library acquisitions departments is assisted by these tools and also by products such as *Books in Print Plus*, *Bookbank* and *Bookfind-CD* which provide details of publications which are in or out of print and enable orders to be placed in electronic format.

Indexing and abstracting services, although they accounted for 17% of all CD-ROM databases in 1992 compared to 48% in 1987 (Nicholls and Sutherland, 1993), have had the greatest impact among libraries and their users. Library users, particularly in academic organizations, commonly need to find out what has been published about a subject in the journal literature. This requirement has become much easier to satisfy through the more powerful and flexible retrieval facilities offered by the CD-ROM equivalents of printed tools. Most of the major abstracting and indexing services now have CD-ROM equivalents. Leading examples are *Biological Abstracts on Disc*, *COMPENDEX Plus* (*Engineering Index*), *Medline* (*Index Medicus*) and *Social Sciences Citation Index*. A popular database with no printed equivalent for business and management literature is ABI/INFORM. Some of the larger databases, e.g. *Medline*, ERIC (education), are available from more than one publisher, increasing the choice available to libraries. Databases of narrower subject scope are also published in this category, examples being CITIS (construction), TREECD (forestry) and PSYCLIT (psychology). Specific document types are the focus of some databases, e.g. *Dissertation Abstracts Ondisc* (theses), NTIS (reports) and ESPACE (patents).

Full-text information has increasingly been published on CD-ROM, with 45% of the total in 1992 compared to the 1987 figure of 28%. This category places the whole text of original works, for libraries typically journals, newspapers, books or literary works, on disc. The whole text of journals may be published individually (e.g. *British Medical Journal*, *American Journal of Public Health*) or, more usually, as a compendium of full-text articles from a number of journals (e.g. *Business Periodicals Ondisc*, covering more than 300 journals indexed in the ABI/INFORM database, and *General*

Periodicals Ondisc which reproduces articles from 200 general interest periodicals). A product of particular interest is the ADONIS service which contains the whole text of almost 500 biomedical journals, from 1991 onwards in most cases. This service is updated weekly and offers libraries a genuine alternative to print subscriptions for journals in biomedicine.

Newspapers have been a popular CD-ROM application and British titles include the *Guardian*, *Independent*, *Times*, *Financial Times* and *Northern Echo*, a regional newspaper whose production and distribution is described in Chapter 14. CD-ROM, with its search facilities and compact size, is certainly an attractive proposition compared to microfilm in this area. Textbooks and literary works on CD-ROM are found in some libraries, and examples are the *Oxford Textbook of Medicine*, the *Bible*, *Shakespeare on Disc* and *English Poetry*, a four-disc product featuring the works of 1350 English poets. Some products of this type have been criticized for failing to add value to their printed versions or, as in the case of the *Oxford Textbook of Medicine* and *Shakespeare on Disc*, excluding tables or figures and critical apparatus respectively (Dorrington, 1991; Wiliams and Armstrong, 1991).

The distinction between full-text and reference CD-ROMs is sometimes blurred. 'Reference' is taken here to indicate factual or numeric information, for example definitions, addresses, guidelines, statistics, values or legislation. This type of information is commonly found on CD-ROM and has increased its market share from 24 to 39 per cent between 1987 and 1992 (Nicholls and Sutherland, 1993). Products such as the *Oxford English Dictionary*, the *Hutchinson Electronic Encyclopedia* and the *World Almanac and Book of Facts* typify general-purpose reference material on CD-ROM. Of more specific application are the *Natural Products* CD-ROM, with chemical and physical data for 65 000 organic substances, *Material Safety Data Sheets*, containing 35 000 data sheets for chemicals in regular use, PDQ (*Physicians Data Query*), which includes details of cancer treatment protocols and a directory of individuals and organizations involved in cancer care, and *Kompass Top 20 000*, a source of company information. Statistical data on CD-ROM includes *International Financial Statistics*, *World Currency Monitor*, *United States Census Data* and *Small Area Statistics for England, Wales and Scotland* from the 1981 UK census. CD-ROM has also proved to be a good medium for storing legislative material, e.g. JUSTIS, containing the whole corpus of European Community legislation, and SI-CD, with details of UK statutory instruments, including full text for those published by HMSO from 1987 onwards.

It has been pointed out (Tenopir, 1990; Nicholls and Sutherland, 1992) that the CD-ROM medium has been unadventurously used by many publishers simply to distribute established print or online products in another form without added value in terms of content. The products highlighted in this section so far tend to support this view. Such products are certainly easier to market to libraries since their content is familiar and user demand for them is known, the retrieval power of the CD-ROM software adding sufficient value to clinch a purchase provided that the price is affordable. However, it is worth mentioning some original products. One approach has been to combine different types of data on the same disc. An example is the *AIDS Compact Library* from Macmillan New Media which contains the full text of AIDS articles from 10 medical journals, bibliographic references and abstracts from two different databases and reports of drug trials. Similarly Bowker's *SciTech Reference Plus* disc comprises bibliographic, biographical and directory information from a number of bibliographies and directories. Another approach is to include software for purposes additional to information retrieval. Thus software for data analysis and graphical representation is provided with the FAME (Financial Analysis Made Easy) product from Jordan, while SAM-CD (formerly CONSULT) from Scientific American Medicine includes, in addition to the full text of the publisher's encyclopedia, a series of patient management tests for use by medical students.

Some interesting multimedia CD-ROM products have also been developed, sometimes to support computer-assisted learning. An example is an interactive tutorial titled *The Nature of Genes* which includes simultaneous text, graphics and voice and allows users to manipulate genetic structures on screen. On a more general level are products such as *World Atlas*, combining textual and statistical data with maps, *Mammals: a Multimedia Encyclopedia*, with photographs, maps, film clips, vocalizations and a mammal classification game, and Compton's *Multimedia Encyclopedia* which includes sound, graphics and animation sequences. The emergence of multimedia products in other compact disc formats is discussed in the concluding section of this chapter.

CD-ROM publishers and distributors

In parallel with the increase in the number of CD-ROM products has been the growth in the number of companies involved in the CD-ROM industry. *The CD-ROM directory* (Finlay and Mitchell, 1992) recorded 48 organizations in 1986 and 2826 in 1992. Many of these companies are involved in disc production, performing functions such as premastering, mastering and replication, and are not in direct contact with the library market. Libraries deal mainly with publishers and distributors.

CD-ROM publishers play a similar role to online hosts in that they act on behalf of information providers whose data they publish in CD-ROM format. The information provider will compile and own the data published on the disc but the publisher will provide the necessary retrieval software and will market and distribute the product at a one-off or, more usually, annual charge. SilverPlatter Information, CD Plus, DIALOG OnDisc and MacMillan New Media are well known examples of companies which operate arrangements of this nature with information providers. The first two publish data in CD-ROM format exclusively, while DIALOG is an established online host which has moved into CD-ROM publishing also and MacMillan was formerly Maxwell Electronic Publishing, an offshoot of the Maxwell Online host. The H.W. Wilson Company is another organization which serves as both an online host and CD-ROM publisher. It differs from DIALOG and MacMillan, however, in that it acts as its own publisher, distributing on CD-ROM many of the indexes which it has long compiled and published in printed format. Oxford University Press and R.R. Bowker also publish their own information products on CD-ROM, although neither has ever been an online host.

Libraries can also elect to deal with distributors rather than directly with CD-ROM publishers. Companies such as Microinfo, Optech and Cambridge CD-ROM act as UK agents for products from a number of publishers. They offer libraries the opportunity to consolidate all their subscriptions with one company instead of dealing with several. Some companies whose original function was to handle periodical subscriptions for libraries have now expanded to include CD-ROM subscriptions also, examples being Ebsco and Faxon.

CD-ROM in libraries today: a qualified success

The CD-ROM medium has proved hugely popular among library users. It has established itself with remarkable speed as an essential information retrieval tool and can be said to have fulfilled many of the high expectations which librarians had of it when the first products began to become commercially available in the mid-1980s. Many libraries have been revolutionized by CD-ROM, both in terms of their appearance, as evidenced by the presence of banks of computer workstations, and in the nature of the services which they can offer to users who now commonly expect to perform their own literature searches and to handle large quantities of text in electronic format. This medium has been primarily responsible for an electronic information revolution (Cox, Dawson and Hobbs, 1992) which has 'ensured that library and information services will never be the same again' (Biddiscombe, 1991). The importance of CD-ROM to libraries is reflected in the large and fast-growing body of professional literature which it has spawned (Cox, 1991a), characterized by journals such as *CD-ROM Professional* and *CD-ROM World* (formerly *CD-ROM Librarian*) in which the favourable impact of CD-ROM on libraries is frequently reported. Certainly one does not tend to see articles describing disillusionment among CD-ROM users or documenting the large-scale cancellation of subscriptions.

CD-ROM has won its place in libraries by providing a cost-effective means of bringing computerized literature searching and powerful data retrieval facilities to library users. Fixed subscription costs have made it possible to budget for unlimited end-user searching of electronic information services in a way which online databases, with their pay-as-you-use charging mechanisms, could not permit. Their search interfaces are much more comprehensible to the end-user than are online command languages, while the ease of access to electronic data without any requirement for telecommunications networks has been a major boon, especially for developing countries (Ali, 1990). For libraries themselves, the introduction of CD-ROM databases and the opportunities which they have provided for the development and expansion of new information services have resulted in greater prestige and in enhanced status within their parent organizations (Cox, 1991b). A visit to the library to see CD-ROM facilities is now a common inclusion in a tour of the parent organization for visitors or potential employees. The strong position which CD-ROM occupies in libraries bodes well for suppliers to this marketplace.

Nevertheless, there are problem areas both in terms of the medium itself and in relations between libraries and other players in the market. The problems inherent in the medium itself include the limited capacity of the discs in relation to large databases such as *Medline*, the slow access speeds compared to magnetic storage devices, the currency of the data with, at best, monthly updates, and the lack of interface standards such that library users need to become familiar with many different systems and methods of searching. These issues are discussed more fully in Chapter 20 which discusses the future of CD-ROM in relation to competing alternatives.

Another major problem area is that of licensing agreements and networking. The vast majority of CD-ROM products are leased rather than sold to libraries. Librarians have had to get used to the fact that, whereas the printed version of the same information is owned when a subscription is paid, the often more expensive CD-ROM edition is only on loan. The loan period will only be extended on renewal of the subscription to it, usually on an annual basis. Worse still, the loan is subject to terms and conditions imposed in license agreements drawn up by the CD-ROM publisher (Nissley, 1990; Jensen, 1991). These agreements are considered necessary by publishers due to the vulnerability of data published in electronic format to copying, republication and resale. License agreements therefore commonly include clauses which specify restrictions on where and by whom the product may be used, the nature of use, downloading of data and the use of superseded discs. Some of these provisions, notably in the case of downloading, are phrased in very general terms. Others clearly require that use should only be by employees of the subscribing organization and should be for non-commercial purposes.

Taken literally, these agreements essentially mean that librarians are expected to monitor usage in ways which are not practical. In general, they are weighted heavily in favour of the licensor rather than the licensee, for instance the former, but not the latter, being protected against claims arising from the use of the database or its associated software and documentation. Librarians face a conflict between the desirability of introducing CD-ROM databases, with their many advantages in terms of information service delivery, into their organizations and an unwillingness to submit to restrictions which they may regard as unreasonable and which, if not observed, could result in litigation. Publishers have shown no inclination to issue CD-ROM products without licenses or to make these agreements less restrictive for the licensee. License agreements undoubtedly influence the market for CD-ROM products and can result in lost or cancelled subscriptions. It would seem, however, that they are here to stay and that anyone who subscribes to a CD-ROM database thus protected, must at least be prepared to take reasonable action to stay within the specified conditions. Equally, publishers need to be aware of the limited extent to which the enforcement of some conditions can be guaranteed by the subscribing organization.

Networking of CD-ROM databases within subscriber organizations has naturally been an area of concern to publishers and information providers and is frequently addressed in user agreements. The popularity of some CD-ROM databases and the presence of local or wide area networks in many organizations, along with the increasing availability of networking solutions designed specifically for this medium, have provided librarians with an impetus for exploring the feasibility of simultaneous multi-user access. Many publishers and information providers are willing to accommodate local networking of databases as long as networks are secure from access outside the subscribing organization. Not surprisingly, given the potential loss of individual subscriptions involved, most publishers make an extra charge for networking their products. A few companies, however, make no additional charges, a notable example being H.W. Wilson. Other companies impose their own charges, either according to the number of terminals licensed to access the database, or based on a specified maximum number of simultaneous users where this is feasible.

Charges vary from company to company, as does the ability of subscriber organizations to pay. In general, there is no standard practice among publishers with regard to networking and charges are typically based on what the market is likely to stand. It is, of course, possible for companies to price networked access to their databases beyond the reach of even larger organizations. For instance, the databases of the Institute for Scientific Information (ISI) have proved too expensive for many organizations to network locally, and this has contributed to the popularity among UK academic institutions of access to the four ISI databases currently available at a fixed annual subscription via JANET (the Joint Academic NETwork in the UK).

Conclusion

This chapter has sought to provide a snapshot of the library CD-ROM market, its products, players and the factors which have shaped its growth and will influence its future development. CD-ROM has quickly established itself in libraries and critical mass has been achieved as hardware and product prices have become gradually more affordable. There are now plenty of products and companies in the market. Production of CD-ROMs has become a much faster and less expensive process in recent times, and the continuation of this trend in the future should be assisted by industry-wide implementation of the Standard Generalized Markup Language (SGML) for coding electronic documents (Anon., 1990; O'Connor, 1992). SGML provides a standard for marking the different structural elements of text (e.g. main headings, subheadings, footnotes) in electronic documents. The application of a standard promises to reduce greatly the amount of conversion required and to make it easier to output text in multiple electronic formats, including CD-ROM. There is therefore every reason to expect that the rapid growth in the number of commercially available CD-ROM products in recent years will continue.

The major impact of CD-ROM in libraries has been to play the lead role in establishing computerized information retrieval by end-users as a routine activity. Nevertheless, it is by no means the only medium suitable for end-user searching, as shown by the emergence of high-capacity magnetic disks for local database storage and the use of the JANET network to provide free access at the point of use to major data sets. These alternative media offer advantages in terms of speed and currency. At present, however, they are not applicable to many databases and the immediate future of CD-ROM at least looks secure. Even if some of the larger databases migrate to other media, CD-ROM will continue to appeal to libraries for coverage of narrower subject areas or full-text and reference sources.

The future of the medium may be further cemented by moves towards a common user interface or the implementation of a data exchange standard. The control which the latter promises to give the user over the interface employed for accessing different databases, would be indeed welcome. Another helpful future development may be the emergence of a degree of inter-operability between some at least of the various compact disc formats (Howorth, 1992). These formats, notably CD-ROM Extended Architecture (CD-ROM XA), Compact Disc-Interactive (CD-I) and Digital Video Interactive (DVI), provide a platform for multimedia and interactive video applications in libraries (Desmarais, 1990; Bonime, 1991; Brandt, 1991) and could build upon the primarily textual focus of CD-ROM to propagate electronic books and tools for computer-assisted learning. There is, unfortunately, little incentive at present for libraries to experiment with the possibilities offered by these formats, due to the different hardware platforms required by each. Only one, CD-ROM XA, can be used with a CD-ROM drive and even this requires the use of a special interface for most drives.

There remains the possibility that some new data storage medium will emerge to leave CD-ROM trailing in its wake and it is for this reason that the long-term future of CD-ROM cannot be predicted with any certainty. After all, one need only recall that the term CD-ROM meant nothing to librarians until as recently as 1985 when online held sway as the route to primarily bibliographic information stored in electronic databases. Since that date CD-ROM, despite some obvious limitations and imperfections, has left an indelible mark on libraries and established a presence in the information marketplace which will not be yielded lightly.

References

Ali, S.N. (1990) Databases on optical discs and their potential in developing countries. *Journal of the American Society for Information Science*, **41**, (4), 238–244

Anon. (1990) What is SGML and why is it important? *Information World Review*, **50**, 17

Arnold, S.E. (1992) Checking the pulse of developers for the library market. *CD-ROM Professional*, **5**, (4), 91–92

Biddiscombe, R. (1991) Networking CD-ROM in an academic library environment. *British Journal of Academic Librarianship*, **6**, (3), 175–183

Bonime, A. (1991) The promise and the challenge of CD-I. *CD-ROM Professional*, **4**, (5), 17–30

Brandt, R. (1991) CD-ROM, CD-I, multimedia and reality. *CD-ROM Librarian*, **6**, (8), 23–25

Buddine, L. and Young, E. (1987) *The Brady guide to CD-ROM*. New York: Prentice Hall

Capers, R. (1991) CD-ROM: the advantages and barriers to market growth. *CD-ROM Professional*, **4**, (4), 88–89

Cox, J. (1991a) *Keyguide to information sources in online and CD-ROM database searching*. London: Mansell

Cox, J. (1991b) Making your electronic information products promote and pay for each other. In *Online information 91. Proceedings of the 15th International Online Information Meeting, 10–12 December 1991*, ed. D.I. Raitt, pp. 421–428. Oxford: Learned Information

Cox, J.J., Dawson, K.J. and Hobbs, K.E.F. (1992) The electronic information revolution and how to exploit it. *British Journal of Surgery*, **79**, 1004–1010

Desmarais, N. (1990) Multimedia CD-ROMs: a perspective. *CD-ROM Librarian*, **5**, (3), 10–11

Dorrington, L. (1991) Oxford Textbook of Medicine. In *CD-ROM information products: the evaluative guide. Volume 2*, eds. C.J. Armstrong and J.A. Large, pp. 297–313. Aldershot: Gower

Dreiss, L.J. and Bashir, S. (1990) CD-ROM: potential and pitfalls. *CD-ROM Professional*, **3**, (5), 70–73

Finlay, M. and Mitchell, J. (1992) (eds.) *The CD-ROM directory 1993*. London: TFPL Publishing

Hendley, T. (1988) An introduction to the range of optical storage media. In *CD-ROM: fundamentals to applications*, ed. C. Oppenheim, pp. 1–38. London: Butterworths

Herther, N. (1985) CD-ROM technology: a new era for information storage and retrieval. *Online*, **9**, (6), 17–28

Howorth, R. (1992) Ending compact confusion. *Byte*, **94UK**, 11–14

Jensen, M.B. (1991) CD-ROM licenses: what's in the fine or nonexistent print may surprise you. *CD-ROM Professional*, **4**, (2), 13–17

Nicholls, P.T. (1988) Statistical profile of currently available CD-ROM database products. *Laserdisk Professional*, **1**, (4), 38–45

Nicholls, P.T. (1989) Information resources on laserdisk: statistical profile of currently available CD-ROM database products. *Laserdisk Professional,* **2,** (2), 101–108

Nicholls, P.T. (1991) A survey of commercially available CD-ROM database titles. *CD-ROM Professional,* **4,** (2), 23–28

Nicholls, P.T. and Sutherland, P. (1993) The state of the union: CD-ROM titles in print 1992. *CD-ROM Professional,* **6,** (1), 60–64

Nicholls, P.T. and Sutherland, T. (1992) CD-ROM databases: a survey of commercial publishing activity. *Database,* **15,** (1), 36–41

Nicholls, P.T. and Van Den Elshout, R. (1990) Survey of databases available on CD-ROM: types, availability and content. *Database,* **13,** (1), 18–23

Nissley, M. (1990) CD-ROMs, licenses and librarians. In *CD-ROM licensing and copyright issues for libraries,* eds. M. Nissley and N.M. Nelson, pp. 1–17. Westport, Conn.: Meckler

O'Connor, M.A. (1992) Markup, SGML and hypertext for full-text databases. Part II. *CD-ROM Professional,* **5,** (4), 123–125

Pooley, C. (1990) CD-ROM licensing issues. In *CD-ROM licensing and copyright issues for libraries,* eds. M. Nissley and N.M. Nelson, pp. 31–43. Westport, Conn.: Meckler

Saffady, W. (1992) *Optical storage technology 1992: a state of the art review.* Westport, Conn.: Meckler

Tenopir, C. (1990) CD-ROM in libraries: distribution option or publishing revolution? *CD-ROM EndUser,* **2,** (2), 56–59

Udell, J. (1993) Start the presses. *Byte,* **18,** (2), 116–134

Wiliams, I. and Armstrong, C.J. (1991) Shakespeare on Disc. In *CD-ROM information products: the evaluative guide. Volume 2,* eds. C.J. Armstrong and J.A. Large, pp. 367–385. Aldershot: Gower

CHAPTER THREE

Management issues

Kath O'Donovan

Introduction

'We hate CD-ROM!'. This statement by Peter Lyman, Librarian at the University of Southern California, caused a sharp intake of breath amongst an audience of UK librarians at a seminar in June 1992[1]. Everyone who is closely acquainted with CD-ROM has shared this view at some time of crisis, when the new software wouldn't work on the existing equipment, or the network refused to respond. Mr Lyman was referring to the US librarians' preference for networking databases loaded onto hard disk, rather than using CD-ROM. For a number of reasons, libraries in the UK have not gone down this route, and on the whole our feelings about CD-ROM are rather more positive than this. It is salutary to remember that CD-ROM, exciting as it is, is not a universal panacea for library problems, and can be a troublesome cuckoo in the library nest. This chapter gives an overview of management issues raised by CD-ROM, many of which are dealt with in more detail in other chapters.

CD-ROM should be seen as a method of delivering information, and not as the information itself. For example Sun, manufacturers of UNIX workstations, use CD-ROM to distribute software. Librarians have tended to think in terms of bibliographical databases which enable them to offer a more sophisticated and acceptable service to their readers in the field of information retrieval and feed in to internal library activities such as acquisitions and cataloguing. As the market expands, more categories of product provide opportunities for libraries, but each presents a range of management issues. For example, in printed format newspapers are cumbersome to search, but on CD-ROM valuable information is easy to locate and the resource becomes much more useful to a surprisingly wide range of library users. However, costs are high as each title is on several discs, and it is unlikely that the current issues of the hard copy can be cancelled. Statistical databases, such as the census, offer facilities which are outside the range of most library services in the past. There is a heavy overhead in terms of training both staff and users, but the benefits in terms of level of service are great. Dictionaries on CD-ROM offer sophisticated searching techniques, but casual users may not wish to learn how to use the software just to find a definition.

As with any service, a range of factors affects how a particular library manages CD-ROM. For example:

- the library's strategic view of information provision, and how CD-ROM fits into that strategy;
- the physical attributes of the library such as size, geography and number of sites, determine location of CD-ROM access points;
- the size of the library budget and how much control the library has in redistributing expenditure or gaining new funding for computerized information sources dictate which and how many products are made available;
- particular enthusiasms and skills of staff influence how the service is implemented, promoted and run;
- sophistication and enthusiasm of library users determine how quickly the service is taken up;
- in almost any situation, the availability of CD-ROM on a network transforms a useful but limited single user resource into an essential service.

Patterns of management

Rapid change and development characterize all IT provision in libraries and CD-ROM is no exception. We are currently in a period of transition, when IT based techniques are spreading throughout the library but the scale of the change may not yet be reflected in management structures, or in the level of IT skills amongst staff. The pattern of administration will evolve as CD-ROM, along with other computerized information retrieval tools, is incorporated as an accepted part of the library service, and as the CD-ROM market itself matures and becomes more predictable. Libraries and their staffs need to be flexible and responsive, matching the management structure to changing needs.

A range of management patterns is possible, from establishing CD-ROM as a separate department, to complete integration within other functions. In the real world the situation is likely to lie somewhere in between, and in a small library issues will centre on how much outside expertise will be required.

Issues arising from different patterns of management

CD-ROM as a separate responsibility	CD-ROM integrated within departments
Complete overview should lead to service responsive to user needs	Fragmented management may lead to less coherent service to users
Complex issues running across the library, e.g. relationship to inter-library loans, may not receive adequate attention	The place of the service within the range of library services will be discussed throughout the library
Straightforward decision making	Decision-making process may be complex, as differing viewpoints are reconciled
Expertise and skills may be lacking if relatively few staff involved	Wide range of expertise and skills can be called on throughout the system
Isolation may lead to conflict within the library	Integration should enable all staff to have a stake in CD-ROM

Aspects of CD-ROM management

In large systems with several departments it may be difficult to pin down who has the responsibility for various aspects, particularly as the range of products widens. A library staff united in their enthusiasm for this medium, will overcome these issues. But if there is stress or rivalry between departments or subject areas, then the potential for misunderstanding and conflict is manifest.

In smaller libraries these management issues may be easy to resolve, as the aims and objectives of the service are more focused, and with a smaller staff divisions between departments may be less rigid. However, budgetary issues may be more difficult as the cost of CD-ROM products and the associated equipment is proportionately higher. Many smaller libraries, particularly in the medical field, have been successful in raising additional funding for CD-ROM initiatives and the prestige of the library has risen considerably as the benefits to the service have been recognized.

A major issue in smaller libraries, particularly one person units, is the range of skills required to implement a service. These skills can be acquired given time, but in such a library time is the most precious commodity of all. Cultivation of IT experts within the organization will pay dividends. A part-time medical librarian with no computing experience at all obtained *Medline* on trial. Within hours of receipt, thanks to her contacts in the computing centre, it was networked, quite illegally, throughout the hospital, putting the library on the map!

Selection

It is perhaps significant that the word 'product' is used in connection with CD-ROM, rather than 'title'. We may or may not like the term, but it does hint at the variety of services contained within this format. Selecting a product involves evaluating the content of the database and its potential contribution to the library service, as well as issues of ease of use and supplier. Most publishers offer to supply copies of their products for evaluation, and it will be helpful to take this up for most, if not all, products. Suitable equipment is required but may also be loaned by the supplier. Library users will welcome the opportunity to take part in trials, and this is a useful way of publicizing the service and forging links with users and their departments.

Selection of CD-ROM products can involve the addition of new titles, in which case funding must come from new money or savings elsewhere. When replacing an existing printed bibliographical service, the more sophisticated features of the CD-ROM will often make the decision to change relatively straightforward. Where the choice is between a printed reference book, or its CD-ROM equivalent, the library will need to consider ease of use and equipment availability. Library users may prefer immediate access to a printed directory if the alternative is a 30 minute wait for a machine to use the CD-ROM version.

Funding

Unless new money can be found to provide CD-ROM, then funding must come from existing budgets which are probably over-stretched already. Subject librarians, particularly those who are less than enthusiastic about IT, may be unwilling to sacrifice books and periodicals. Eventual savings from cancellation of hard copy abstracting and indexing journals may take time to filter through, and are in any case unlikely to match the cost of CD-ROM. Library management will need to decide where the responsibility for these difficult decisions lies.

Budgeting

Many CD-ROM purchases are committed expenditure in the same way as periodicals. But all services, even one off purchases of textual databases, carry recurrent equipment and maintenance costs. Networking databases will further increase costs, and staff dealing with suppliers will need to sharpen up their negotiating skills. The CD-ROM market is maturing quickly, but there are likely to be substantial price variations for some time, and the attitude of vendors to networking remains unpredictable. Spreadsheet software can be enormously helpful in showing the pattern of expenditure and predicting the effects of different strategies.

Summary statements will help management to monitor the pattern of expenditure.

Ordering and recording

Once a decision has been made about the supplier and any network agreements have been made, then ordering, receipt and recording may logically reside in the periodicals department, with its facilities for regular receipt of items. However, as more non-serial products are made available in the library, this should be kept under review.

Relationship with other parts of the library

Introduction of CD-ROM services will have knock-on effects on other parts of the library.

Enquiry desk

Enquiry desk staff will need to train in using CD-ROM products, and in basic technical trouble-shooting. Staff will need to consider whether they should leave the desk, possibly for extended periods, to give instruction in databases located some distance away. For networked databases, a terminal at the desk is invaluable for brief demonstrations.

Online services

CD-ROM databases in the library will reduce the number of online search requests. This may lead to reorganization of the service to concentrate online skills in a smaller number of staff. Online service staff may already be involved with CD-ROM, but if not their skills equip them to contribute to this area very easily.

Inter-library loans

Most libraries experience an increase in the number of inter-library loan requests with the introduction of bibliographical databases on CD-ROM. Libraries may need to re-evaluate their ILL policies to keep numbers under control. For example training users how to use the service responsibly, or introducing mechanisms, such as (increased) charges.

Circulation desk

Extra traffic will be generated at the circulation desk if a decision is made to lend CD-ROM discs across the counter for use within the library. Information services staff will need to check with their colleagues in reader services that this is feasible and acceptable.

Location of the service

Library clienteles are increasingly 'information users' rather than 'library users', and so the question: 'where do we locate the CD-ROM service' soon becomes: 'how can we network this to all parts of the library and to all branches', and indeed in academic and special libraries: 'how can we network this to the user's desk', because this is undoubtedly where the user finds it most convenient to access such services.

Nevertheless, there remains the question of where the library terminals for network access are to be located, and there will always be a number of products which are not networked either because the level of use does not justify the cost, or because of licensing restrictions.

Ideally a CD-ROM workstation requires:

- Electric sockets
- Suitable lighting
- Desk space for papers and note taking
- Access to a printer
- Access to the network
- Access to library staff for help and advice.

Many libraries will find it difficult to find any space at all for CD-ROM workstations, let alone a large quiet area for a cluster of workstations with easy access to library staff, and initially accommodation may be unsuitable. Those responsible for the service will need to draw up good specifications for furniture and space requirements, make a strong case for improved accommodation, and be ready to press this need when reorganization of any part of the library is under consideration.

The criteria for location of CD-ROM workstations are examined separately below, but external factors will play a part in decisions, and a mixture of approaches is increasingly likely.

Subject floors

Dispersing CD-ROM workstations through the library on subject floors or subject areas brings services into the mainstream of provision in the subject. Specialized subject staff will be on hand to introduce the resource to new users. On the other hand, this support may not be available throughout library opening hours, and technical support, if it cannot be offered by subject staff, may not be on hand immediately.

Near the enquiry desk

Locating CD-ROM workstations by the enquiry desk will ensure that assistance is available throughout library opening hours, although, realistically, expertise will be spread more thinly across the available products. Technical support may be available more easily. This location will facilitate loan of discs for stand-alone databases.

Importance of technical support

Let's not be mealy mouthed about this, technical support is not an issue or a challenge, it's a downright problem. But it is not unique to CD-ROM services. It relates to any form of IT in the library, whether for staff or reader use. Libraries have managed technical support for major library systems very well. Usually only one suite of software is involved, and all administration is handled centrally by a small group of staff. Access by other staff and library users can be strictly limited by function. As the number of individual microcomputers and peripherals has grown and the variety of software has mushroomed, technical support for both staff and users has become crucial. Some technical support issues relating to CD-ROM in particular are:

Variety of interfaces

Staff who work on enquiry duty irregularly are faced with a wide array of interfaces and will need at least a brief introduction to each one, which can amount to a lot of extra training where large numbers of staff are involved. Some staff will find no difficulty with this, but others will be quite overwhelmed. The same is true for readers. Many younger readers will welcome the chance to try out skills gained at school, but less confident readers may need a lot of hand-holding.

Troubleshooting

'The printer won't work.' 'The cursor is stuck.' 'I can't find anything on my subject.' All these are regular queries, and each can have a variety of causes, from the online button on the printer, to a fault on the network. Once again, training staff to become confident in dealing with these issues can be time consuming, particularly as diagnosing the fault can take a lot of experience. Staff can be helped greatly by the provision of troubleshooting checklists and manuals of database quirks. Regular maintenance of printers, including changing ribbons and checking that there is plenty of paper, is an effective way of keeping queries to a minimum. An alternative tried in some libraries is not to provide a printer at all!

Networking

CD-ROM is essentially a single user medium, and all attempts at networking have to overcome this. Couple this with the novelty and fluidity of much of the search software and there are the makings of a very complex system. Inevitably the skills associated with such complexity are not yet widely available, and libraries will have to consider whether they can develop and support a CD-ROM network.

Many libraries have the staff and skills to handle technical support very well independently. But where skills are limited the obvious route to regular support is through the computing section of the organization, and indeed the impetus for the development of CD-ROM services may well come from this area. The success of this approach will depend once again on personal and organizational factors. There are honourable exceptions, but in many organizations the progress of co-operation between computing service and library staff has been slow. In a small library within a business environment, library staff may simply not have the time to build up the technical skills necessary. Here, the commercial imperative should ensure good co-operation. In a larger organization, such as an academic institution, such links may need to be nurtured. Good relationships between heads of service and strategic definition of respective roles will help to avoid misunderstanding.

Collection and use of management information

In any library, CD-ROM services remain expensive in terms of purchase of products, purchase and maintenance of equipment and in staff time, and could take a large proportion of the budget. It makes sense, therefore to monitor the cost and the benefits of CD-ROM products.

Library staff must think through what management information is required and how it is going to be used before deciding how it will be collected. Information on use of databases can contribute to purchasing, retention and networking decisions. The amount of time a product is used, and the number of simultaneous log-ons for networked products, indicate the level of demand and whether access should be reduced or increased. It will help to show if a stand-alone product should be networked, or if a networked product is earning its licence fee. Carefully chosen software will also control access to the products, restricting users to the licensed number. As with budgeting for CD-ROM, spreadsheets can be used to tabulate data collected and to produce predictions and summaries. Combining data from these two exercises will give good information to support decision making.

Manual collection

Carefully designed booking sheets to collect information from stand-alone workstations will provide a lot of useful data, such as use of individual products, and, from the number of forward bookings, how much demand there is for the service. Users may be asked to give their department, as well as the product they are using, and could even be asked to comment on the products themselves. The disadvantage of this method is that inevitably some information will be missing.

If discs are lent across the counter for use at stand-alone machines, then information about users can be collected at this point.

Logging software

Access to networked databases will be controlled through a menuing system, such as Saber LAN Manager or SiteLock, and these programs will yield much information about levels of use. Unless passwords are used for access, then there will be no information about users (department, etc.). Libraries will have to consider whether the information and security gained from using passwords is worth the amount of staff time involved in administering them.

Controlling access

Ideally, access to CD-ROM databases would be available to all users as and when required. For a number of reasons access will continue to be controlled for some time.

Level of demand

We have not yet begun to approach the limits of demand for computerized information retrieval, including CD-ROM. In the British academic environment the amount of 'search time' available grew out of all recognition with the introduction of nationally networked services via JANET (Joint Academic NETwork) in 1991 (the ISI databases and later *Embase*, the computerized version of *Excerpta Medica*). In the space of 12 months in my own library, searching went from about 300 online searches each year carried out by library staff, to some 1200 ISI accesses per month by users across the campus. As each new CD-ROM workstation is added to the library system, it is used throughout library opening hours, and workstations are booked days, and sometimes weeks, ahead. Librarians must recognize this level of un-met demand from our users as a challenge for the future.

Cost

The cost of equipment, CD-ROM subscriptions, network licensing fees and staff input is such that hard choices face all libraries when deciding on where CD-ROM access ranks in importance in relation to other 'traditional' library services.

Licensing restrictions

Some database suppliers set generous limits on networking and user groups. Others are more restrictive, and may limit use to one workstation, or to particular groups.

Rationing

Where demand outstrips supply in any context, then control will be required to ensure fair distribution of the scarce resource. Booking for stand-alone CD-ROM workstations could be done centrally, at the enquiry point for example, so that all details can be taken by library staff. An alternative is to place booking forms beside workstations, allowing readers to book ahead themselves.

Passwords

Access to networked databases can be restricted by password, giving the library control over who has access, as well as information about users. However, administration of such a system is a heavy overhead and libraries will need to consider if enough information and control are forthcoming to make the effort worthwhile.

Loan of discs

Discs which are not networked can be held at the counter and lent for inhouse use via the circulation system. This will ensure that only authorized groups have access, and will give some data on levels of use.

Charging

Libraries will need to examine licence agreements carefully before adopting any charging mechanism for CD-ROM access. If charging is in order, then time on machines can be charged out using for example, photocopy charge cards. These cards can also be used to control access to printers. Note however, that there will be a considerable cost involved in installing such a system, which will have to be covered before the system will generate revenue.

Receipt and loading of updates

The technical requirements of new products should be addressed before ordering:

- Is the available hardware appropriate?
- Is there enough memory?
- Does the product require a windowing environment?
- Are there enough CD-ROM drives?
- Will the budget support the purchase of new equipment if necessary?

When the product arrives, it will be loaded onto the appropriate machine, or onto the network, and tested before it is made available to library users. Staff will be informed and trained in using the new service. The library's documentation will be updated, and some libraries will prepare a help sheet in line with existing documentation.

Most databases have regular updates, both to the data on the discs, and to the searching software. When new discs arrive in the library, procedures will ensure that the disc is added to the system, and the software is updated, in a timely way. Communication between the library service staff and technical support staff may need to stress the importance of this.

Particular problems may arise with software upgrades. As the searching software for bibliographical databases has grown more sophisticated the specification of the equipment required has increased. This can cause dismay when a carefully planned funding bid is sabotaged by the requirement for a more expensive machine with the next software upgrade. The moral must be to specify the biggest machine you can afford, and keep your fingers crossed.

It is not unknown for suppliers to cause further havoc by releasing software before it has been fully tested, so that it has to be withdrawn from use. This is bad for the library in two ways: time is wasted in trying to solve problems, and bad public relations with users. The plurality of suppliers and interfaces can work in the consumer's favour, as it is possible to change to a different supplier if such problems occur. Suppliers should be left in no doubt that such sloppiness is not acceptable.

Conclusion

This chapter has dealt with a range of management issues which libraries will confront when developing CD-ROM services. With careful planning the issues can be resolved successfully, and the library will reap the benefits of providing a highly valued service to library users. The following are paramount in the successful implementation of new computerized information services:

The library must know what it is trying to achieve. CD-ROM can be a difficult medium, and a strategic view is required to provide a framework for rational decision making and to set CD-ROM within the overall context of information provision.

The library must respond flexibly to the demands of staff, users and the technology itself. Communication across traditional departmental boundaries is essential.

Library staff must be prepared to train, experiment and adapt their skills to the new media, of which CD-ROM is such an important and fascinating part.

Note

1. The Electronic Library: Challenges for the 90's. Imperial College London, 9th June 1992.

CHAPTER FOUR

Resourcing issues

Christine Abbott and Nick Smith

Introduction

According to marketing theory, purchasers of new products can be divided into five broad groups – the innovators, the early adopters, the early majority, the late majority and the laggards – each of whom display different characteristics in their buying behaviour (Rogers, 1962). The process by which Library & Information Services (LIS) managers have adopted CD-ROM conforms to this model. For the small percentage of the profession who were the innovators, the potential offered by CD-ROM was perceived to outweigh the financial risk. For the early adopters, the principal concern was to find ways of resourcing the purchase from within tight budgets. As time has elapsed, and the sceptical majority, and even some of the laggards, have come to adopt CD-ROM, it has become clear that questions of resourcing and acquisition are much more complex than simply 'finding the money'. Integrating CD-ROM into the resourcing process has become a major strategic issue which, potentially, requires the reallocation of resources across the whole of the LIS budget.

The penetration of CD-ROM and other electronic products into UK academic and public libraries has been well documented recently by East (1991). He makes it clear that, with a few exceptions, most LIS managers' reactions to this shift have so far been tactical rather than strategic. No doubt this is partly because the sums of money concerned have represented a relatively small proportion of total acquisition budgets. As long as CD-ROM penetration into a particular library remains slight, this seems a reasonable approach to adopt. In some cases, however, a considerable shift has already taken place from print to electronic sources, and significant amounts of money are already being committed. For example, Aston University now spends on electronic sources an amount equivalent to more than twice its spending on printed abstracting and indexing sources; an amount that represents some 15% of its total acquisitions budget. Similarly, at UMIST (University of Manchester Institute of Science and Technology) the amount committed is between 7% and 8% of the acquisitions budget (Day, 1992). At this sort of level, adoption of CD-ROM clearly has strategic implications which must be addressed. The strategic issues primarily concern resourcing, but also involve the conceptual questions raised by the changes in the methods of information delivery. Once these issues have been resolved, however, the strategic impact of further purchases will diminish (unless these additional products represent radical alternatives to current information retrieval and delivery mechanisms). In due course, then, the process of CD-ROM selection should become seamlessly integrated into the library's overall 'collection' development policy.

It is our contention, then, that there is some kind of 'strategic threshold' involved in the introduction of CD-ROM and other electronic products, at which the LIS manager will have to confront strategic, rather than just operational, decisions associated with their introduction, but beyond which they can be managed within the new operational framework. Where does this threshold lie? We suspect that the answer will vary from library to library. At Aston, that threshold was probably crossed at somewhere around 10% of the acquisitions budget, representing the cost of some 10 products (including their networking fees). However, perhaps a more important indicator that the threshold has been reached may be the number of users (or uses) of the systems. How many users constitute the 'critical mass' needed to cross the threshold, though, we do not know. Clearly, more research is needed into this topic.

Funding issues

Any decision to invest in new services poses similar operational questions. Does the new service represent value for money? What is the cost benefit? Can we afford it? Where will the money come from? Since the first CD-ROM titles to come on the market were straightforward electronic substitutes for existing (mainly bibliographic) serial titles, the purchasing decision tended to be based on the perceived advantages of the new format, and upon crude cost comparisons: if to subscribe to the title on CD-ROM was cheaper, or only a little more expensive, than its equivalent in print, then the purchase was likely to be approved, despite the fact that, in many cases, the printed equivalent was not initially cancelled as a 'trade-off'. However, a true comparison between the relative costs of a CD-ROM and a serial title in hard-copy should entail life-cycle costing (Stephens, 1989), as well. To the cost of a serial subscription in hard-copy need to be added the 'hidden' costs of acquisition, such as processing, binding, shelving and reshelving. In libraries which operate as autonomous cost centres the cost of the space occupied by that title needs to be taken into account. Even in situations where this does not pertain, the opportunity cost of housing serial backruns should be considered. Cost comparisons should also include a consideration of the likely effects of inflation on the cost of the hard-copy subscription in future years. This, of course, is a problematic area, since inflation is extremely hard to predict from year to year. Furthermore, while costs of subscriptions to CD-ROMs have remained relatively stable in the recent past, it is still uncertain what pricing strategies publishers will adopt towards CD-ROMs and their networking in the future.

If CD-ROM costs were to follow serials and begin to show year-on-year increases in excess of standard inflation, then methods of cost containment would have to be found. In some cases, LIS managers have had to find savings on serial costs by reducing or completely eliminating binding. A comparable option does not exist for CD-ROMs. One answer to constrained resources might be to charge for printing (as discussed below). However, in institutions in which information is free at the point of use this may be an unacceptable move. If funds become so constrained that a CD-ROM title has to be cancelled, then additional problems face the LIS manager. If one cancels a serial subscription, one is at least able to retain the back issues. In many cases, as we shall see later, if a CD-ROM is cancelled the subscriber is forced to return even the previous years' CD-ROMs to the publisher.

Just as the decision to purchase a serial title brings with it associated acquisition and life cycle costs, the acquisition of a CD-ROM title poses questions of capital and recurrent funding beyond that of the CD-ROM subscription itself. The introduction of just one CD-ROM normally requires the purchase of a personal computer (PC) and associated equipment. This equipment will, in turn, need maintenance. Its capital cost should be amortized over its notional lifetime, and a provision built into the costings to allow for its eventual replacement. It has become accepted practice in most libraries that use of a hard-copy journal is free, but that users pay to photocopy an extract from a journal. Similar decisions need to be made in relation to CD-ROMs. For example, who pays for the printing costs? Should print-outs from a CD-ROM be priced so as to recoup all the costs of the printer consumables, or should the library only demand a contribution towards these costs? Furthermore, offering a CD-ROM service normally requires a significant input of professional time: to prepare explanatory leaflets and manuals, to train other LIS staff who may be involved in supporting the service, and to train users. The continuing requirement for staff support, which is likely to be greater than that required for the serial in hard-copy, should not be forgotten when working out the cost equation; neither should the requirement for training facilities and equipment. Finally, there will be additional equipment and subscription costs incurred if the product is eventually networked.

When seen as a substitute for mediated online searching, CD-ROM has much to commend it from a budgetary point of view. The difficulty of estimating the cost of an online search makes online a difficult area to monitor and control. By contrast, CD-ROM costs (once pricing structures for printing are decided) are generally much more predictable and controllable by the individual manager, hence contributing to the attractiveness of the product. Furthermore, the high unit costs of mediated online searching, and the amount of staff time involved, make it practically impossible to extend such services to all users. In general, subscription-based, end-user-oriented CD-ROMs do not suffer from such disadvantages. However, this situation does not necessarily extend to the case of electronic journals on CD-ROM.

CD-ROM products such as ADONIS, *Business Periodicals Ondisc* (BPO) and *IEEE/IEE Publications Ondisc* (IPO), which contain the scanned images of printed journals, are document-delivery or on-demand publishing systems. For ADONIS at least, a royalty must be paid whenever an article is printed out (the IPO subscription does allow for up to 25 000 pages to be printed by academic institutions before royalty costs are incurred, and there is no per article royalty charge for BPO at present). However, in calculating the financial desirability of such systems, one should also take into account possible trade-off factors, such as cancellation of the titles, covered by the service, that the library already holds; the associated savings incurred by the elimination of the life-cycle costs of those titles; and the potential for income generation by supplying documents within copyright to other users in the locality. Nevertheless, if the ADONIS royalties precedent prevails, one of the major advantages of CD-ROM products – their financial stability and predictability – may be lost, and the spectre of the 'bottomless-pit', which was often invoked in arguments against the subsidization of mediated online services, will rear its ugly head once again. This could lead to the ironic situation in which, just as the increased sophistication of these products is beginning to make them more attractive to the end-user, the difficulty of cost control is reducing their appeal to the LIS manager.

When CD-ROMs have no direct equivalents in hard-copy the decision to purchase must be based primarily on the potential benefits to clients from doing so (assuming that funds can be found). It is in such cases that LIS managers can expect to have the most difficulty in persuading their users, and those who control the finances, particularly if use of the service requires a change to the orthodox method of information retrieval or study. In such situations the existence of 'pump-priming' funds becomes valuable. For example, over the last three years or so, Aston University has used non-recurrent money to introduce a number of additional CD-ROMs. During this period, CD-ROM and other (online) electronic services have won the acceptance of the academic community to such an extent that academic staff now set undergraduate projects based around their use. Discontinuation of any of these services would, therefore, be viewed with dismay by academic staff and students alike. However, had we not been able to use non-recurrent funds to test the water in this way, it is questionable whether the relevant academic staff would have been sufficiently convinced of the value of these services at the outset, to find the money themselves from within their own departmental budgets; neither is it likely that they would have agreed to cut serials or book expenditure to finance them. This dilemma has already proved to be a stumbling block for those institutions which operate rigid formula-funding with little by way of contingencies and little flexibility within the formula. Continuation of such 'pump-primed' services may become a problem, of course, but their success can be used to argue the case for additional funding to maintain them. In future, though, the substitution of electronic for printed resources is likely to be the main way in which most academic libraries will be able to increase the proportion of electronic services that they offer, while remaining within constrained budgets. If the cost equation between the electronic and printed equivalents does not balance, then this substitution will only be achieved by sacrificing other 'marginal' titles as well.

Practical issues of monitoring and control of expenditure also arise with the introduction of a wide range of CD-ROMs into a library. While most library housekeeping systems contain acquisitions modules that adequately control the serials acquisition process, their design may be less well adapted to cope with integrating new types of facility such as CD-ROMs. To separate off purchases in CD-ROM format into their own cost centre may have implications for the accuracy of the library's management information, such as analyses of expenditure by material type (serial, standing order, monograph, etc.). Conversely, the practice of purchasing serial titles on CD-ROM from the serials fund can greatly complicate analyses of changes in materials costs over time. For example, at Aston University, until this year, certain CD-ROMs that had direct equivalents in hard-copy abstracts or indexes were purchased from the serials budget. Gradually, titles became networked and the networking fees were also charged to the serials budget. As the number of CD-ROM titles of this sort multiplied, so this system of allocation became increasingly misleading, with the potential for distorting the average cost of 'real' serial titles and year-on-year inflation data. As a consequence, from this financial year onwards, all recurrent CD-ROM costs for all titles have been allocated to a special electronic information services budget head.

To summarize, then, as increasing proportions of libraries' acquisitions budgets are spent on CD-ROM products, the traditional distinction between equipment (capital expenditure) and supplies (recurrent expenditure) becomes harder to sustain. This shift is not easy to manage, particularly in those institutions where finances for equipment and supplies are governed by different resource allocation processes, and where funds are not interchangeable between the two areas. So, the adoption of CD-ROM, particularly when multiplied several times over, blurs the traditional divisions between heads of budget to such an extent that a re-examination of whole areas of resource allocation may be needed.

Product selection

Many libraries now possess written collection development policies upon which their selection decisions are based, and it could be argued that in such cases CD-ROM products should not be treated any differently from printed or microform media. Ideally, that would be the case; however, unless the policy explicitly addresses the particular issues raised by the introduction of CD-ROM (and other electronic) products, some guidance is still likely to be necessary for the LIS staff responsible for selection decisions or recommendations. As the above section illustrates, the selection of a CD-ROM product is likely to have a more far-reaching impact upon users, staff and the library's budget than most traditional media. Some considerable investment of staff time may therefore be necessary to produce a convincing case for the allocation of funds.

Checklists are a generally applicable means of aiding the selector to make his or her recommendation. Such checklists can encompass all the relevant issues that need to be taken into account in the selection process, including implementation and monitoring of the resulting service. Aston University LIS uses checklists in its selection and implementation processes, and Haar *et al.* (1990) give an example of a selection checklist used at the Virginia Commonwealth University. A typical checklist might cover the following broad areas:

1) Customer issues relating to the size and composition of the intended audience; their status (whether teaching/research staff, undergraduate or postgraduate student, etc. in an academic library); potential applications of the product (specific research projects; known coursework, etc.); and so on.
2) Budgetary and acquisitions issues, including both capital and recurrent expenditure; trade-offs from cancelling printed equivalents; possible savings or increased expenditure on inter-library loans; additional cost of networking; etc.
3) Product and supplier issues such as comparisons of the same product offered by different suppliers (*Medline* is a good example); comparisons of the printed, online and CD-ROM versions; quality of documentation and support from the supplier; and so on.
4) Technical issues covering the software and hardware needed; ease of use of the interface software; networking compatibility; etc.
5) Implementation issues listing all the stages necessary for a successful launch of the product to users, followed by continuing support and monitoring of the service by LIS staff.

Purchasing, leasing and licensing agreements

Most LIS managers are accustomed to purchasing and owning the majority of materials that comprize their collections. Subsequently, those materials are normally made available for users to enjoy without restriction, and without further financial commitment to the supplier. Inter-library loans (document delivery) and mediated online searches have been the main exceptions to this rule – in these cases the library acts as an intermediary between the supplier and the user, but does not usually retain the information itself;

furthermore, charges for obtaining the information may be passed on to the user.

CD-ROM products add a new dimension to the concept of 'access, rather than acquisition', as many CD-ROM versions of printed or online bibliographic sources are available under licence conditions that permit only leasing of the product, rather than purchase. Although the source is locally accessible, it has not been truly acquired, for the library may only be able to retain it so long as it continues to pay the annual subscription. A typical arrangement might involve leasing a five year 'moving window', with archival discs being retained, either free of charge or for some further non-recurrent fee. The licence conditions usually also pertain to the archival discs, and if the subscription is terminated all of the discs revert to the supplier. This poses a real dilemma for LIS managers – should they retain the printed equivalent, assuming that they already subscribe to it, or should they cancel it and risk a substantial hole in their collections at some later stage, if finances become constrained?

As CD-ROM product penetration into libraries increases, it is possible that most libraries will find themselves with 'collections' of secondary sources that are leased rather than owned. In the case of collections of primary material such as ADONIS, the situation is even more complicated, because, although the information may be purchased and retained on site, it is not accessible in printed form without the payment of a royalty charge. It may be that the market is still in its infancy and that many of these inconsistencies will be ironed out. Then again, it may be that a diversity of 'purchasing' arrangements will persist, thereby increasing the complexity of the acquisitions manager's job.

Apart from the leasing aspects, licence agreements may impose a range of other restrictions on how the information may be used and distributed. Networking is usually only permitted provided that further fees are paid according to the number of users, or the number of designated workstations, allowed to access the database simultaneously. There are exceptions to this rule, and some databases may be networked free within educational environments. Furthermore, it is clear that some suppliers still have not formulated a policy on networking charges, and many have just followed the lead of those suppliers who were first in the marketplace. This means that there may well be scope for LIS managers to negotiate deals to suit their local circumstances, and it is certainly the case that suppliers need to consider more flexible options than the usual one of banding, i.e. charging for a base subscription, plus 2–10 simultaneous users, or 11–20, and so on. Networked CD-ROM systems may be configured to restrict the maximum possible number of simultaneous users of a product (either through the networking software, for example Novell, or through the optical networking software, for example OptiNet), so institutions will be able to monitor the usage of particular products and should be given the option to pay fees that reflect actual, rather than potential, usage. A further restriction on networking may confine it to a single site (for example a campus, not just a single building), so there are obvious cost implications for multi-site institutions.

Restrictions may also be placed upon the way in which the information is used, once retrieved. Needless to say, resale, or repackaging for resale, without permission is almost always prohibited, but limits may also be placed upon the re-use of the information, particularly if it is subsequently stored on magnetic media. As many users now routinely download information from databases, and personal bibliographic retrieval systems are becoming more popular, this almost certainly means that many users are breaking the suppliers' licence conditions by storing at least some of the results of their searches permanently. As it is extremely unlikely that this practice can be stopped, it would be sensible for the suppliers to recognize that it happens, even that it is desirable, and provide facilities for it to be done legitimately, as has been done with the downloading option on some online systems. This might well have cost implications for LIS managers, if the option carried an additional fee with it. However, while price increases would not be welcomed by LIS managers, it would remove the need to worry about copyright implications, and would stimulate the re-use of the information in group teaching and research situations.

In the particular case of financial databases on CD-ROM, access by third parties may not be allowed, unless a further fee is negotiated. It is obviously in the suppliers' interests to ensure that companies do not by-pass direct subscriptions with them by relying on academic institutions for cheap-rate access. However, it does put academic libraries in something of a quandary, especially if they already offer some form of business information service to local companies, or if they have replaced a previously open-access source with one that is now restricted to members of the institution. On the one hand, they may find it difficult to control access to the service by outsiders, or by legitimate users on behalf of outsiders, while on the other, companies may not be able to afford to pay the subscription fees for a service that they may use only infrequently. The obvious solution is for the suppliers to offer some additional third-party option at a realistic fee, thereby increasing their overall income and satisfying a wider range of customers.

Finally, LIS managers should check carefully the details pertaining to termination of the contract for each product. The notice required to terminate the contract, by either side, is usually at least one calendar month before the renewal date, but may be as much as three months prior to that date. As it is unlikely that all contracts will have been entered into at the same time of the year, a review mechanism must be established to ensure that a contract can be terminated without penalty, if required – e.g. for financial reasons, or in favour of another product. The best way to ensure that this happens is to build into the LIS's operational plan a review of each contract at the appropriate time of the year.

'Acquisition' arrangements

For purchases of serial titles, it is normally the case that libraries prefer to deal with one or two agents, rather than with a large number of individual publishers. Although conventional serials agents do handle CD-ROM products, specialized agents also exist (e.g. SilverPlatter, MicroInfo, Optech, KimStacks and so on). CD-ROM product penetration into UK libraries is still relatively limited (compared to numbers of serial titles held) – on average somewhere between 12 and 20 products per academic library (Day, 1992). This number is small enough to be manageable by dealing directly with the suppliers as, no doubt, many libraries still do. But there are both advantages and disadvantages to this method of trading. On the one hand, it offers the possibility of negotiating locally favourable conditions directly with the supplier, but on the other, one loses the negotiating strength of an agent or consortium acting on behalf of a large number of customers. If the number of CD-ROM products per library increases dramatically over the next few years, it is likely that using one or two channels for purchasing will become more efficient and effective, and hence increasingly common.

However, when considering negotiating strength, perhaps the correct comparison to be made is not between CD-ROM agents and agents for printed materials, but between both of these and CHEST (the Combined Higher Education Software Team), which, in the UK, has been responsible for negotiating a number of deals with suppliers for the wide-area networking of online databases to the academic community; most notably the Institute for Scientific Information's databases, which are provided by the Bath Information and Data Services (BIDS).

It is probably true to say that the jury is still out on the question of whether local area networking of CD-ROM databases, or wide area networking, such as BIDS via JANET (Joint Academic NETwork), is technically and financially preferable. In each case, LIS managers will need to weigh up the relative advantages of three main factors: pricing, transparency (visibility from different types of workstation), and ease of use of the interface. The costs of the licences negotiated by CHEST are comparable to those of networked CD-ROM products (at least, if the latter are limited to about 10 simultaneous users), all being in the approximate range £4K to £8K. The CHEST products, however, have the advantage that they are normally easily accessible from any type of terminal, including Macintoshes, whilst the CD-ROM products are at present largely confined to IBM-compatible PCs only, and networking may pose additional problems. Another advantage of the CHEST deal is that it allows a high number of simultaneous users from any one institution; for example, access to the BIDS database is currently limited to 120 simultaneous users, within which there is no limit on the number of simultaneous users from a given site. This advantage rapidly turns into a disadvantage, though, if the global upper limit is frequently reached, because institutions do not have local discretion to give priority to certain users. This can cause difficulties, for example when running training classes. However, perhaps the most crucial factor is the nature of the interface, which has to support a wide spectrum of users, from the totally naive to experienced searchers. Command-driven interfaces are likely to require far too much support from LIS staff to be a realistic option, so menu-driven systems will probably be the norm until more sophisticated, but intuitive, graphics-based systems become widespread.

A third option to those of local CD-ROM networking and wide-area networking, is local or regional area networking, from hard-disc, of a database distributed initially either on magnetic tape or on CD-ROM. This option is particularly prevalent in the USA, but is now being introduced in the UK as well. However, costs appear to be significantly higher than for the other two options, which may make it viable only in the context of local or regional collaboration between institutions.

Processing implications

CD-ROM products should not have any major implications for the acquisition and cataloguing processes. In general, they can be treated in the same way as books or serial titles, as appropriate. However, some modification to these processes is necessary, as CD-ROMs, unlike books and serials, cannot simply be placed on the shelves once they have been processed. They will either have to be loaded onto a stand-alone workstation or, increasingly, onto a 'tower' or 'jukebox' system coupled to an optical server. They may also incorporate, or come with, updating software that will have to be loaded onto the CD-ROM workstation or fileserver. Superseded discs may have to be returned to the supplier or destroyed. Thus some form of 'routing' information will have to be included in the acquisitions record for each title, to ensure that post-acquisitions processing is carried out by the designated person, be it information specialist, computer officer, or whoever.

Furthermore, for services like ADONIS, which allow large numbers of printed periodical titles to be replaced or supplemented by their electronic equivalents, and new titles to be added, but only in CD-ROM format, catalogue entries for each title will have to be amended or created to show their availability in the new format.

CD-ROM as a medium for full-text and image databases

Although, so far, the main impact of CD-ROM on libraries has been as a substitute for secondary (bibliographic) sources, CD-ROM has also proved ideal as a medium for distributing primary numeric and textual information. Thus we have seen the emergence of CD-ROM versions of printed or microform products containing company financial information, law reports, census data, cartographic data, and so on. Not only is it easy to retrieve this data, it is also possible to manipulate it in ways that were not possible before without rekeying the data into a computer. In this context, CD-ROM may be considered to be an enhanced replacement for microform, in the sense that information may be archived securely (especially if networked), retrieved more easily than on microform, and copied in a form that is susceptible to transformation, if necessary. In most cases, however, what has been stored is not an exact facsimile of the original product, but merely an ASCII representation of the text.

More recently, CD-ROM products have emerged that carry facsimile copies (scanned digitized images) of the original printed pages of journals. Typical examples, as mentioned before, include ADONIS, BPO and IPO. These pose new challenges for both LIS staff and users. Even the phenomenal storage capacity of CD-ROM (relative to its size) is currently insufficient to cope easily with the volume of data produced by digitizing images of periodical articles. Thus four or five hundred periodical titles require something of the order of 50 or 60 discs per annum, when distributed on CD-ROM. This number of discs is only easily manageable using jukebox technology (although BPO does offer a manual carousel option), which is still in its infancy and relatively expensive – approximately £7K for a device that will store 100 discs and has a single read-head. All in all, the initial outlay for equipment may be of the order of £10K to £15K. In addition to this, as we have already seen, there are the recurrent subscription costs, royalty charges (if any), and trade-offs to take into account.

Furthermore, the networking of digitized images presents a new technical challenge – it may well be the case that most current networks are simply not capable of carrying this sort of information without significant degradation of network speed for all users. Thus, the concept of the distributed library, apparently offered by CD-ROM technology, once again recedes over the horizon, at least for image databases. In the future, though, as institutions install, or upgrade to, networks that have much wider bandwidth, then distribution of digitized images will become much more common. In addition, there are already plans to implement this kind of upgrading on the UK's national academic network, JANET. We will then be faced again with the alternatives of local area networking of digitized images from CD-ROM or other sources, versus wide-area networking from central databases. It is clear, then, that these new CD-ROM products present an even more complex situation for the LIS manager to deal with, than the 'traditional' CD-ROMs do.

For the user, too, the advantages of such systems may also appear to be mixed – at least with the current state of the technology. Certainly, they offer users a vastly expanded set of periodical holdings sited locally, but unless the system can be networked, it may act as a bottle-neck, by restricting access to one user at a time. Furthermore, those periodicals are now in digitized form and must be retrieved by searching an index of some sort first (the digital image, itself, is not searchable). Once retrieved, the image may not be easily readable on-screen, in which case it will have to be printed-out, perhaps at a cost to the user. More importantly, the traditional features of printed journals – portability and browsability – have been largely lost, and the latter has been shown to be an important factor to take into account when making judgements about the feasibility of trade-offs between printed and electronic journals (MacDougall et al., 1986). It is essential, therefore, that the views of the potential users of these systems are sought by suppliers, when designing them, and by LIS managers, when contemplating their introduction.

Conclusions

The implications of CD-ROM for resourcing in libraries is both operational and strategic. At the operational level the LIS manager has to consider issues such as the additional equipment required, its maintenance and eventual replacement. There are also staffing issues related to training of LIS staff and users, and continuing support for the service. Issues connected with the costs of printing have to be considered, and may be analogous to those raised by charging for photocopying. Many of these and the other operational issues to be considered are similar to those involved in the introduction of, for example, microform equipment, albeit on a different scale, and so do not represent conceptually new problems for LIS managers. However, there is a threshold at which CD-ROM becomes so important as a medium for information provision that it ceases to be a purely operational matter, and its strategic implications need to be addressed.

The obvious popularity of non-mediated electronic services, whether distributed on CD-ROM or wide-area networks, means that our traditional concept of the library as a collection of materials that are purchased, stored locally, and owned, will need to change radically. CD-ROM is one of the key elements in the new paradigm that emphasizes libraries' primary concern as being with information access, retrieval, and management, whether that information is stored locally or remotely, and whether it be purchased in advance, paid for at the point of use, or leased. The challenge for the LIS manager is to bring about the transition from the old to the new, efficiently and effectively.

References

Day, M.P. (1992) *CD Networking*. Preliminary report on a joint IUCC/SCONUL-directed project entitled 'The assessment and evaluation of networked CD-ROMs as academic information sources'. Presented at CD Impacts 1992, 24th November 1992, Church House Conference Centre, London

East, H. (1991) *Balancing the books: resourcing electronic information services in academic and public libraries*. CCIS Policy Paper no. 3; British Library R&D Report 6057. London: Centre for Communication and Information Studies, Polytechnic of Central London

Haar, J. *et al.* (1990) Choosing CD-ROM products. *College & Research Libraries News*, **51**, 839–841

MacDougall, A.F. *et al.* (1986) *Modelling of journal versus article acquisition by libraries*. British National Bibliography Research Fund Report 23. Loughborough: Pilkington Library, Loughborough University

Rogers E.M. (1962) *Diffusion of innovations*. New York: Free Press. Quoted by

P. Kotler. (1988) *Marketing management: analysis, planning, implementation, and control*. 6th edn. Englewood Cliffs, NJ: Prentice Hall

Stephens, A. (1989) The application of life cycle costing in libraries. *British Journal of Academic Librarianship*, **3**, 82–88

Case study: Use of a full-text product in a library: *Business Periodicals Ondisc* at the University of Warwick Library

Geoffrey E. Cleave

Introduction

Libraries have usually set themselves two principal objectives, to provide a document delivery service to satisfy the formulated needs of their users, and, secondly, to provide a support service to enable researchers to identify particular documents containing information of value. In general, libraries have struggled to meet these objectives, especially it would seem simultaneously. Information searching in the pre-computer age was laborious and distinctly unfriendly. With online access it became efficient, but too expensive to be more than a limited facility operated by intermediaries. CD-ROMs offered solutions to the information retrieval problems, but came when libraries were facing increasing pressures on internal funds and a propensity for external services to become slow and costly. A new crisis was emerging which linked easy access to good bibliographic records with a collapse in document supply. It seemed that readers again would not be satisfied.

Business Periodicals Ondisc (BPO) offers a radical solution to this dilemma in that it brings together a searching system (ABI/INFORM) with a collection of full-text periodicals on a set of CD-ROMs. It is mounted on a dedicated workstation with a high-resolution monitor, twin CD-ROM drives for the index and image discs, and two printers, one of which is a laser printer for the output of the full text. It is a partial system in two senses. Firstly, only 330 of the 800 journals in ABI/INFORM database are actually included in the full-text service, though this 40% is still a remarkably large collection. Secondly, searching is only conducted on the bibliographic record (including abstract) and not the whole of the article. There are several published descriptions of the system (e.g. Thompson and Evans, 1989; Klein, 1991; and Stewart, 1991).

The purpose of this paper is to describe the experience of the University of Warwick Library in using BPO over a trial period and the first year of operation. It will, therefore, make some contribution to the discussion of the issues surrounding such a system. In a sense this paper cannot be impartial, since Warwick became a subscriber to the system. However, as BPO is one of a whole portfolio of information systems in the Library, including some potential competitors to BPO, the system is under constant comparison and evaluation.

Overview of Warwick's BPO experience

Warwick was one of the first UK libraries to have BPO on a trial. This took place in the early summer of 1991, and Warwick became the first UK subscriber in August 1991. The trial was obviously important in establishing the answers to operational questions. Did the system work reliably, in an end-user situation, and in a large university library? Was the system accepted by the potential clientele? The trial aimed to display the system in its future possible mode of operation, and to acquire additional information by means of evaluation sheets and demonstrations to academic and library staff.

Alongside this operational exercise, there were other important issues to be explored and possibly determined. The Library had to form a view on BPO's contribution to its collection building, mostly in relation to subject coverage. Given the high opportunity cost of BPO, would the periodicals collection benefit? This question was to be answered by a straightforward comparison of the periodicals in BPO and the Library's existing provisions and currently expressed needs, and by user reaction to the information retrieved.

There were also important service issues. Did the system fit with the periodicals and inter-library loan (ILL) services operated by the

Library? Would the system operate within budget, and provide positive benefits for other budgets? Whilst some of these questions would be answered by the end of the trial, it was always recognized that many savings would only be possible in the medium period, though some pointers could be obtained.

In the event, the trial was completed successfully. BPO and its supporting organizations were shown to be reliable. Users accepted, indeed welcomed, the new technology. In the decision process, therefore, the other issues came to the fore, and it is these issues which are discussed in more detail in the rest of the paper. The Library made every attempt to include as wide a group of users as possible in the evaluation of BPO, and, therefore, believes that it was thorough and effective as an exercise in evaluation; (for a discussion of such processes see Bawden, 1990). It was, therefore, pleasing when the financial settlement for 1991–92 made purchase possible. The cost was born jointly by the Library and the Business School, a feature of many developments in the Library over the last decade.

Collections and subject coverage

The dominating feature for the business part of the Library from 1985 had been the doubling of staff and students involved in business and management education. Warwick's School of Industrial and Business Studies (SIBS) became, as the Warwick Business School, one of the leading business schools in the UK and with it a whole series of new demands were made upon the Library. Undoubtedly a feature of this expansion had been the increase in research activity by SIBS culminating in the formation of the Warwick Business School Research Bureau. Though the University Library had some notable research collections (Statistics, Working Papers and the Modern Records Centre) the main requirements for this research-led growth were a better periodicals collection and better databases.

However, the Library's experience with periodicals, like other UK higher education institutions had not always been expansionary. There had been two review exercises leading to reductions in periodicals expenditure, and, though SIBS as an expanding department had largely been protected from these cuts, after yet another review in 1991, there were still over 50 titles on its 'desiderata list'. BPO, therefore, offered an attractive solution to this problem. Superficially it provided 330 journals, complete with backfile to 1987, at a stroke! But was it providing the right titles? Was the Library acquiring too many unwanted titles in the overall package?

Undoubtedly, the depth of the periodicals collection changed dramatically, and in practice the benefits of BPO were much better than the 'superficial view'. The emphasis of BPO on US titles meant that the Library could offer two collections that were basically complementary, the UK-based hard-copy collection and the US-orientated CD-ROM collection. It was found that there were 71 journals common to both collections but since these were not all 'management' journals there was overall more benefit to the management collection. BPO was also strong in the fields of management engineering, information technology and database design. BPO was used effectively by students from the Engineering and Computer Science Departments, both for management and technology in their fields of study. This was important, as it increased the overall acceptability of BPO. It was not simply a single-discipline initiative, however demanding the particular group for which it was intended.

Warwick's pattern of management education was not particularly US-orientated, and it was a subject of some concern that BPO was not likely to fulfil the information requirements of case studies and projects which had an increasingly European emphasis. However, during the trial it became known that BPO was intending to improve its European coverage and was seeking consultation with European business school libraries on this point. Some suggestions were compiled from the evaluation sheets. However, it meant that Warwick could not abandon any of its European indexes, and has had to investigate the proposals of other information providers entering the European scene. UMI has now announced its *Global Edition* which includes an additional 200 English-language journal titles from Europe, Australia, etc.

BPO has attracted a wide group of users, partly because of its own strength, and partly because of its novel technology. It can provide immediate and full answers to many researchers' needs.

Service issues

BPO was located in the Corporate Information Library (CIL) within the main Central Campus Library. CIL has a long tradition of and emphasis on, providing end-user systems with extensive library support. From 1991, library staff have offered small-group tuition on using database systems, and a regular programme of tutorials is in operation. Advisory services are immediately available during periods of database use.

Normally end-users must use a booking system for the particular database they wish to consult, and search slots of 30 minutes or one hour are allowed depending on the database. BPO, it was decided should be offered on this basis. This meant it would be used both for searching and full-text retrieval in the same operation. This seemed to comply with the way the system was designed, and how it could best meet the information problem described in the introduction. It would have seemed invidious to separate the two functions, though there would be minor operational conflicts in such a pattern of operations. There would be inconvenience to those who simply wanted to use BPO as a retrieval device, since they would have to find a booking slot rather than be given immediate access to the CD-ROM holdings. With the system running at near capacity, delays would be inevitable. Conversely, some slots would not be fully utilized if they were occupied by 'single-item' searches. New users requiring 'single-item' searches also required additional staff support.

The alternative way of working would have been to institute a procedure whereby all searching was undertaken on an ABI/INFORM workstation, and the BPO workstation used only for retrieval purposes. Besides the theoretical objectives to this approach, in BPO's case there were also practical difficulties which meant that this working arrangement was never tried. ABI/INFORM does not provide availability information on BPO, and it would be an inconvenience to readers to insist that after using the computer they make a visual check in a printed contents list. It is possible to load holdings information into ABI/INFORM and this may be an interim solution, though it would not have been cost effective during the trial when the object was to achieve maximum use of BPO. Given a shortage of ABI/INFORM terminals anyway, it would have been inappropriate to let the most expensive terminal remain idle! However, this does indicate some limitations on the usefulness of BPO in its present configuration as a substitute for a hard-copy collection in a busy library environment. It does not permit the necessary multi-user access that can be obtained from a hard-copy collection. No doubt, technology will soon develop solutions, but the limitation is there at present. The system ought to include a higher proportion of the ABI/INFORM database for optimal working.

This does not mean, however, that BPO could not have a role in the rationalization of a periodicals collection. It is not necessary to duplicate all titles between CD-ROM and hard-copy collections, and there will be many titles for which BPO will be sufficient. At Warwick this was seen as a medium-term aim, which is now being implemented. Initially, it was estimated that the value of the overlap was worth over £3500, and it has now been proposed by the Library to SIBS that subject groups should review duplicates with a view to making suggestions for cancellation from the hard-copy collection in order to provide for new titles. All suggestions for new subscriptions will be scrutinized for their inclusion, or likely inclusion, in the BPO full-text collection.

It was hoped, of course, that BPO would ameliorate the demands upon the Library's ILL service. Since 1990 requests to borrow had increased by 25%, and the Library was under pressure to introduce a charging system for use of the service. The increase in demand often meant delays in processing requests, and the delay in receiving material from external sources was increasing. SIBS was a significant, but not excessive, user of ILLs. BPO was expected to be useful in that it increased the number of management journals in the Library system by a factor of 2.5.

In practice, it has proved extremely difficult to measure the effects of BPO on ILLs. Positive effects might be of two kinds: supply of those journals which would otherwise have to be borrowed, and substitution of a BPO journal for a putative requested item as a result of a successful search on BPO. Evidence is only circumstantial, in that the usefulness of BPO only became apparent when a reader failed to identify BPO as a source before completing a request form, and this error was observed during the Library's bibliographic checking.

Regular observation of this failure upon a reader's part to identify BPO as a source for a particular journal implies definite changes to a library's practice. Besides the obvious need to inform all students of the existence of full-text systems, other systems that record periodical holdings must be changed to include holdings of full-text systems available in the Library. It is not sufficient to link BPO to ABI/INFORM searches, but to the normal sources, including Online Public Access Catalogues (OPACs), which contain periodicals lists. It is interesting to contrast this approach with that of libraries which are integrating information about articles into their catalogues from all their periodical holdings. Both BPO and integrated systems are aiming to provide access to articles, that can be found on site. BPO provides the article directly and other systems require the availability of the hard-copy. Most libraries cannot guarantee such availability, and BPO can, therefore, achieve better retrieval performance as well as providing a back-up for hard-copy duplicates which have been mislaid or destroyed. Both kinds of system will provide good searching ability, but BPO will provide information about sources not in the host library.

Warwick has no information which would directly link the availability of BPO as a finding device to the perceived increase in ILL activity. Quite often sources of reference will be given, but no survey of these has yet been undertaken. As stated above, the real change in library behaviour has been the use of BPO to supply some information immediately to meet essay or project deadlines.

Whilst the benefits of BPO to the periodicals and ILL budgets must remain at present unquantified, though they would appear to be positive, there were other costs that were immediately apparent and clearly negative. The BPO contract was dependent upon a service contract for the hardware which constituted the special workstation. During the trial period and the first annual contract (the position has now changed) the Library would have to pay royalty charges for each full-text print. Moreover, the Library wanted to cover the extra running costs of a laser printer. Over the first accounting period, despite the high usage of the system, there was no income from these parts of the service to set against the subscription costs, and marginal costs have only just been met. We were informed that US experience suggested that usage would decline steeply if we exceeded 2.5 times the cost of a normal photocopy. Warwick has stayed below that figure so far, but the financial experience implies that it would be difficult to establish BPO as an income generator.

Networking

The BPO service as described is a stand-alone system requiring the users to come to the single workstation to retrieve and possibly print the article required. Clearly it would be highly desirable for all concerned if the system could be interrogated remotely across a network and the article read on the screen from the personal workstation in the researcher's office and if necessary printed at a local printer or captured first in the PC (if equipped with a FAX card).

For this to be possible a networkable automatic loading mechanism, or jukebox, is needed with a large disc storage capacity and multiple drives so that more than one disc can be loaded at the same time. Such a machine is currently being tested by UMI who have commissioned the design and manufacture from the Canadian company Kubik Technologies. The machine can store up to 240 discs, has up to four drives, and will connect to standard networks such as Novell.

We will watch these developments with keen interest with a view to investment when funds permit and the machinery has been fully tested.

Conclusions

BPO is a major advance in document provision, and its system reliability and technological accessibility mean that it will be extremely popular with library users. In some senses it represents the future, though it is difficult to say because of the coverage limitations and absence of networking capability that the future has arrived.

Library users who want to receive their information promptly, if not immediately, will find that BPO can achieve impressive results.

Not all effects of a system like BPO can be evaluated or determined immediately. A physical trial can establish important facts about an information system, including likely use patterns, but the wider implications of a document delivery system will only be seen when ILL's and accessions policies have settled.

When first seen, full-text systems are dramatic, and when compared with complicated library finding systems are highly attractive. They will attract use from many fringe users, and library systems, especially cataloguing of periodicals, must reflect this. BPO has the design to take over a lot of library use. One early review (Browning, 1991) debated whether BPO was the 'greatest thing since sliced bread'. Warwick would say that if it were not the whole loaf, it was certainly better than half.

References

Bawden, D. (1990) *User-oriented evaluation of information systems and services*. Aldershot: Gower

Browning, M.M. (1991) Is Business Periodicals Ondisc the greatest thing since sliced bread? A cost analysis and user survey. *CD-ROM Professional*, **4**, 37–41

Klein, G.M. (1991) Business Periodicals Ondisc. *CD-ROM Librarian*, **6**, 24, 26, 28, 30, 32, 34–36, 38

Stewart, J.A. (1991) Business Periodicals Ondisc. ABI-Inform on CD-ROM. *Information Today*, **8**, 21–23

Thompson, D.M. and Evans, N. (1989) Business Periodicals Ondisc. *Library Hi Tech News*, **65**, 1–3, 12

CHAPTER SIX

Hardware issues

Phil Bradley

Introduction

When CD-ROM was first introduced into the market-place the choice of hardware involved a much simpler decision than it does today. There were very few drives available, and even four or five years ago the specification of computer was much more straightforward. The software that was used by different CD-ROM applications was also much less memory hungry; many of them would run in a 512K or even 256K RAM environment. Today however, there is a multiplicity of drives – stand-alones, internal drives, jukeboxes, portable drives, and drives which use SCSI (Small Computer Systems Interface) for example. This is mirrored by the number of computers that you can run drives from: 386 based machines are common, 486 based machines are becoming standard; laptops can also make use of drives, and users are faced with a bewildering array of different memory specifications and memory managers to go with them. Consequently, the hardware specifications for different applications have increased, both in terms of required memory and hard disk space, but also, if you wish to use an application that makes use of graphics, in terms of a Windows environment as well. This chapter will address the problem of choosing a computer and drive that will both fit your needs now, and which will also give you room for expansion in the future. The very knotty subject of networking drives will also be discussed, and will briefly cover the choice of networking software and hardware that will be needed if you should decide to follow this route.

Criteria for choosing a workstation

The amount that you can spend has got to be a high priority, obviously. However it is pleasing to note that in this area, if in no other area of life, the price of computers, and the amount that you can get for your money is falling all the time. An entry level 486 based machine can be had for around £1000, while reliable, high specification and good performance 386 based machines can be had for less. While it is possible to upgrade an older machine, such as an XT, by buying more memory and an accelerator board, you may run into compatibility problems, and will, in all probability end up spending more than simply buying a new machine. I would therefore recommend that you should spend your time in persuading your buyer (or manager!) to replace, rather than upgrade an existing machine.

As application software becomes more sophisticated, it will require greater and greater use of more free RAM (Random Access Memory) within which to process the search that you are running. The software will also make greater demands on your hard disk to store temporary data, but this will be limited in size, commonly to around two or three megabytes. Consequently, the size of the hard disk is not critical, but the choice of a machine with large amounts of RAM and a fast processing speed is. I would therefore suggest that you should consider buying a 386 based machine to give you fast processing speed, or if you can afford it, go up a level and buy a 486 based machine. Most of these will have at least one megabyte, and commonly two megabytes of RAM as standard. However, the more that you can purchase, the quicker your search will be processed, and I would suggest that you go for four megabytes if you can afford it. If the application software that you wish to purchase is going to make use of the Windows environment (and this is becoming more and more common) you will need at least this much, if not more; perhaps up to eight megabytes. You will then need a memory manager to allow the computer to access this; a computer is essentially stupid, and unless you have software that will allow it to access a greater amount of memory, it will simply ignore it. One of the most common, and widely used memory managers, is QEMM from Quarterdeck. This is easy to install, and is compatible with CD-ROM applications; if you decide to purchase another memory manager you should check with the supplier to ensure that it is going to be compatible with the application that you wish to use.

The choice of screen may or may not be important to you. However, I would also suggest that you buy a computer with a colour screen with VGA or Super VGA (SVGA) graphical capability. Colour because many CD-ROM applications make good use of colour which assist users in their searches, and SVGA if you are likely to use an application which will make use of graphics, which will be clearer and easier to see in higher resolution.

One small, and perhaps silly, point – but one which has caused a number of users some grief – is the size of the floppy drive. A 5.25″ disk drive looks very inviting to some users, and is just the right size to accept a CD-ROM disc. This will not only damage the disc, but will in all probability render the disk drive unusable. Either buy a computer with a single 3.5″ floppy drive, or tape up or otherwise label the 5.25″ drive clearly to ensure that no-one puts the CD-ROM disc into it. It is worth doing simply to ensure that you do not have the embarrassment of ringing up your supplier and explaining why you need a replacement disc!

Many computers will now come with DOS 6 and Windows 3.1 as standard, but you may, of course, be using, or purchasing a machine which does not. Windows software is not imperative (unless of course you intend using an interface which is Windows based), but I would strongly recommend DOS 6. It makes better use of memory, and frees up more of your 640K RAM for use with your application software.

Choice of CD-ROM drive

Having chosen your computer, you next have to decide on your CD-ROM drive. You will be pleased to know that the choice here is much easier, as there are fewer drives on the market than PC's. The first question to ask, which is really rather academic is 'Does this drive read ISO 9660 standard discs?' The ISO standard is used by virtually all CD-ROM producers, and relates to the way in which the CD-ROM disc is produced, and how data is stored on it. If the drive is unable to conform to that standard, you will find that the majority, if not all of the discs you wish to use, will not work on that drive.

You must then decide if you wish to purchase an internal, or external drive. This depends very much on your own individual circumstances. If you only ever intend to use the drive on one machine, or have a particular concern over security, then fitting an internal drive is a very viable option. Most of the major CD-ROM drive producers will have an internal model of their latest drive available. The physical installation is a little more tricky than for an external drive, but it can still be accomplished without too much bother. However, if you require greater flexibility, or wish to link (or daisychain) several drives together on one machine, you will be better off going for an external version of a drive.

You may also find that manufacturers will offer SCSI (Small Computer Systems Interface) versions of their drives as well. SCSI devices first started life on Apple Macintosh machines, but are increasingly common in a PC environment. With a Macintosh, you can simply plug it into the SCSI port of the machine, but with a PC you will still need to install an interface card into the computer. They have a slight advantage in that it is easier to daisychain drives together, you can quickly put them onto a Macintosh if you have both types of machine available, but they will commonly cost up to £100 more than those that come with a proprietary bus (or interface card).

You will be faced with a rather bewildering array of statistics if you look at the specification sheet for a CD-ROM drive. The three most important to look at and compare are the Transfer Rate (measured in Kb per second), the Access Time (measured in milliseconds) and the Mean Time Between Failure (or MTBF, measured in hours). The most quoted of these is the Access Time, i.e. the time it takes for a computer to read data from the disc into its memory. The fastest drives currently available will have an Access Time of around 200ms. Anything over 450ms will be a rather slow drive. You should however be aware that most portable drives will have a slow Access Time; it is the pay-off for making it light and easy to carry around with you.

Also discover how the drive deals with the problem of dust. This is perhaps one of the largest single reasons for a drive to fail to work, or to work intermittently. Older drives had no way of protecting the laser head from collecting dust, but most new drives will have a double door system, an automatic lens cleaner and a caddy. For preference, purchase a drive that has all of these features, as you will have less recourse to ring up a support department, or send it back for repair or replacement.

One particular drive which is worth mentioning in a little detail is the so called 'jukebox'. This will come with a 'magazine' allowing you to have ready access to up to six different CD-ROM discs. If security is a concern, and/or you do not wish your users to handle discs directly it is worthwhile investigating in some detail. There is however something of a debate on its value in a networked situation as it only has one read-head. This means that only one disc at a time can be accessed, and if you have a number of users on a network all making calls to different discs, it will spend a lot of its time swapping discs, rather than searching.

Whichever CD-ROM drive you purchase, it should come with an interface card, cable and software, though it is always advisable to check. The physical installation of the drive should not cause too many problems, even for a complete novice, taking no more than an hour, or much less if you are confident or have a technician to do it for you. The major reasons for a failed installation are ill-fitting interface cards, incorrect cabling, or wrongly installed software. The majority of these faults can quickly be assessed by the support department of your CD-ROM drive or database supplier. It is worth mentioning that the installation of a drive should not affect any other applications that you may have installed on your computer; the addition of a CD-ROM drive is simply that – an addition; you will still be able to use all of the other functions that you would wish to.

You may well wish to link several drives together in a process commonly called 'daisychaining'. This will have several benefits for you; it will limit the number of computers that you need to dedicate to CD-ROM database searching, will decrease the number of machines that you need to update software onto, and will in some circumstances, allow cross database searching. Drives can quickly be daisychained, simply by cabling the second drive to the first, the third to the second, and so on. You will not need to install a separate interface card for each machine; each card should support up to four or eight drives with no difficulty (depending on the type of interface card). The only other thing that you will need to do is to make a slight change to the software to tell the computer that it has more than one drive available to it. I would not however suggest that you 'mix and match' CD-ROM drives from different manufacturers on a single computer. While technically there is no reason why you should not do so, you will have to insert a second interface card into the computer and make some adjustments to the software. It will also make the task of identifying a problem a little harder.

Alternatively, you may wish to consider the option of buying a tower or '4-pack' of drives. These are a relatively recent innovation into the market and have considerable value. Essentially, a tower will be composed of four internal CD-ROM drives linked together in an enclosure. You simply need to insert the appropriate interface card into the machine, and cable it to the back of the enclosure in exactly the same way that you would with a single drive. It will provide you with greater security and ease of use. However, should one of the drives fail, you may need to either return the entire unit for repair, or remove the failed drive, which may or may not prove to be an easy task.

A few brief words on the software that was mentioned above – Microsoft Extensions. This software (which is easy to install, coming as it will with its own installation program) performs three main functions. Firstly, it tells the computer that a CD-ROM interface card has been installed, secondly, it will assign a drive letter to your CD-ROM drive, and thirdly will help DOS cope with reading very large files. You should be aware that it will make some changes to your CONFIG.SYS and AUTOEXEC.BAT files so that your computer immediately recognizes the existence of the drive. These changes should not have any effect on any other programs that you run, but if you are in any doubt, contact a technical support department who will be able to sort out any conflicts that occur.

Caring for your system

Once you have installed your system it should look after itself. Common sense will dictate what you can and cannot do, but if you follow some simple guidelines you should not have many problems. Take regular back-ups of your system, so if the worst does happen you can restore data quickly and easily. Ensure that the interface card and the cables are securely screwed home. Make sure that the ventilation holes on the drive are not covered, in order to keep the unit cool. Keep your discs in caddies or their jewel cases, and handle the discs as little as possible. Try and keep dust to a minimum.

If you do encounter a problem, don't panic! In the vast majority of cases there will be a simple solution. Take a note of the problem, when and how it occurred, any error messages and so on. Keep a note of your computer, model of your CD-ROM drive, and printouts of CONFIG.SYS and AUTOEXEC.BAT files handy. When you ring the technical support department, try and do so from a telephone near the computer, as they will in all probability ask you to try out various things, and it will be annoying for you to have to keep running across the room.

Networking CD-ROM drives

A network is a method of connecting two or more computers together to allow them to share different resources, such as printers, modems and, of course, CD-ROM drives. A network will give you several benefits: greater access to different CD-ROM databases, updating software applications will be quicker and easier, enhanced security, greater flexibility and the impact of one of your computers going down will be much less. Needless to say, there are also disadvantages: a network is not something which should be considered by someone who is not fully conversant with computers – it is best to get the supplier to install the network, or for preference your own computer department. You will need to dedicate a member of staff to administering the system; they will need to be technically competent, and there will be several hardware considerations to take into account. While it is possible to use an old or slow computer in a single stand-alone situation, it may be undesirable, or even impossible (without upgrading the computer) to use it efficiently in a network. Similarly, while an old CD-ROM drive with slow access time can be used as a stand-alone, its performance will quickly degrade to unacceptable levels if you have two or more users trying to search on it at one time. I would strongly suggest that, if you are considering installing a network the minimum configuration of computer and drives should be that which was mentioned earlier in this chapter, that is to say, a 486 based machine with 4 MB of RAM. Finally, you may also have to take into account other matters such as licensing and so on.

Choosing your CD-ROM networking software

Networking CD-ROM drives and databases is not the simplest thing in the world to achieve. There are a number of very good solutions to the problem, but the first thing that you must do is clearly work out what you want from your network, and how you wish to expand it. The following section gives a list of the criteria that you should be asking yourself and your potential supplier(s) before you buy a system. I have also given some information on potential networking solutions that can be expected to fulfil your needs, but of course, you must expect to have to spend a considerable amount of time investigating all the possibilities.

There are a number of different criteria that you will need to consider when going down the networking route:

- Do you have enough computers, and are they of a high enough specification? Any network software which you put into place will take up a certain amount of RAM.
- What version of DOS are they running? Check the requirements of individual suppliers of networking software for this.
- Are your existing CD-ROM drives going to be fast enough for access by more than one person at a time? A general rule of thumb here is that if they are faster than 400ms they should be quite adequate for the job.
- Will the actual CD-ROM applications work over a network? Some don't, so you will need to check this.
- Where are the workstations going to be physically located? The

distances between workstations can be important, as a network can only reach so far without routers to boost the signal. Again, check with the supplier.

- Do you want to have, or require, a server? A server is basically a large, powerful computer on which you can place the majority of applications, rather than have them loaded on individual workstations. You may also require a separate optical file server, to take care of the CD-ROM drives that are linked into the network.

The point should also be made that, even if you already have an existing network (such as Novell Netware for example) you will probably need to purchase additional software to allow you to use your CD-ROM drives across it. The reason for this is that most LANs (Local Area Networks) can only talk to magnetic drives, and not optical ones (though this is now changing with the recent release of version 4 of Novell Netware). The software will intercept the request to talk to an optical disc and translate it into the format that the CD-ROM drive can understand. The software will often reside both on the file server, and also on the workstation, or it will be split between the two.

You may also wish to consider front-end menus. Some CD-ROM networking solutions will allow you to, for example, limit the number of simultaneous accesses to a database, provide password access, give you statistical information on which workstations access databases, and which databases are used most often.

The use of Microsoft Extensions also needs to be considered. Some networking packages require extensions to be loaded to allow workstations to get access to the CD-ROM drives, while others will provide a method of 'mapping' a drive letter to a particular CD-ROM drive. This may cause problems if a particular application requires the existence of extensions, so you should check with your database supplier to see if there are going to be any problems in this area.

The CD-ROM application software must also be considered. Most applications will require space to store temporary files. Usually, this will be on a local workstation's hard disk. This can, of course, cause problems if you have diskless workstations, in which case, these temporary files must be stored elsewhere, such as on the file server.

This will be acceptable if you only have a limited number of workstations attached, but in an environment where you have a large number of workstations all logging on at the same time and taking up to perhaps two or three megabytes of hard disk space, even on a temporary basis, unless you have a very large file server, you will quickly run out of space. Again, check with your supplier to see what they recommend.

Do you want to be able to allow remote users to get access to the databases? Technically, it is quite easy to allow users who work from home to log into the network via a modem. If this is the case, you need to ask the suppliers if it is possible to do so using their networking software; generally, the answer should be a positive 'yes', but you would be advised to check, just to be on the safe side.

How do you want to expand your network? Users are notorious for wanting more information quickly. You should estimate the number of users you think will want access and at least double it; it will not take long for word to get around, and you will want to have purchased a networking solution that will allow for easy expansion. With this aim in mind, also consider that it is possible to download the data onto very large hard disks (in the order of 6–10 gigabytes) and use the CD-ROM simply as the mechanism for distributing the data, rather than as a means of searching in its own right. If this is the case, or you feel that it is conceivable that you will want this capability, make it clear at the outset, and ask the supplier if it is possible to do this using their software. It is, of course, worth pointing out that the main reasons for doing this are to provide much faster access to the data, and also to allow more users to access that data.

Finally, take into consideration the physical installation of the network software. Are you going to have to do it, get your computer department to do it for you, or does the supplier offer to come in and do the installation and training for you?

Once you have a clearer idea of your needs, you are then in a position to start to look at the various networking solutions that are offered by different companies. The following is a list of some of those which are currently available, and an indication of the kind of network that they suit.

CD Net

Produced by Meridian Data. It is also available as either stand-alone software, or can be incorporated into an existing network. Server Towers are available in a variety of configurations. Software installation allows for a flexible configuration of the system overall, or even of individual workstations. A utility program allows the administrator to set up multiple menu databases. It works easily across a range of different networks.

SCSI Express

Produced by Micro Design International Inc. It is easy to install, and provides quick and efficient access to CD-ROM drives. It can be sold as a software only option, but it is also possible to purchase it with an interface card and drive(s). It is designed to run with Novell Netware version 3.11, and a requirement is that it must reside on a file server which has at least four megabytes of RAM available to it. It makes clever use of the Netware cache device (which ensures extremely fast performance by using memory to help process the searches) and also does not require extra memory on the individual workstations. Unlike some other networking products SCSI Express does not support Microsoft Extensions at all. In many cases, this will not cause a problem, as a lot of CD-ROM applications software can work without them, but some products, which require the existence of Extensions may well refuse to run. If in any doubt, ask the supplier for a list of databases which will not run under SCSI Express. It will also support other SCSI devices, such as WORMs, back-up drives and so on.

OPTI-NET

Produced by Online Computer Systems Inc. OPTI-NET has been on the market since 1986 and was the first software only solution to CD-ROM networking. It is used in a large number of libraries both in the UK and abroad. This product allows usage of drives, and network statistics to be easily monitored. It also has a number of other useful features, including the ability to unload device drivers to free up valuable memory without having to reboot a workstation. OPTI-NET does not require the use of a dedicated optical server, which gives flexibility and reduced costs.

Lantastic

This is a slightly different solution to those mentioned above, as it is basically an operating system in its own right. In comparison to other networks, such as Novell, it has the ability to directly support CD-ROM drives. It also does not require the existence of a separate server; any PC in the network can be used either as a workstation or as a file server; this type of configuration is commonly referred to as 'peer to peer'. It also has a number of utilities to allow interrogation of workstation usage, log-ins, log-outs and so on. Each workstation can 'share' its CD-ROM drive with the others, but the addition of the networking software, extensions and device driver may cause memory problems on computers with limited memory available.

Current and future trends in CD-ROM hardware

Any kind of scrying into the future of computer technology is doomed to failure before you start; the technology moves faster than we can ever predict. However, there are several clear trends that one can see with regard to CD-ROM technology. Firstly, drives are continually becoming faster. Second generation machines were considered to be fast if they could reach an access time of 450ms. Today, with 200ms drives available, this is considered to be merely adequate. Secondly, the price for a drive seems to be coming down, at least in some areas. New machines, which are faster, with more features tend to be priced within the same range band that their older counterparts were two, or even three years ago. Thirdly, the existence of 'multimedia' CD-ROM discs which include graphics, moving images and sound as well as textual data are becoming increasingly common. In most cases, these databases will be compatible with existing drives, although you may well have problems if you wish to access one using a second generation machine.

Portable CD-ROM drives are now becoming more common, and

with the use of various hardware and software utilities can be used with laptop machines. Handheld drives have been produced in Japan and so we should shortly be reaching the situation where you will be able to read a book, or access a database on the train.

The situation with regards to networking CD-ROM drives is even more exciting. At least two suppliers (SilverPlatter and CD-Plus) now offer solutions for copying large amounts of data onto hard disk, thus increasing access times, and giving much greater numbers of users the possibility of searching databases simultaneously. Users can search databases, regardless of the CD-ROM capability on their own workstation, simply by accessing the network. We are now in a position to search databases with the same huge files at the same sort of speed over the network as previously we were only able to do by going online with all of its attendant problems.

CHAPTER SEVEN

Case study: The University of Birmingham's CD-ROM network

Michele Shoebridge and Morag Watson

Introduction

The University Library

The University Library contains over two million volumes, and has 31 000 registered borrowers. In addition to the Main Library and its remote store, there are nine site libraries: the Barnes Library, the Clinical Teaching Block Library, the Harding Law Library, the Education Library, the Barber Music Library, the Barber Fine Art Library, the Shakespeare Institute Library, the Baykov Slavonic Library and the Public Policy Library.

The Library is organized into five functional divisions: Collection Management, Public Services, Sites, Research Libraries, and Administration and Systems. The Library has an extensive and long-standing commitment to automation, being a founder member of BLCMP (Library Services). It has its own dedicated minicomputer which supports over two hundred simultaneous connections and which is used to run the integrated BLCMP library management system BLS. The Library supports three PC based microcomputer networks, including a public cluster for casual student use, an internal administrative network and a CD-ROM network. There are also a number of stand-alone PC applications.

The CD-ROM network

The Library has been providing networked access to databases on CD-ROM using Novell and OPTI-NET software since 1990. This case study describes the Library's objectives in installing the network, the decision-making that went into selecting the hardware and software, the administration of the network and future plans for development.

Adopting a network strategy

Stand-alone CD-ROM workstations were installed in the Library in 1989 and proved to be very popular with users. Databases initially provided were ABI/INFORM, *Science Citation Index* and *Social Sciences Citation Index*. As more titles became available on CD-ROM Library staff recognized that considerable time would have to be devoted to maintaining the different information retrieval software required to run them. CD-ROM technology was a relatively new topic, but already networking CDs was being discussed and implemented at a few sites in the UK. The Library decided to investigate this as a long-term strategy, chiefly because of the opportunities it offered for providing more access points to the data. Other benefits included cutting down on resources by enabling printers to be shared and less staff time spent in installing software. There were also security benefits in restricting access to the operating system. Obvious disadvantages were the fact that the information retrieval software had not been written to be networked, the lack of technical expertise offered by the CD vendors, and the confusion over licensing which has still not been resolved.

Once a network strategy had been chosen, there were three possible options for its implementation: inhouse, the University's Academic Computing Service (ACS) or an outside company. Since a Systems Unit had only recently been set up at Birmingham, there had been little time to develop inhouse expertise in the complicated area of networking. Relations between the Library and ACS, although in existence, were not very well developed at this time, and their staff had no knowledge of CD-ROM technology. A local

CD-ROM Databases currently mounted on the CD-ROM network

ABI/Inform 1987–1993 (2 discs)
Bookfind
CINAHL
Dissertations Abstracts 1981–1993 (2 discs)
ERIC
ESTC
Humanities index 1984–1995
JUSTIS
MEDLINE
MLA Bibliography 1984–1993
Sports Discus
UKOP

Other Databases available on the CD-ROM network

IMMAGE

Databases to be added to the network

ASSIA
Boston Spa Conferences
Boston Spa Serials
CAFOLD English Dictionary
Chemical Abstracts Index
Dissertations Abstracts Archive 1851–1983
EC Infodisk
English Poetry Database
Harraps Multilingual Encyclopaedia
Microview

Current Stand-alone Databases

Main Library

CD Atlas de France
CD MARC Bibliography
CENSUS 1981
CENSUS 1991
Dissertation Abstracts 1851–1981
Elsevier Catalogue
Encyclopaedia Britannica
English Poetry Database
Greek and Latin CD's
Move
Oxford English Dictionary
Science Citation Index 1986–1991
Social Sciences Citation Index 1981–1991
Shakespeare on Disc
Springer-Verlag Catalogue
Standards Infodisk

Education Library

ICDL
NERIS

Clinical Teaching Block Library

MEDLINE

Shakespeare Institute

English Poetry Database
Oxford English Dictionary, 2nd Edition

Figure 1 List of networked and stand-alone databases on CD-ROM

company which had been providing the Library with PCs and PC support was approached but, although they had the networking experience, they had little knowledge of CD technology at that time. Consequently Attica Cybernetics, a relatively new company based in Oxford who claimed to have in-depth knowledge of CD-ROM technology and which was heavily promoting itself, was approached and after a period of lengthy negotiation was commissioned to install the network.

Installation

The initial installation took longer than expected, possibly because Birmingham was one of Attica's first big projects. Work began in August 1990 with the installation of cabling and setting up of the file server. The applications software was then loaded and this took a considerable amount of time, particularly because it had not really been written for a networked environment. Fine tuning of the server continued until the end of 1990, with a succession of visits from Attica's engineers.

A number of problems were still outstanding by February 1991, one major one concerned printing. Each CD-ROM workstation shared a printer and the print queue was controlled by the 'pserver' program in Novell. This was not sophisticated enough and was replaced by a separate piece of software, LANSPOOL, which solved most of the problems users were experiencing with printing across the network. When the networking software was upgraded to Novell 3.11 the pserver program was found to be much improved and was used to control the print queues again.

Initial configuration

The installation comprized a 16 bit thin-wire Ethernet network with Attica supplying the wiring and all the hardware:

- a 386/20 file server, with an 80MB hard disk and 2MB RAM running Advanced Novell Netware 2.1 with a 250 user licence and DOS 3.30;
- a 286/20 optical server, 40MB hard disk, 4MB RAM, and 8 Hitachi

3600 CD-ROM drives, running OPTI-NET 1.2 with a 100 user licence;

- 7 hard diskless workstations with 3.5" disk drives, 286/12 CPU, lMB RAM, VGA colour monitors, remote boot roms, and DOS 3.30;
- 4 Epson SQ850 inkjet printers shared between workstations (purchased from a local supplier);
- All CD-ROM applications software was loaded on the network file server along with inhouse devised front-end menus.

Current configuration

Twenty-six additional drives configured in three optical towers have been added over the last 12 months making a total of thirty four. This necessitated an upgrade to the file server which was replaced by an Apricot 486 FTE with a 380MB hard disk, 8MB RAM, 3.5 disk drive, running Novell Netware 3.11 with a 250 user licence.

The old file server, an Attica 386 with 80MB hard disk, 8MB RAM, has been used as an additional optical server to run 10 of the new drives. The original optical server has been upgraded to a 386/20 with 16MB RAM to improve caching. The optical server software has been upgraded, first to OPTI-NET 1.3 and then to OPTI-NET 2.1.

Why choose OPTI-NET?

When the Library was selecting the hardware and software there was little choice for optical networking other than OPTI-NET. There is more choice now e.g. Lantastic and SCSI Express (see Chapter 6).

What is OPTI-NET?

OPTI-NET is a software package that runs on top of Novell Netware and allows access to optical drives as if they are local drives. It supports most types of CD-ROM hardware and allows a number of users to share CD-ROM databases over a network in the same way as the files on a hard disk can be shared over a network. The CDs are accessed through DOS, using Microsoft Extensions, or by reading directly from the CD. OPTI-NET 2.0 permits simultaneous database access to each optical server on an optical storage network.

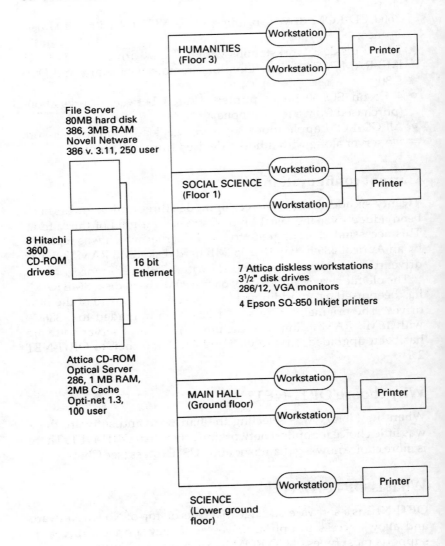

Figure 2 Original hardware configuration

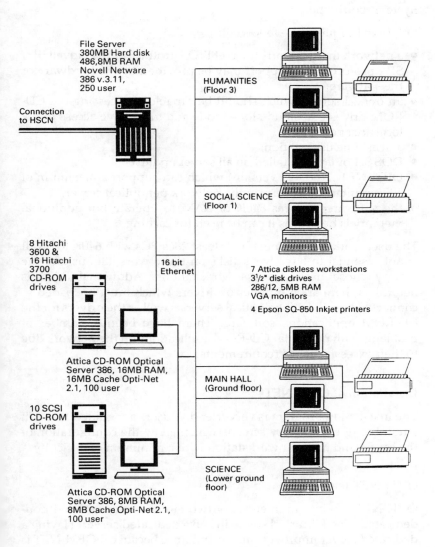

Figure 3 Current hardware configuration

System requirements

OPTI-NET requires the following:

- a network that supports the Net BIOS protocol or the Novell IPX/ SPX protocol; this support may be provided by the hardware or the software;
- an optical server which should be capable of accessing the CD-ROM drives in a stand-alone mode and must have access to the local area network;
- at least one user station;
- DOS 3.1 or later installed on all server and user stations;
- OPTI-NET 2.0 (DOS version) which can support a maximum of 100 simultaneous users on the network per optical server;
- the software requires 640K of RAM to operate but additional memory is helpful as it can be used for caching.

The user workstations must be at least 286s PCs with 640K RAM. It is not essential to have hard disks on these workstations and the Library chose hard diskless workstations. Additional RAM is helpful as there are a number of drivers which must be loaded to connect to Novell and the optical server as well as the drivers for the CD-ROM applications software. There have been a number of problems with particular CD-ROM applications on the network due to their excessive RAM requirements.

Installation of OPTI-NET

The installation program is very friendly, users are guided through a number of explanatory screens which allow the configuration of the server and the user workstation with a minimum of difficulty.

OPTI-NET features

OPTI-NET can be run in either of two modes: dedicated and non-dedicated. The Library chose to install a dedicated server. Having a dedicated server improves the performance because if OPTI-NET is run as a non-dedicated optical server, it results in a slower service, slower local applications and reduced reliability. In addition, if the local application crashes it can crash the optical server as well. The advantage of a non-dedicated server is that it reduces hardware costs, as workstations can be used to run other applications because OPTI-NET is run as a TSR (Terminate and Stay Resident, meaning that the program is loaded into memory and used when needed but stays in RAM even when not in use) program which can be invoked by the use of a 'hot key' or convenient single keystroke.

- ADMINISTRATOR MODE

In administrator mode it is possible to change the configuration of the optical server and databases and to view and alter the hardware configuration (e.g. view the current parameters for the system cache, whether it is caching with the system or expanded memory), the bypass values and the size of the memory available for caching. However, it is not always advisable to do this as it blocks all optical storage network activity, with requests for access to the optical disk being queued but not processed.

Once in the administrator menus it is possible to specify the name of the optical server to be used, enable the log file, assign CD-ROM drives to particular databases and set the number of permitted concurrent accesses to individual databases. It is possible to add, remove, dismount and mount databases or cause a database to dismount automatically when there is no activity. All data is written to the OPTI-NET configuration file and OPTI-NET automatically configures the optical storage network, with user station access to the databases assigned to CD-ROM drives in the OPTI-NET configuration file.

- MONITOR MODE

The optical server is generally left with the monitor mode active. This permits the monitoring of the current status of the optical server and the network. Monitor mode allows feedback on optical server usage, errors and other problems. Typical commands that appear are: x = request executing, s = request received, f = request failure.

● OPTI-NET SERVER ACCESS FROM A USER STATION

Before the user can access a mounted database an optical storage network session must be initiated at the user station and the database must be opened at the user station.

OPTI-NET includes a utility to initiate and end the optical storage network session at the user station, to open and close a database, to query server status, to set user name and to release and remove the Microsoft Extensions and drive letters from memory.

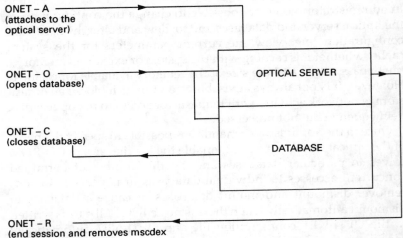

ONET – A
(attaches to the
optical server)

ONET – O
(opens database)

OPTICAL SERVER

ONET – C
(closes database)

DATABASE

ONET – R
(end session and removes mscdex
netusr from memory)

ONET – S
(shows current status of attached server
& databases loaded)

Figure 4 How OPTI-NET works

System features

● OCONSOLE

The OCONSOLE utility is one that came with OPTI-NET 2.0 and is very useful in allowing the network supervisor to log-in across the network and monitor the optical server or change the configuration. This method negates the need to use the administrator mode which blocks user access.

- CACHING

When the network was first installed the cache size was 4MB and it was soon apparent that this was not sufficient since only approximately 20% of requests were being met by cache. When the network was upgraded in 1992 the RAM was increased to 16MB in the hope that it would increase performance. Casual observation of the optical server suggests that approximately 60% of requests are now being met from cache.

OPTI-NET provides a considerable amount of information about the cache: the RAM allocated to cache, cache used, number of kilobytes of RAM that are currently occupied by CD-ROM data, number of cache hits, percentage of read calls retrieved from the cache, and the total number of requests serviced by the cache.

Management information from OPTI-NET

- LOG FILE

OPTI-NET can be configured to keep a log file. This logs which workstations are accessing the network, what time of day it was used, how long the database was used for, which database was accessed, and reports an error code for any failed accesses to the CD-ROM network.

This log file in its raw state, i.e. as OPTI-NET log, is however, a little impenetrable and requires some manipulation to produce acceptable management information. The Library has made little use of it so far, but has recently obtained a copy of a QBASIC program from Alan Neville, Information Officer at the John Rylands University Library of Manchester, which produces much more meaningful data, including cumulative statistics of number of sessions on each database and total access time for that database. It also provides cumulative statistics for total number of sessions on the CD-ROM network and total connect time of users for the whole network. The program can be set up to print these data automatically.

Usage data obtained from this program will be used to determine which databases are the most heavily used and should remain on the network, and which should be mounted on the stand-alone PCs. They may also influence future purchasing decisions.

● LICENSING CONTROL

It is possible to define how many simultaneous accesses can be permitted to individual databases. This number can vary from 1 to 100, with 100 being the default value. When a user attempts to access a database that already has the permitted number of users attached they are refused access and returned to DOS.

This facility has never been fully enabled at the University of Birmingham. When the network was initially established, licensing for seven copies of each product was arranged, a figure which reflected the number of workstations then available on the network. There was no need to limit connections as there could never be more than seven simultaneous accesses.

Now that the CD-ROM network is bridged to the University's high speed campus FDDI network, the number of simultaneous accesses will have to be controlled because there will be a large increase in the number of potential users. Secure methods of controlling licensing and simultaneous access have been investigated. A number of options currently under consideration include the OPTI-NET licensing control feature, the use of a specially purchased piece of software, or using the concurrency control built into Novell Netware. A decision has yet to be reached.

Administration of the CD-ROM network

The network is technically supported by the Systems Unit. Staff in Public Services provide user support, including training, documentation and promotion. A small group of staff from Systems and Public Services, chaired by the Head of Collection Management, co-ordinate suggestions for the purchase of new titles.

Technical support

It became apparent soon after the installation of the network that the increase in PC-based activities in the Library would necessitate additional staff being appointed to the Systems Unit to support PCs, rather than the traditional area of library housekeeping. This recognition led to the appointment of a Deputy Systems Librarian in December 1990. In 1992 the Library was restructured and a new division 'Administration and Systems' created which has responsibility for the Systems Unit (the Unit had traditionally reported directly to the Deputy Librarian). When the post of Systems Librarian became vacant in that year, it was replaced by two Assistant Librarian posts – one to head up a housekeeping team, the other to lead a PC networks team. These posts are supported by two professional librarians, a software assistant (jointly funded by the Library and ACS), 0.5 clerical assistant and 0.25 Faculty Computer Officer assigned to the Library by ACS.

When the network was first installed Attica provided front-line telephone support at a cost of £600 per year. This reliance on Attica often resulted in breaks of service, and frustration on the part of both staff and users. As Attica took on more customers their support became increasingly unreliable because of the workload being taken on by their technical personnel. Over the last year inhouse expertise has grown to an extent that the Library no longer feels it necessary to pay for Attica support. With the spread of CD-ROM networks an informal support network has emerged. Electronic discussion lists, bulletins, and the awareness seminars organized by the 'CD-ROM and Information Networking Group' (set up by the Joint Network Team in 1991) on trends in CD-ROM networking have also helped.

User support

User support is provided by staff in Information Services and the subject areas. All staff on evening and Saturday duties are expected to answer basic questions on how to use the databases and this has meant a considerable amount of staff training. Some staff have adapted to these demands better than others.

Training

Training systems staff

Attica did some very basic training for those members of library staff directly responsible for supporting the network when it was first installed but it really was not very detailed. A more formal one-day training course followed in 1991, run by Attica at their Oxford offices. It included an overview of the Attica CD-ROM network server, some basic Novell training, maintenance of the server and network in general and the principles of networking applications and how to install them. Its aim was to make their customers more self-sufficient. One spin-off was the useful contacts made with people doing similar work in pioneering areas. Apart from this course most training has been very much 'on-the-job'.

Training users

Mention has already been made of the need to train library staff. Training sessions have also been organized for the academics and students. These have usually been targeted at specific subject areas. User guides have also been written for all the databases subscribed to.

Future developments

The CD-ROM network has recently been bridged to the High Speed Campus Network in order to make databases more widely available. Initially access to this service has been limited to public access PCs in the site libraries. Eventually access will be given via the Campus Wide Information Service.

Network access, whilst welcomed by users, does have implications for systems staff since more technical assistance and user support will be required. It is envisaged that technical questions about the network will be referred to ACS. Staff in the Library's Information Services will have to provide more training and documentation than has previously been necessary.

The Library is also beginning to explore searching across more than one disc with the mounting of *Medline* on the CD-ROM network (previously it has been available stand-alone). OPTI-NET

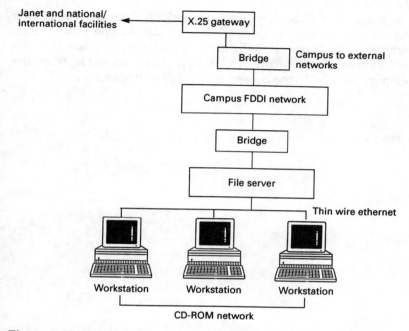

Figure 5 Diagram of the campus network, with CD-ROM network attached

can be configured to search across multiple discs simultaneously but there have been some problems getting the applications software to recognize that there are multiple discs and allow searching across them.

The growing trend to offer large bibliographic databases on magnetic media as well as on CD-ROM may make the use of OPTI-NET redundant. However, it is more likely that the two systems will run in parallel for some time because not all databases are suitable for the magnetic approach, which works best for larger, heavily used databases. Smaller, less sophisticated and less popular databases may well continue to be offered on CD-ROM. The Library has discussed Magnetic *Medline* with SilverPlatter but the high cost has prevented the project progressing.

There is also an argument for leaving the less popular databases on stand-alone PCs rather than networking them and the Library has continued to provide databases on stand-alone PCs in cases where the software is difficult to network or the licence costs prohibitive. Traditionally, these have been bookable from the enquiry desk, with the consequent use of staff resources.

CHAPTER EIGHT

Case study: CD-ROM networking at Templeton College Oxford

David Perrow and Laurence Fouweather

Introduction

Templeton College (Oxford Centre for Management Studies) is a management studies centre which runs short post-experience courses for practising managers, and management courses at undergraduate and postgraduate level for Oxford University. The College's Information Centre and Library caters for a throughput of over 1500 managers each year and a permanent population of around 250 students and academic staff, and therefore serves two quite different types of demand.

Information needs

Executives

Executives are on programmes which are typically one to two weeks in length, though some are as short as three days or as long as nine weeks. These are intensive periods of study, lasting from early morning to late at night and based in teaching and seminar rooms away from the Information Centre. Though executive teaching relies heavily on the presentation and use of information, in the past this has usually been pre-packaged in the form of handouts and case studies.

As executive education changes, there is growing demand for more sophisticated presentation of information by course leaders, and projects which draw upon current information to analyse markets, competitors and corporate strategies. Executives are also more interested in learning information and IT skills, having a 'hands-on' approach, and guiding their own learning.

These trends all point towards more sophisticated information systems being networked to allow simultaneous multi-user access. Executives are not interested in whether the information is on CD-ROM, online or held as local databases on PCs or mainframes. The information matters, not the technology, and the main requirements are accessibility, reliability and ease of use. Whilst networking information services within the Information Centre is important, from the start Templeton's requirement was to deliver these services into the teaching and seminar rooms. This is not a CD-ROM strategy, but an information plan in which CD-ROMs are one vital element.

Student and faculty information requirements

The information requirements of teaching staff are more diverse. They may need company information, market research and news to support their executive teaching, but also require bibliographic sources for both research and teaching. Their information behaviour over the last five years has changed significantly, and whilst there is still a high degree of dependence on printed sources, the demand for electronic desktop delivery is significant. Some are adopting home working, and wish to extend dial-in to E-mail and catalogue systems to database searching – possible for personally controlled password systems like BIDS and online, but excluded by licence from most CD-ROM network services.

Student demand is more Information Centre based (though there is demand for dial-in to overcome short Information Centre opening times). Networking of information services here overcomes queuing problems which build up on single workstation installations.

The information service

The Information Centre and Library (IC&L) developed automated services from 1988 when the first CD-ROM, ABI/INFORM, was installed on a stand-alone machine. Shortly after, the College laid down an Ethernet network and installed 2 VAX 3800 mainframes supporting 100 terminals/PCs. Using the All-in-One office management software and PCSA (now Pathworks), an environment was created which integrated a number of software functions within one menu structure. Locally this is known as the Nautilus Network.

Information Centre and Library

GSA	Guide to services available	AED	Access Other Catalogues and Database
ATC	Access Templeton Catalogues	RIC	Requests to Information Centre Staff
LPL	Periodicals Holdings List	BFS	Books for sale from College Bookshop
LCI	Company Information List	MRP	Templeton Management Research Papers
LVA	Video and AV Materials List	RLM	Reading Lists in Management Studies

Figure 1a Information Centre & Library: Main menu

Taking the IC&L environment as an example (see Figures 1a, 1b, 1c), Nautilus users are able to access the catalogue (which uses CAIRS software), connect to remote catalogues available on JANET, or send E-mail by filling data onto forms (including reservations, suggestions for stock, etc.). Online systems such as Datastar Focus

Access Other Catalogues and Databases

Books and Periodicals

OLIS   Access Oxford University Union Catalogue
          (OLIS)
OTHER   Access UK Academic Library Catalogues
ABI   Access ABI INFORM
BIDS   Access BIDS – Social Science Citation Index
HEL   Access Helecon

Market Research, News, Company Information and Case
Study

Figure 1b Books and periodicals sub-menu

(which gives access to Textline and other company, market and stockbroker databases) are offered via the COM option.

The CD-ROM network, which was installed in 1991, is nested within this system, but is not presented as CD-ROM technology. The IC&L environment is designed to answer information needs, and the technicalities of the information source are not particularly relevant to the user. Hence the IC&L user doing a bibliographic search might search a remote database such as BIDS (subject to password authorization), an internally created periodicals index held on the VAX, or ABI/INFORM on the CD Network. A company database may be online, on CD-ROM, or loaded weekly from data received on floppy disk (see Figure 2).

For network users, the IC&L services are integrated with personal All-in-One menus (see Figure 3), and All-in-One is one choice on personal PC screens, so that users can move easily from use of word-processing, spreadsheets or E-mail into and out of the Nautilus/IC&L environment.

Public terminals in the IC&L are predominantly dumb terminals,

Access Other Catalogues and Databases (2)

Market Research

MRL   Templeton Market Research Holdings List

PRE   Predicasts

News Databases

FILES   Templeton News Information Files

TIMES   Times and Sunday Times Fulltext

PRE   Predicasts

Company Information and Case Study databases are on the next page

Figure 1c Further sub menu for market research and news databases

so PC options are not available and the system is locked into Nautilus All-in-One, with menu options restricted to free public information (e.g. catalogue, CD-ROM network, JANET). Online connections are available, but with password control, so users must either have their own password (BIDS) or be logged on by IC&L staff (Datastar Focus, FT Profile, Colis).

At present there are some information services which are available only in the IC&L and not offered via the Nautilus Network. *Business Periodicals Ondisc*, the image-based full text underlying the ABI/INFORM management index, is popular with both executive and academic users, but cannot yet be networked because of technological constraints. Other services have interfaces which are not considered sufficiently user-friendly or network fees which cannot be justified by use.

Access Other Catalogues and Databases (3)

Company Information

COMP   Templeton Company Information Holdings List

LOTUS   Lotus One Source CD/Private UK (UK Companies)

MICRO   MicroExstat (UK Companies)

DATA   Datastream (UK and International Companies)

Case Studies

CASE   Templeton Case Studies Holdings List

COLIS   Cranfield Case Study Database

Figure 2 Company information and case studies sub-menu

Managing the network

The IT Manager was recruited to set up the Nautilus system, and the IT Department has responsibility for all hardware management and software upgrades.

Since the CD-ROM system (including the drives) resides physically in the computer room, IT staff change CD-ROM discs when update discs arrive. The Information Centre is responsible for product selection, subscription maintenance and training and publicity.

Selection of CD-ROM hardware and software

When starting the search for a CD-ROM networking system, the following technical constraints were identified:

● It had to fit in with the College's IT strategy, both from a hardware and software viewpoint. This meant that it had to be either DEC

TC	College Information
ICL	Information Centre and Library
WP	Word and Document Processing
EM	Electronic Messaging
DM	Desk Management
COM	External Data Communications
CAP	College Applications

CONF	Electronic Conferencing
M	More
EX	Exit

Figure 3 Nautilus system menu

VAX/VMS or networked MS-DOS based (using Digital's PATHWORKS (a modified version of Microsoft LAN Manager)).

- The system had to be accessible from any college workstation (from basic IBM PC/XT's upwards) and in addition, preferably VT320 series terminals.
- It had to run the commonly used business information CD-ROM databases.

In addition the system had to work within the following aims:

- The system had to be accessible from any network access point around the College.
- It had to be reliable, secure, easy to administer and robust.
- It should not involve the IT support staff having to support another operating environment.
- The interface presented to the users had to be, as far as possible, consistent with other systems.

At the time the College was looking (1990), the market for CD-ROM networking was in its early stages of development and two main types of system were identified:

- PC server based. This included OPTI-NET and Meridian CD-NET in their first incarnations.
- VAX/VMS based. There were two main systems, Logicraft CDWARE and Virtual Microsystems V-Server. The V-Server was not available in the UK at that time and so was not considered further.

It quickly became apparent, that because of hardware constraints imposed by the large number of older (8088/8086) workstations in use in the College at that time, it would not be possible to use a PC based CD-ROM server system to achieve the project aims. Once these systems had networking and CD-ROM software loaded, the memory left was insufficient to run the desired applications. It would have been possible to add expanded memory to these machines, but this was not considered cost effective, in view of their expected life.

It would have been possible to offer a limited network service only in the Information Centre and Library, but it must be remembered that a primary aim was to be able to deliver the information to any part of the College to existing workstations. For this reason, the Logicraft system was selected for further investigation.

Technical description of the Logicraft system

The Logicraft system is a basic PC style platform with a large power supply into which various options are installed. It can have different size floppy drives or local hard disks. It has no screen or keyboard, and doesn't need one in normal operation although an asynchronous terminal is needed from time to time to change the configuration (e.g. to change the amount of memory or number of slave cards (see below)). A 286 processor card controls the system and performs all the screen i/o (input/output) remapping etc. This processor is not used to run any application programs. It boots its control software (which appears to be modified MS-DOS) from the floppy drive on power up.

The system takes standard PC/AT bus cards (ISA). To start with you need a Logicraft slave card containing a 386 processor and 4MB memory. The basic system has one slave card, the maximum number per server being four cards giving 16 users. It can have any standard PC peripheral controller cards (e.g. CD-ROM controllers, serial or parallel I/F's). The memory used by a DOS application can be selected from the VAX at run time. The four user slots can use expanded memory and it is normal to run the MS CD extensions in expanded memory with as much disk caching as possible. There are a number of extra commands that are used to map user sessions to disk areas (either on local hard disks or virtual hard disks on the VAX disks) in read only or read/write mode.

To use the system, the sequence of events is:

1) Log-in to the VAX system.
2) Invoke the Logicraft software to connect to the box. This runs a program on the VAX which connects across the Ethernet to the software controlling the box. In invoking this software a number of parameters can be set including output destination (e.g. VAX file, VAX printer queue).
3) An MS-DOS session is then booted (with its own CONFIG.SYS) on one of the slave processors in the box. The AUTOEXEC.BAT file is executed to set up the environment, connect any real or virtual disks etc. and can, as usual, enter a DOS application if you want to keep users from seeing the MS-DOS prompt. Note that you can have different boot configurations for different software. These are stored in virtual disks on the VAX, although they do consume VAX disk space. All screen i/o is remapped via the VAX to your terminal.
4) On leaving the application a BYE command is executed which

returns control to the VAX process and resets the slave processor to await the next user.

5) The VAX process then exits to DCL level.

This product was well established as a means of offering PC based software to a DEC VAX/VMS based environment. The CD-ROM variant was not in use in the UK at that time, although there were many US installations and several in Europe. Tests were carried out to establish that the CD applications we wanted to use would run on the system. With help from Logicraft tech support ABI/INFORM and Lotus One-Source were installed on a test system with two drives connected to the College network, so that functional and performance tests could be made.

Timing trials were carried out which showed that for one user the response time to a large search was faster than on a stand-alone system. With two users accessing the same CD the time was equal, and three or four users accessing the same CD began to show a degradation, although this was heavily dependent on the application in use.

Using two different CDs at the same time showed that the contention was in the access to the CD, very much as expected, and not in the performance of the server. (Functional tests were also carried out using the X-Windows interface on a DEC VAX station. This was most impressive). These tests showed that for a small installation this was a viable solution.

Technical problem areas

One area for decision was highlighted as a result of these tests. The keyboard mapping for the terminal sessions on the server could be:

- set to emulate a PC keyboard, but then the other systems (library catalogue, E-mail etc.) would not work as documented;
- left as standard (VT200 mapping) in which case the CD-ROM applications keys would not work as documented.

As Logicraft could supply keyboard templates for the second option, it was decided to follow that route.

Another problem was that the CD-ROM systems running on the

server could not access the floppy drive on a desktop PC, although data could be transferred to a virtual disk accessible from PCs connected to the College network. As the system could print to any printer (either network or PC attached), and one or two stand-alone systems in the Library were to be retained, it was felt that this problem could be tolerated. The system was purchased and a service offered to end-users in Spring 1991. Since then the number of CD drives has been increased to eight, with further additions now being planned.

Performance and reliability

The system has performed without any hardware or software problems. The only major disruption has been following a momentary interruption to the main power supply, when the Logicraft server and the main VAX systems did not resume interaction properly. This was solved by a cold restart of the server system.

Future developments

As the workstations around the College are progressively upgraded to more modern and powerful systems, it is planned to investigate moving to a 'conventional' PC server, with the Logicraft system still in use, but accessing the CD-ROMs on the PC server, rather than directly attached. Suitable PCs would then have the option of direct MS-DOS access or as now via the terminal emulation route.

This approach has already been adopted by some Logicraft sites, and enables them to offer access to CDs on VT ASCII terminals, MS-DOS, MS-Windows, X-Windows and MAC workstations.

The present configuration is shown in Figure 4a and the upgrade path in Figure 4b.

The development of the CD-ROM network is less technically constrained than it is hampered by the high price of disc based services in business, where a company database can cost around £4000 p.a. Competition is growing, but as yet prices have not fallen significantly and a great deal of time is devoted to evaluating new discs and re-evaluating existing subscriptions.

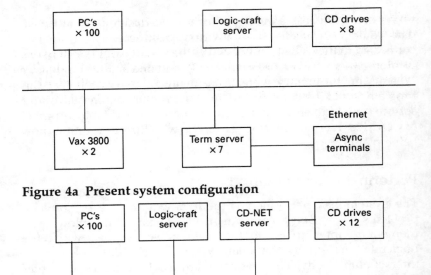

Figure 4a Present system configuration

Figure 4b New system configuration

A second 'soft' problem relates to the management of change. The lack of uniformity in CD-ROM software means that even without budget constraints there is a limit to the number of services a small information centre staff can support, or users know and exploit successfully. Once a CD-ROM (or online end-user) service is adopted the training and publicity attached to its introduction and maintenance is a significant resource commitment, and to change to a rival product which may be marginally superior in terms of content, software or price must be a considered decision.

Increasingly online vendors are responding to CD-ROM competition and stagnant markets by offering attractive academic packages. If online costs can be lowered and controlled by fixed-price agreements, and end-user interfaces improved, the advantages of CD-ROM over online will be eroded, and technical systems have to have the flexibility to respond.

The Logicraft system embedded in the Nautilus VAX network gives Templeton the possibility of using CD-ROMs, locally mounted databases and online through one interface so that we can react sensibly to the shifts in the information marketplace and changing user needs.

CHAPTER NINE

Case study: CD-ROM networking at the University of Portsmouth using SCSI Express

Terry Hanson

Introduction

The University of Portsmouth Library made its first investment in CD-ROM in 1988 with two titles, *Medline* and PAIS. Like many other libraries we were attracted by the technology because of its potential for end-user searching. In early 1989 further titles were purchased and the number has grown steadily ever since to a current total of 28. Also in common with other libraries was the desire to provide multiple-access to these services from a variety of locations via a local area network (LAN) when possible and affordable.

Though it was clear from early experiments with CD-ROM networking that there were considerable problems we began, in late 1989, a planning process that placed CD-ROM as a technology in a key position. In this case study I will describe this planning process and how the early phases of it have been implemented, in particular a CD-ROM network using the SCSI Express software, and look at some of the management issues involved.

The University

Portsmouth is fortunate among former polytechnics in having its buildings concentrated on only two sites (two miles apart) and in having a centralized library policy. This makes the planning and implementation of all kinds of library services easier than if there was a multi-site situation. However, even though there are no major library facilities on the smaller of the two sites (Milton) it would of course be necessary to provide the staff and students there with networked information services. Indeed the need to provide an improved library service to this site was considered to be of strategic (political) importance.

There are six faculties in the University and all major areas are covered with the exception of medicine, though biomedical sciences are well represented with strong research groups and teaching programmes in pharmacy, biology, medical chemistry, etc. Law has not been well represented in the past but there is currently a planning committee looking at new courses in this area. There are some 10 000 students in total, the vast majority of whom are on full-time degree level (or above) courses.

The Frewen Library

The Frewen Library is the central library of the University. It is a modern building built in 1977 with a second phase added in 1988. There are some 450 000 volumes and about 3500 journal subscriptions. A fairly typical subject librarian system is in operation which emphasizes liaison and independence within a vertically integrated structure. Collections are organized on three floors by subject: science and technology, social science, and humanities. Each floor is self-contained in that all books, journals, abstracts and reference books pertaining to the subject area are located on the appropriate floor.

In our planning process these organizational factors were very significant in determining how we were going to implement electronic information services. The most fundamental question we had to address was whether to integrate CD-ROM databases into the locational arrangements already in existence or whether to centralize them in one location. The former option meant there would need to be four physical locations for CD-ROM; the three subject floors plus the General Reference area on the ground floor. Clearly this approach would be much more difficult to administer but we thought that it would nevertheless be the logical and consistent solution.

University networking strategy

As in many universities there has been a strong move towards a decentralized model of computing services at Portsmouth and away from the mainframe-based strategies of the past. And though this is generally recognized as a good thing there is still a valid role for a centralized computing service. In particular there is a need to establish networking standards that all departments can adopt. Whether they are compelled to adopt them or encouraged to is a difficult question. At Portsmouth the approach is to indicate the advantages of following the recommended Novell standard and the consequences of not doing so. In particular the range of information services envisaged in the report mentioned in the next section acted as a powerful inducement to accept the recommendation from the centre. Most departments have followed the advice though a few have still some adaptation to do.

The network strategy at the institutional infrastructure level has concentrated on the establishment of an FDDI (Fibre Distributed Data Interface) ring. This involves fibre-optic cable connections between all buildings and will have the effect of speeding up the inter-departmental network traffic significantly. The standard Ethernet transmission speed is 10 Mbps (Megabits per second) whereas the FDDI standard is capable of speeds of up to 200 Mbps. The remote Milton site is connected to the main campus by megastream bridges with a combined speed of 4 Mbps. An early priority is to upgrade this connection to fibre as soon as possible.

The planning process

In 1990 I wrote an internal discussion paper (Hanson, 1990) on the development of the electronic library. This paper envisaged a campus-wide virtual library whereby all staff would be connected to a powerful network and thus to a range of information services presented by the Library. We identified bibliographic databases, full-text services and other types of information sources such as statistical information and ultimately graphics, sound and video. The paper identified CD-ROM as a key technology as it was clearly having a major impact in all of these areas, but other technologies, such as local loading of data on hard disks and databases mounted on JANET, were also considered important. It was clear that the question of the most appropriate technology mix would be a constantly shifting one and that whatever the strategy it would have to be flexible and adaptable to circumstances.

The paper also made clear that the focus of the strategy had to be on the end-user. In many ways the most important aspects of current networking technology is the potential offered for providing information services direct to the user via the desktop workstation. This of course obviates the need for the user to visit the Library but the convenience of the user has to be paramount.

This paper contained the proposal that a working party be established to consider the overall plan and how best to make progress on implementation. This was accepted and the group was set up with a representative from each faculty and staff from the Library and Computing Services. After two meetings I presented a revised plan which went beyond the original brief, to make recommendations on a Campus-Wide Information Service (CWIS) and on electronic mail information services such as online discussion lists, and services such as bulletin boards and electronic journals. Eventually, after four more meetings, a final report was issued (Hanson, 1992).

The main purpose of the report was to market the ideas and the vision to the University community as a whole and, hopefully, to make them receptive to funding bids at the various implementation stages. The first phase of implementation was to be the establishment of a CD-ROM network which, after a suitable period of satisfactory operation, would be connected to the campus network for remote access to a range of bibliographic databases. A funding bid had been placed for this project during 1991 and this proved successful to the tune of £60 000.

For a variety of reasons everything then began to grind to a halt. The money promised was frozen pending the deliberations of another working party on information technology strategy. When the money was released in February 1992 we still had two major problems to address before implementation of the network could begin. We had no technical support in the Library. Without this we could not contemplate a CD-ROM, or any other kind of network.

Also we needed extra money to cover network licences for the databases that we wanted to put on the network. Both of these problems were raised in the final report of the working party but without response.

In the meantime the Computing Service came to the rescue on the technical support front and some money was 'found' from existing Library sources to pay for some network licences, so that by early 1993 it was possible to begin the implementation.

Hardware and software

Decisions had been made in early 1992 about the software and hardware to be used for the CD-ROM network. The University standard for Novell Netware as the primary networking software was adopted but there was no Ethernet cabling available such that Novell could be used. Our first task was thus to wire the building with data-grade 10BaseT (UTP) Ethernet cabling. This work was done over the summer vacation 1992. On top of the Novell software we then needed to add one of the several CD-ROM networking software packages. This is because, at that time, neither Netware nor its main competitor LAN Manager from Microsoft, could recognize CD-ROM devices directly. Now, however, the long-awaited version 4 of Netware does include support for CD-ROM thus obviating the need for additional software. Indeed the Netware version 4 software is itself distributed on CD-ROM.

In the meantime, however, we had to make a decision from among the available products. The market leader in the UK appeared to be OPTI-NET and there were some users of MultiPlatter, CD-PlusNet, and CD-Net etc. Then along came SCSI Express which appeared to offer a significant advantage over OPTI-NET. The latter required the CD-ROM drives to be attached to a separate server from the network file server. It was thus expensive in hardware. SCSI Express on the other hand is integrated directly into the Novell software and allows the CD-ROM drives to be attached directly to the file server as 'Netware Loadable Modules' (NLMs) (Leman, 1992; McQueen, 1992). Not long after we made the purchase however, an NLM version of OPTI-NET was released.

As well as being less expensive in hardware terms this solution also seemed more elegant and likely to offer better performance. This was borne out in the first major comparative review published in *PC Magazine* in December 1991 (Perratore, 1991) where SCSI Express was the top rated product. This 'seal of approval' was the final confirmation of our decision and the order was eventually placed.

The hardware configuration at the time of initial installation was:

- Dell 486DX 50MHz EISA server with 16 MB RAM and 120 MB hard disk running Novell Netware 3.11.
- 22 workstations. 8 Philips 286, 1 MB RAM, 20 MB hard disk; 14 Dell 486SX, 4MB RAM, 50+MB hard disks. All with 3.5" diskette drives.
- 14 Toshiba CD-ROM drives attached to 2 Adaptec 1542 SCSI interface cards.
- 2 printers shared between workstations in one location. 1 Canon Bubble Jet 300 and 1 Epson SQ850. The printers are shared using buffered printer switches.

In April 1993 we purchased a third 7-drive tower and an additional 8MB RAM.

In addition to the networked services, several of the workstations have access to stand-alone CD-ROM products through built-in drives (mainly Hitachi) or attached Pioneer jukeboxes.

Implementation

By October 1992 we were ready to start testing the network and with the help of the Computing Service's resident Novell expert we soon had things working well. The installation of the SCSI Express software on the server and the mapping of the CD-ROM drives all proved disarmingly straightforward. However, it wasn't until six months later that the network was configured and made available for public use. By this time decisions about which products to network and the locations of networked machines had of course been taken. The most popular titles were, and still are, *Medline, Compendex, Inspec, Georef, PsycLIT*, ABI/INFORM, ASSIA, ERIC, and the *MLA International Bibliography*. With the exception of *Compendex* which was then considered too expensive to network and which was about to be made available within the BIDS service, the others were duly mounted.

The 24 workstations were distributed between the four reference areas according to user demand and product popularity. The Science and Social Science areas each had eight machines while the Humanities floor and the General Reference area each had four workstations. During the early implementation it was decided to offer printing facilities in one of these areas (Social Science) as a trial to gather experience of problems and user behaviour. Where possible the CD-ROM software was configured to allow no more than 25 references to be printed. When users wanted more than this they were encouraged to download and take their disk to the general purpose computing room where several of the PCs had a menu option for printing downloaded CD-ROM references.

The CD-ROM products that have not been networked are made available on stand-alone machines using separate drive units or Pioneer jukeboxes. However there are a few machines which have menu access to both networked and non-networked products. The consideration here is with traffic control. It may not be desirable, for example, to restrict access to a stand-alone product by allowing access to very popular networked databases from the same machine.

The implementation plan envisaged an initial phase of satisfactory operation inside the Library only, before attempting to provide access from other buildings. Thus from April 1993 the 14 drive network was 'launched' for access within the Library and within a month the seven additional drives were mounted. Almost immediately, experiments commenced with test connections to the network from other buildings on the campus. These have been restricted to sites that have followed the recommended Novell path and thus far the experiments have been successful and it is hoped that the remote access arrangements will be formalized during the summer vacation 1993.

The question of access by means other than Ethernet connections has been considered. The policy is to provide the strongest possible encouragement to each department to adopt the preferred network strategy and consequently asynchronous connections have not so far been attempted. It may still be necessary, however, to provide this service and in the meantime staff are investigating the various options available to achieve this: the Novell Netware Access Server, Cubix cards, etc.

The performance of the network in the first few months of operation has been very satisfactory and though there have been teething troubles staff have been very pleased with the early experience. The improved access arrangements, and the 'experimental' introduction of (free) printing facilities, have, not surprisingly, been welcomed with great enthusiasm by the users.

Management and support

The CD-ROM network and other database services, apart from the BLCMP library system, are the responsibility of the Sub-Librarian: Electronic Information Services. The BLCMP housekeeping systems are the responsibility of the Deputy Librarian who, since his promotion to that post has retained his earlier systems responsibility. The need for co-ordination is recognized and the Library's Information Technology Advisory Group (ITAG) has been charged with this responsibility. This body is chaired by the author and meets frequently to discuss IT matters affecting all Library operations and makes recommendations to the University Librarian on policy, purchasing and training needs, etc.

At the technical level the Library now has a technical support team, provided by the Computing Service. This team comprises three staff and has a brief to provide support for IT in all areas in the Library, staff computing, seminar room computers, student general purpose computers, as well as those designated for CD-ROM access. Two of the team have expertise in network management and all are familiar with PCs and Macintoshes. As mentioned earlier the Library was ready in all other respects, other than technical support, to make the CD-ROM network available some months before the eventual launch date. Technical support was considered essential for such a service to be made available.

As CD-ROM networking is not yet as reliable and standardized as networking with hard disks it is inevitable that problems would arise that were not predictable and for which there was no obvious solution from either the SCSI Express, Novell or individual

CD-ROM software manuals. Resort then is to the software supplier (CD-ROM Systems for SCSI Express), to colleagues in other institutions with similar configurations or to the various, and invaluable, online discussion lists such as the US based CD-ROMLAN.

Training and guiding

When libraries begin to make their services available across institutional networks they enter uncharted territory as far as training and guiding are concerned. They have to start thinking as online hosts rather than traditional libraries. In the past, the user needed to be in the library physically and thus in close proximity to a source of help should any be needed. How then should the library respond in the network situation?

The online host comparison is in fact a good one and the response of hosts provides a good model to emulate. Thus the library at Portsmouth provides specific database guides, equivalent to DIALOG Bluesheets, and sends them to those who may be interested. One obvious difference however is that the library's guiding has to take account of the different interfaces used in the variety of databases available. In some cases a database will be of very obvious interest to all staff in a certain department and hence a batch of guides will be sent. Some CD-ROM producers provide excellent single sheet guides themselves which may obviate the need to produce them locally. On the other hand some libraries, such as Portsmouth, will have established a house style for their guides and therefore prefer local production.

The other standard host response is to provide a telephone help desk service during advertised hours. This is a difficult service to provide because it requires the person on duty to be capable of helping the user with a great variety of databases and procedures. If, on the other hand, the help desk is decentralized by subject then it requires guaranteed staffing at all three subject enquiry areas during the advertised hours. Though it is difficult to provide such a guarantee the library has opted for the subject approach, and early experience suggests that this was the correct decision though it has emphasized the need for more staffing.

Training in the use of databases and in related areas of information management and personal databases is provided by Subject Librarians throughout the year. This has increased each year since the acquisition of CD-ROM and now that network access is possible the demands will go on growing. The author is currently working on a project to design a course module on information management and the use and creation of bibliographic databases, to be offered, in suitably customized form, to all departments. It is hoped that in the light of newly decentralized access to information via the campus network the departments will recognize now, if not before, the need for assessed coursework in this area. However, even the most optimistic enthusiast for this approach will recognize the need to provide improved assistance at the point and time of need as well.

Future developments

Early experience with stand-alone CD-ROM was enough to convince staff in the Library that there was great demand for end-user searching and for extending access across the campus network when possible. This was true of both academic and research staff as well as students. With network access now established, the Library has begun the long and hazardous journey towards an electronic or virtual library as described in the working party report referred to earlier in this paper, and the user population has had its collective appetite whetted.

The next step is to ensure that access is possible from all departments and to expand the network by the addition of a second server and extra drives. At the same time the Library is also very interested in the hard disk option for some important products such as *Medline*. However the higher price prohibits early experimentation.

In common with other universities, staff at Portsmouth are very interested in the CHEST/BIDS database access developments and look forward to more databases being made available in this manner. In the meantime, the University's connection to JANET is about to be upgraded and local access restrictions removed. Thus it is intended that during the summer of 1993 the Library will start subscriptions to the ISI databases, the British Library Inside Information current awareness database and, possibly, Compendex.

References

Hanson, T. (1990) *The development of the electronic library: a discussion paper*. University of Portsmouth

Hanson, T. (1992) *A strategic plan for electronic information services: final report of the Electronic Library Working Party*. University of Portsmouth

Perratore, E. (1991) Networking CD-ROMs: the power of shared access. *PC Magazine* (US edition), 31 December, 333–363

Leman, P. (1992) Journey to SCSI Express. In *CD-ROM networking in practice*, eds C. Moore and N. Whitsed, pp. 65–67. UKOLUG/LITC

McQueen, H. (1992) File server-based CD-ROM networking using SCSI Express. *CD-ROM Professional*, **5**, (6), 66–68

CHAPTER TEN

Marketing CD-ROM in libraries

Eileen Elliott de Sáez

Marketing strategy

Does CD-ROM in libraries need a marketing strategy? Do Kellogg's cornflakes, do Hoover for their vacuum cleaners? Of course they do. Hoover want more people to buy their equipment, Kellogg want more people to eat their cereals and more of them. Librarians and information professionals want more and more users. They particularly want users who are so delighted with services that not only will they come back for more, they will be articulate in voicing their approval and make demands for the resources to support such services.

'Delighting the user' may not be a phrase which comes readily to the lips of librarians or information professionals, but Philip Kotler, the expert's expert of marketing, insists that 'delighting the customer' is what we need to aim for:

> When I am asked to define marketing in the briefest possible way I say marketing is meeting needs profitably . . . Marketing is the homework that you do to hit the mark that satisfies those needs exactly. When you do that job... the word gets out from delighted customers that this is a wonderful solution to our problems. (Kotler, 1991)

CD-ROM – a wonderful solution? Certainly CD-ROM represents a revolution for researchers and students, in that it provides powerful and immediate access to major information sources, without the problems attached to over restrictive and expensive online systems. However, CD-ROM is already proving that the benefits which it can provide permeate far beyond the market of online users, to a developing market 'with its own metaphors, rhythm and expectations', which Rigglesford addresses in his paper, *CD-ROM – the answer for end-users?* (Rigglesford, 1992). Community information services, education databases for schools, multi-lingual products, systems which allow the user to link searches using a windowing system across several databases, the CD-ROM environment is expanding fast, of 3500 titles available worldwide, 1520 new titles appeared in 1992 (Finlay and Mitchell, 1993). Why should CD-ROM services need marketing given this apparent phenomenal rate of success? CD-ROM *is* wonderful, the potential *is* far reaching, and marketing concepts and techniques are the vital tools which will effectively ensure that:

- potential markets are identified, reached and satisfied;
- CD-ROM products will match the needs of these markets;
- resources will be available to support the CD-ROM environment;
- libraries and information services and their users will benefit, develop and go forward.

Strategic planning is vital for all aspects of library and information service activities and marketing must be a very strong element in the planning and implementation process.

The institution or organization may well have a published corporate mission, vision or strategic plan. The library and information services described in the Case Studies emphasize that strategic planning and specific objectives within their own sphere must be in tune with those corporate strategies to achieve resource support and ultimate success.

Library mission statements tend to include statements such as:

- the library services will play a key role in the social, educational and economic life of the community by providing information in all forms to individuals, groups, organizations and businesses;
- the library aims to meet recreational, cultural and educational needs;

- the library will provide collections which reflect the breadth of human experience, knowledge and imagination;
- the library aims to disseminate information to meet personal, recreational, educational and business needs.

The grandest mission statement of all comes from the British Library (1989) with its evocative title 'Gateway to Knowledge'. CD-ROM provision is arguably one of the more important gateways to knowledge that the information age has forged. It is certainly more than capable of supporting all the facets of the mission statements listed above and it is this type of evidence which needs to be fed to the decision makers who are formulating policies. The executive function may be in the public or academic library domain, the competitive worlds of business and commerce, the fast changing school or college environment, or the voluntary sector. They all need to be convinced of the value of CD-ROM.

Part of the public relations strategy in marketing CD-ROM will be to ensure that the library is represented on relevant committees, working groups and quality control circles. The library's representative should be well versed in the benefits of CD-ROM provision and must take every opportunity to demonstrate those benefits. The agendas of these committee meetings are a perfect forum for introducing CD-ROM; new products can be announced, changes in service times discussed, training sessions can be arranged and support asked for in terms of department heads releasing or supporting staff or encouraging students.

Networking potential will be a perennial item for such agendas and gradually a knowledge and understanding of the CD-ROM environment will build into ownership of the institution's CD-ROM provision. This is a long term policy but if resources are being sought from general budget heads, then CD-ROM has to be seen as an organization or institution wide asset.

CD-ROM is still a comparatively new information provision model and the costs associated mean that there may have to be significant sacrifices, both perceived and real, in the institutions investing in it. Abbott and Smith highlight marketing diffusion theory in Chapter 4. Behaviour patterns in the way that products are taken up by segments of the market were identified by Rogers, the innovators (2.5% of the market) who try new products immediately take on the attendant risks, finances among them. The early and late adopters, who in libraries and information services waited to see, were in a better position to plan strategy and allocate resources to CD-ROM, whilst Rogers' laggards (16% of a market) should have no place in the information world of today (Rogers, 1962).

Many of the strategic decisions made will be based on marketing information. CD-ROM should fit into the strategic marketing plan as a specific piece and not be lumped in with a products and services general policy. CD-ROM is too important as a marketing tool in its own right to be merely a facet of a portfolio of offerings. As the technology develops, in for example, the potential for standard user interfaces to all databases, (described in Chapter 20), the increasing ease of use of CD-ROM makes it even more effective in attracting users.

The marketing plan

Marketing audit

A marketing audit must be one of the first steps in a marketing plan; both the macro-environment and the micro-environment must be covered. Information and trends from a macro-environmental scan will produce a clearer context in which forecasts can be formulated and decisions made. The uncontrollable variables identified as having a potential influence on libraries and information services will be political, economic, social and cultural and technological (the PESTs of marketing theory). CD-ROM is obviously going to effect and be affected by technological change. As society becomes more attuned to home entertainment, teletext, tele-shopping, tele-banking and working from home via computer networks (telework), CD-ROM services will become an acceptable part of social and cultural life. The economics of, for example, changing birth rates, unemployment, women returners, service rather than manufacturing bases, are ensuring a ready audience for a plethora of CD-ROM network products. On the political scene, the freedom of information debate, the fate of our public library service, the changes in education structure at all levels, all have a significant influence on types of CD-ROM need, provision, products and access.

SWOT analysis

An easy to follow primer in formulating a marketing plan is Malcolm McDonald's *The marketing planner* (1992) which includes a step-by-step approach to the preparation of a strategic marketing plan and an operational marketing plan.

Essentially, the next step is a SWOT analysis, that is, an honest appraisal of the strengths, weaknesses, opportunities and threats afforded by CD-ROM. The comparative ease of use which CD-ROM affords the end-user appears to be an obvious strength, but it could well be a weakness. Terry Hanson of Portsmouth reports that senior academics in most universities will not take kindly to having their searching ability tested. In truth, it is quite possible that they do not know that the opportunities are wider than information searching, Hanson describes downloading and post-processing in the university library (Chapter 16) and a number of schools are downloading bibliographic records from the British Library's BNB, Whitaker's *Bookbank* or *Bookfind* from *Bookdata*. Community information services are becoming more widespread as producers of CD-ROM services.

Threats will undoubtedly list costs, staff training budgets, increasing demands on terminal provision and even user education might be seen as a poisoned chalice; in a do-it yourself gone mad world, libraries and information professionals might disappear. Day's Chapter 11 on user training should lay that ghost to rest and indeed, user education programmes should be an opportunity to enhance the promotion of CD-ROM.

The SWOT analysis will have different elements and emphases depending on the institution involved, but it will provide a clear framework and identify key issues if it is handled as a consultative process and as many staff as possible are involved.

Marketing objectives

Marketing objectives can be set usefully at this stage, but may be amended in the light of market research and evaluation procedures. The library or information service may decide to examine its portfolio of products and services relative to the competition and, for example, CD-ROM could well be considered in comparison to online, or community service or CD-ROM provision could be measured against telephone advice systems. One of the standard models for portfolio management is that from the US Boston Consulting Group, and other models too are well illustrated by Wilson and Gilligan with Pearson (1992).

The BCG model demands that all products or services are classified as follows and dealt with accordingly:

- 'Cash cows' are the steady profit makers or in library terms attracting users consistently.
- 'Dogs' are not producing any benefits and should be shot; kind hearted professionals may call for a stay of execution and resuscitate such services with renewed resources or different user bases, but it will be difficult if not impossible and nor should it be sought in most cases.
- 'Question marks' are self-explanatory. Is it worth taking the risk, are the markets big enough, is the potential benefit worth it?
- 'The stars', expensive but worth it, value will increase as resource support diminishes and they become the cash cows of the future.

The classification for CD-ROM would seem to be unquestionable.

Marketing mix

The set of marketing strategies developed by Igor Ansoff (1957) also merit close consideration before deciding on appropriate marketing mixes. Ansoff suggests a matrix based upon existing and new markets and existing and new products. Essentially:

- 'Market penetration' would involve existing users using CD-ROM services more than at present.
- 'Market extension' would be finding and attracting new users.
- 'Product development' would look to enhancing CD-ROM services.

- 'Diversification' strategies suggest you go in a completely new and totally unrelated direction.

The marketing mixes designed to support these strategies will need to be pretty powerful instruments.

A marketing mix is a set of strategies aimed at moving potential users from a state of awareness of a service through to actually using it and preferably continuing to use the service or buy the product. A useful starting point is the AIDA model; the acronym refers simply to the actions of potential users:

- Making the potential user AWARE
- Attracting further INTEREST
- Creating DESIRE
- Encouraging ACTION

The idea of the marketing mix and its widely acclaimed four Ps was developed by E J McCarthy (1978) from earlier work by Borden (1965). McCarthy's four Ps are a seller's paradigm of product, price, place and promotion. Philip Kotler suggests that we use, more properly in the customer oriented world of today, four Cs:

- Customer value
- Cost to the customer, which includes energy and time cost
- Customer convenience
- Communication, or dialogue rather than promotion (Kotler, 1991).

There are any number of marketing mix variables in reality, but the four Ps or four Cs are invariably elements. The emphases of the marketing mix will depend upon where CD-ROM is positioned according to the market segment targeted. A high-value, technologically packaged service for senior academics or perhaps a user friendly, press-the-button operation, for community information seekers would demand different approaches in presentation, accommodation, guides available, staff to hand and so on.

Market segments

One of the most important market segments initially will be colleagues in the institution who will all have their own patch to defend and promote. So that marketing CD-ROM may well have to start with library or information service colleagues as a priority. Donovan's chapter on *Management issues*, stresses the importance of integrating responsibility for CD-ROM into existing management structure. This is a marketing ploy in itself, since staff ownership of a product or service area is a high motivational factor. A confident user base, well able to operate CD-ROM information, benefits library staff by freeing them for other more sophisticated professional responsibilities. Bibliographic downloading again offers exciting possibilities in creating new information tools, as well as reducing routine record making. If the library has access to the services of JANET and the Internet navigation tools, such as Gopher, WAIS and World Wide Web, possibilities are endless for a seamless, browsable continuum and information addiction could become the disease of the new century.

To emphasize benefits, whether inside the library or to the users and potential users, it is essential to identify who the users and potential users are and to investigate their needs, perceived as well as real. Market segmentation and market research, therefore, needs to be considered in conjunction with marketing mix preparation. Market segments will differ naturally for each library offering CD-ROM provision. The academic library will include the Senate or Academic Board, senior management, tutors, research students, postgraduate students, undergraduates, disabled, part-time, mature and overseas students, administrative and technical staff and probably, local businesses and professional organizations. The public library range will include students from school through to higher education, ethnic minorities, local businesses, community organizations, the unemployed, the bored, the young mother, the new man, the ever expanding third generation and many other segments too. The school library, or more probably, the learning resource centre today, will need to reach pupils, teachers, parents and governors. Reachability is vital, a market segment must be accessible, homogenous and worth the effort. This may sound ruthless, but in the continuous battle for resources it is essential that priorities are decided and acted upon. Success breeds success and from a position of strength in the future, the library will be able to focus on activities which perforce have to come later in the queue at present.

Promotional activities

The CD-ROM directory (Finlay and Mitchell, 1993) has a product to meet user needs at different stages, but the marketing mix will need to be different in each case. The same information will be useful to any number of market segments, but will need to be packaged differently. Academic staff and research students may be offered facilities physically apart from the undergraduate population, similar to the Club Class beloved of airlines. The CD-ROM provision for school children may be centred in the school library to persuade them to use other materials and facilities, but the system may be networked to allow access by the head teacher, other staff in the staffroom, the school technician and perhaps other schools in the area. The public library will need to enhance text to suit elderly eyes or provide toys to keep small children quiet alongside the access point their parent is using.

General publicity leaflets extolling the virtues of CD-ROM are a waste of energy; segments need to be targeted specifically: demonstrations and practice sessions, videos showing the benefits of information found, open sessions with incentives thrown in, these will work. As will invitations to special events where CD-ROM can play a visible and vital part, or readers' queries answered with a demonstration, not just a printout and a flourish. Articles for student magazines or the local media will be readily accepted, they have acres of space to fill and libraries too rarely feature. Try to find a relevant, local connection or amusing or heart rending example to draw attention to the service, 'job search successful' is a good one and library staff could be alerted to note media-worthy items.

The promotion element of the marketing mix includes personal selling as well as publicity and every member of staff is part of the sales team. Paid for advertising is unlikely to be a real proposition since it is so costly, but a Public Service Announcement is worth considering. PSAs are no longer the dreary public warnings of yesteryear. Commercial television companies now allocate professional staff to the making of these advertisements for local community organizations and activities. Again it will be necessary to be creative in providing interesting images, a screen on the screen is not the most riveting object in the world, but multimedia CD-ROM products include all singing all dancing graphics today. Nevertheless, it is the personal selling which will work most effectively, the introduction by a well informed, enthusiastic member of staff, the user training programmes, the seminars to introduce new products, the visits to relevant department or authority heads and then the message spreads. Kotler's delighted users will spread the word for you.

Place, or access point, is important; the awful paradox for the librarian is that where CD-ROM is part of extensive network provision, the user's need to visit the library reduces dramatically; success can be a double-edged sword. What is vital in this situation is that the library ensures it is credited as the source of the service, a compelling logo or service name is a promotional necessity. CD-ROM lends itself to a host of interesting possibilities, and competitions are a time honoured way of refreshing tired creativity banks. Try not to be too humorous, humour dates rapidly but do aim for pronouncability, it engenders affection, especially if the name or acronym is short. Marketing lore tells you to use a K or an X, Aston University's Project, ACCENT, must be the most tortuous acronym imaginable, but we don't forget it.

Price cannot be ignored, cheaper than online ostensibly, but again, the more successful CD-ROM is, the greater the demand, and the provision of extra service points and more and more relevant products dramatically reduces the financial distance between the two – a distance which will only marginally be covered by improved efficiency in the service. The price to users is their time and energy, where previously a librarian would have provided all the relevant sources and information, now the user is in control, just as the inexperienced newly qualified driver is in control, however, and we cannot escape the reality, that the real cost to the user is a potentially inadequate, even if unrecognized as inadequate, delivery. How can we turn the L-driver into the advanced motorist and should we even try?

Evaluation and market research

Evaluation is so mixed up with market research as an ongoing process, that it is a joy to greet a new text from Peter Chisnall, whose *Market research: analysis and measurement* (Chisnall, 1981) is used on marketing courses everywhere. *The essence of marketing research* (Chisnall, 1991) contains concise but comprehensive information about the nature, scope, tools and techniques of marketing research and evaluation, and the academic references have deliberately been kept to a minimum.

The best advice on market research that can be given to librarians and information professionals is to go to a market research supplier. It will be more effective and less costly in the long run and the more a market research organization is used, the better the understanding and relationship which builds up, leading to a more effective decision-making machine. However, the reality is that most libraries will attempt inhouse research or more correctly, investigation. Questionnaire design is a science, it can be learned, but it is not easy and if this is to be an investigation method, read the books, take advice and use a pilot study. Even then be prepared to accept the error quotient which has been built in inevitably.

Exit surveys, beloved of the political election polls, are calculated to fail in the library situation. Who wants to be stopped, having made the decision, probably for excellent reasons, to leave the library? Use the technology, introduce interactive modes at regular intervals on screen. Question users at the approach or even in the middle of a search, having warned them in advance by posters or cards near the terminal points or even better, on-screen messages. Remember, that the user's perception of a satisfactory search may not be yours, but remember too, what your own tolerance levels are and how they change over time and depending on circumstance. When did you last weed your personal authority file, wipe no longer needed files, check shelving, dust the top of the wardrobe?

Take it for granted that searching skills of users will need updating or refreshing, as professionals we attend seminars on new developments in CD-ROM, do we feel threatened? Golf and tennis professionals charge for polishing skills, evening classes are full of adults enhancing their motor maintenance, cookery, first aid or self defence skills. In an information world, information seeking skills are survival and life enhancing skills. The objective of the CD-ROM marketer is to ensure that the relevant market segment perceives information seeking in the same light as the aforementioned.

A clinic advertized to relevant E-mail boxes and offering an appointment system will target senior academics effectively. An open day, or open evening, invitation to members of the local community, councillors, organization leaders etc. will help in the public library – the library should normally be closed at the time of this event. These proceedings can form part of the evaluation procedure, although ostensibly advanced training or public relations events. Focus groups, or discussion groups, are a well established method of seeking user views, the major drawback is the accurate recording of such views, and video rather than audio is increasingly being used.

The value of sampling populations, whatever method is used, cannot be over estimated. Search quality will of necessity be problematical, but well designed structured interviews can be constructed and the reference interview looms large in professional literature to help. Having ascertained a reader's actual needs, it is then relatively easy to check the user's success rate against a librarian's hit rate. There are other aspects of CD-ROM provision which must be investigated and which, fortunately, are rather more tangible: knowledge of products available, ease of access arrangements, menu structure, ease of use, guidance materials availability and quality, downloading facilities, training sessions, quality and effectiveness of help-desk or trouble shooting services, among them.

The objectives in collecting such information need to be clearly formulated, there is no point in collecting information on a 'nice to know' basis. Collect what is needed, calculate the acceptable shortfall in accuracy and build the information into a decision making tool to enhance the CD-ROM provision on offer and make a case for more resources.

Conclusion

The purpose of this chapter has been to examine the way in which marketing concepts and techniques can support the CD-ROM environment effectively. Contributors elsewhere in the volume, particularly in the case studies, naturally incorporate marketing thinking in their papers, pointing to the pervasive nature of marketing philosophy and its vital function in library and information service provision. If we are to delight our users and serve them effectively, CD-ROM will undoubtedly be a quality element in that provision. It is only by accepting the fundamental need to put into practice effective marketing strategies that the battle for resources will be won and that need must be a continuing one to ensure the protection and development of our services.

References

Ansoff, H.I. (1957) Strategies for diversification. *Harvard Business Review*, **25**, (5), 113–24

Borden, N.H. (1965) The concept of the marketing mix. In *Science in marketing*, G Schwartz, pp. 386–97. Chichester: Wiley

Chisnall,P.M. (1981) *Marketing research: analysis and measurement*. New York: McGraw-Hill

Chisnall, P.M. (1991) *The essence of marketing research*. Hemel Hempstead: Prentice Hall International

Finlay, M. and Mitchell, J. (1993) *The CD-ROM directory 1993*. London: TFPL Publishing

Kotler, P. (1991) Silent satisfaction. L. Mazur. *Marketing Business*, 24–7

McCarthy, E.J. (1978) *Basic marketing: a managerial approach* 6th edn. Homewood Illinois: Richard D. Irwin

McDonald, M. (1992) *The marketing planner*. Oxford: Butterworth-Heinemann

Rigglesford, D. (1992) CD-ROM-the answer for end-users? In *Information systems for end-users – research and development issues*. London: Taylor Graham

Rogers, E.M. (1962) *Diffusion of innovations*. New York: Free Press

Rogers, E.M. (1983) *Diffusion of innovations* 3rd edn. New York: Macmillan

Wilson, R.M.S. and Gilligan, C. with Pearson, D.J. (1992) *Strategic marketing management*. Oxford: Butterworth-Heinemann

CHAPTER ELEVEN

Training end-users of CD-ROM

Joan Day

Introduction

CD-ROM has been the most exciting thing to happen in libraries for years, bringing the power of interactive searching to users and library staff in general, not just a privileged few professionals. No other recent innovation has affected so many members of the library community so quickly. It is ironic that what was launched as an end-user medium is now placing such demands on libraries for user instruction far beyond any experienced for print based materials. More than one conference goer has referred to 'the great CD-ROM con', as initial euphoria has given way to sheer panic at how to stop demands for help in using CD-ROM products from swamping the information service. This book is being prepared as we enter a third stage, with the realization that end-user searching is here to stay, not a nine-day wonder, and that the way in which it is introduced and supported has to be part of a library's overall strategic and operational plan for user service.

Many of the issues arising from the introduction of single user CD-ROM workstations apply to the growing number of alternative forms of end-user access – networking and dial-up access to CDs and other databases available within the library, or online access to major databases at a fixed cost such as those available to the academic and research community via JANET (Joint Academic NETwork) in Britain and Internet in North America.

What end-user interfaces have done is to create the illusion that searching, often complex, databases is easy. What is difficult is getting a quality result, not least by choosing the most appropriate database to search, and understanding the underlying concepts involved in interactive searching. The problem with end-user systems used in isolation is that they remove the safeguard of a professional intermediary to offer such advice. This is not to say that formal training has to be offered to all CD-ROM searchers in order to use every product. If this is proving necessary, send the CD back and say why you are doing so! The user friendliness of much CD-ROM search software has changed dramatically as a result of feedback from librarians, but unless a single CD-ROM product offers the absolute solution to users' information needs, then there are much wider education and training issues to address.

Why train?

Most libraries offer some direct support to enable users to get the best out of their services. The level and type of support will depend on the interaction of three main variables in the training triangle:

- the overall aims of the library service in relation to its users;
- the complexity of the information system;
- the level of staff resources.

The level of support is likely to relate directly to the extent to which users need or want to be self-sufficient in information seeking. CD-ROM is no exception; the extent and nature of training needed, if any, will be dictated by the complexity of the CD-ROM product, the types of users and their expectations of the library service, and the level of staff resources available to offer user support. A library will already have a policy on how much direct user support it gives in using the service and the sources within it. This should be part of its mission statement or may develop by custom and practice and this will influence its approach to training for CD-ROM. Public libraries do not have a captive audience for training programmes; academic libraries do. There are, nevertheless, features of the CD-ROM medium which have clouded the picture and led to reactions like those quoted by the librarian in Chapter 3 – 'we hate CD-ROM'.

Popularity and over expectation

The novelty and instant popularity of CD-ROM with users has no parallel with print based sources of information. The visibility of computer screens, particularly when well designed with sensible use of colour, attract attention in a way in which printed sources cannot do. Once information has been retrieved on one topic from a relevant CD-ROM, user expectations rise. Why cannot all problems be solved in this way? Despite the exponential growth in available titles outlined in Chapter 2, they represent a tiny proportion of available information resources, and users need to realize this limitation and be willing to use complementary sources, usually in print. Because the data is well packaged, with the added features of flexible access and immediate output, the quality of data and its appropriateness for the particular purpose are easily ignored. Even library staff can be guilty of this; early reviews of CD-ROM products tended to concentrate solely on the search features, quality of documentation etc. and ignored the content. Users need to understand what they are searching within the context of the information available to them.

Range of databases

The increasing variety of data available on CD-ROM presents a further problem. Searching a full-text newspaper with immediately usable output contrasts with the need to seek the documents traced in a bibliographical database, particularly an index without abstracts. The ability to add local holdings onto some commercial CD-ROMs, and the increase in provision of source material on CD-ROM to support a bibliographic index goes some way to solving this problem, but the user needs to know what is beyond the CD search (see discussion of *Business Periodicals Ondisc* in the Templeton College case study in Chapter 8).

Diversity of software

A more serious issue in a training context is the diversity of search software in use, and this is unlikely to change significantly beyond a general improvement in user friendliness. It does not make commercial sense for rival producers to harmonize, unfortunately. Techniques learnt in searching one interface may not, therefore, be transferred easily to another, unless the user is aware of the underlying principles involved in formulating a search strategy.

Unless the search software is largely intuitive as, for instance, the latest version of CD Plus's software OVID is designed to be, then it helps if the user understands something of the nature of the search process. Most systems still work on the now dated concept of Boolean logic, and where it has been possible to monitor end-user searches, the misuse of the Boolean operator OR for AND has been the commonest cause of poor search results (see the Cairns Library case study below). The ability to browse through large numbers of retrieved records, as many end-users seem happy to do, allows the problem to be overcome to some extent, but is not the best use of the user's time or of the equipment which may be in heavy demand. Use of the context specific help provided on the majority of CD-ROM products is the commonest method used in the first instance by most users surveyed (Culbertson, 1992), but the quality and extent of this varies widely between products. Few users are prepared to work systematically through the ondisc tutorials offered by some producers like SilverPlatter particularly before using a database for the first time.

Access

The library can affect the need for training in a number of ways. Location of workstations in a cluster, particularly if networked, might justify time tabling a roving trouble shooter and avoid constant interruptions at the enquiry desk. As case studies in Chapter 12 and at the end of the volume will demonstrate, the approach can and should change as users become more experienced, staff resources are overstretched, or control is lost as CD-ROM access moves away from single user workstations in sight of the enquiry desk to networked access within and without the library.

Who to train?

User categories

Users are not a homogeneous mass, and it is often difficult for the librarian to know if a satisfied customer is actually in a state of blissful ignorance. Can we categorize CD-ROM users? Each is a unique individual with a complex mix of personality traits and level of experience as an information user and computer user, with varied motivation towards accomplishing the task for which the CD-ROM might be used. Individual instruction might seem the ideal solution but it is beyond most library resources, and is not as effective as might at first seem, as will be discussed.

Some common factors can be considered in categorizing users and their training needs, and, wherever possible, account should be taken of the level of previous experience and likely patterns of use.

- The NOVICE user tends to have low knowledge of database and search concepts and may also have computer anxiety, so requires a system that is easy to use and gives quick rewards.
- The KNOWLEDGEABLE BUT INTERMITTENT user has a good basic knowledge but may be out of practice and/or is new to a particular system, so will appreciate a simple interface but with the potential for shortcutting menus.
- The FREQUENT user is likely to retain good search practices once learnt, and may want to learn more sophisticated features.

These categories have been adopted by most CD-ROM software designers, with the default software level in novice mode, or the chance to choose either menu or command driven software as with DIALOG OnDisc. The same approach should be borne in mind in preparing training sessions, writing support documentation or even giving point-of-need help. Royan (1992) similarly categorizes end-users as NAIVE (New And Infrequently Venturing End-user), REGULAR and SUPER. What levels of user are you dealing with? If in doubt, aim for the novice and keep it simple, aim to build confidence; ensure the user knows how to find out more when needed.

Where the user population is high in relation to staff resources for training, it makes even more sense to concentrate efforts on those users most likely to benefit. Hepworth (1992) uses Plutchak's matrix (Plutchak, 1989) as a basis for developing an end-user information course. Plutchak analysed results from a survey carried out by the US National Library of Medicine at 21 test sites using between them eight versions of *Medline* on CD-ROM. By concentrating on two variables – the subjective satisfaction of the end-user of a CD-ROM system or the 'feel good factor', and the degree of skill or 'eptness' with which the end-user manipulated the search systems, he identified four categories of user. The two categories of DISSATISFIED user are not a serious problem – although they mean work, they identify themselves fairly readily. The DISSATISFIED EPT – will complain that there are no abstracts, or full text. They don't need training as much as patience in explaining why they must be more realistic. The DISSATISFIED INEPT are ripe for training – strike while the iron's hot and with luck, you help them join the third category – the SATISFIED EPT. It is the SATISFIED INEPT who represent the real challenge to the librarian, since they are difficult to identify and when you do, they may not wish to accept that with a little effort on their part, their search time will be used much more effectively.

A good reference librarian or information officer develops a second sense for the satisfied inept and intervenes, a skill even easier to employ if the CD-ROM workstation is placed near an enquiry point where you can casually observe what is happening on screen. This approach may solve the dissatisfied inept user's specific problem, to find relevant information, but this is likely to be achieved by the librarian taking over the search while the user learns little in the way of transferable skills for the next time. The user will either join the satisfied inept, muddling through in future, or more likely, revert to dissatisfied inept, and so the cycle goes on. Suggestions for approaching this type of situation more effectively are given below.

Staff training

Staff training must come first, and is an ongoing commitment. It must include anyone likely to be on a public service point where users might seek help. Not everyone will need to know all databases in depth, particularly in a broadly based service, with clear distinction between professional and non-professionally trained staff in giving user support. However, understanding the nature of CD-ROM products, the common technical problems and what help aids are available is a minimum requirement. A training strategy should identify what level of knowledge and skill is needed by each staff member.

Staff as end-users

Royan (1992) identifies a fourth category of user – librarians: professionally qualified librarians with online expertise who find CD-ROMs frustrating; retrieval is slow, menu systems are cumbersome and a disc may cover only a fraction of an online database. Such attitudes are not a good starting point for training genuine end-users, who compare CD searching with the tedium of using printed sources at best, or serendipity browsing through the shelves at worst. It is from the real end-user's point of view that training needs must be assessed and a training strategy devised.

Approaches to end-user training

Training needs assessment

There is no 'right' way to solve the dilemma of the extent to which you train end-users. The 'best' approach for an individual library will depend on the balance of the training triangle.

Most people learn skills like database searching by practical experience, so insisting that everyone attends an introductory presentation before hands-on experience may put some off altogether. This may be an appropriate model for training end-users of high cost online systems, but the need to accept the change in approach has been successful in at least one pharmaceutical company with experience of end-user training for online databases (Sullivan, 1992). Optional training after an initial search if required was shown to be a better use of resources.

Setting aims and objectives

The development of a training strategy with clear long term aims and specific objectives needs to be agreed at the outset. A survey of UK medical librarians showed the common aim to be to train end-users to the extent that they could search effectively without continual help from librarians (Steele and Tseng, 1992). Objectives in relation to this might be to offer regular demonstrations to acquaint users with *Medline*; to plan workshops at novice and intermediate level; to provide point-of-need help sheets; to refer all enquirers to the appropriate source of further assistance.

There is always a danger when assessing needs that library rather than user objectives are set, leading to overkill. What the librarian feels the novice user needs to know to carry out 'effective' searching is often more than the novice user actually requires, for example a few informative abstracts to supplement lecture notes as a basis for a student essay. Analyses of end-user searches have, not surprisingly, shown room for improvement. A survey of academic end-users of scientific and technical databases analysed 1633 searches. Only 20% used any special features beyond selecting search terms and printing results. Just over half used Boolean operators, in all but one case AND. Print was the most commonly used feature, mainly to dump results into a print queue rather than select from a display (Culbertson, 1992).

There is no doubt that, assuming a suitable database has been chosen and the user is happy to use a computer keyboard, a reasonably intelligent end-user should be able to find something of use from many of the commercial CD-ROM products available in libraries. If this is adequate for their needs, you may question seriously whether you ought to put staff resources into offering more, and your 'training' activity may be confined to adequate publicity and marketing, and sorting out queries on demand. After all, individual attention is the preferred method by users, and is perceived to be most effective by library staff (Whitaker, 1990). However, it is the least cost-effective approach in terms of staff time, and its long term value to users can be questioned, as will be shown.

Training methods

Most libraries have found that a combination of approaches to training end-users is necessary, involving two or more of talks and demonstrations to raise awareness of training need, formal taught sessions, small group workshops aimed at different user groups, and the preparation of support materials, as well as point-of-need help.

A clear training strategy will lessen the chance of unnecessary duplication of effort. Where several staff are involved it is useful to set up a working group to agree on a standard approach wherever possible from developing a house style for support materials like hand-outs and prompt sheets, preparing 'scripts' for staff to use when giving advice or running a more formal session, to 'troubleshooting' hints to help solve recurring problems. This standard approach is not only cost effective for the library, but encourages understanding of basic concepts and the development of transferable skills between CD-ROM products.

Troubleshooting

Recurrent problems experienced with CD-ROM use are well rehearsed in other chapters and case studies, and some can be overcome by forward planning. Creating standard menus for choosing titles can include instructions on loading discs: clear instructions will help avoid the most basic questions on getting started; networked CD-ROMs avoid the user handling discs, but create other problems as there is more chance of the user choosing the wrong database, or thinking they are searching the library catalogue and can find all references in stock. A telephone help line may be useful in such cases (Jaros, 1990).

Checklists of the regular problems that arise and how to deal with them can be prepared for both staff and users, with a manual of database specific issues which regularly crop up for staff. Knowing how to identify the 'fault' can take time, so it is sensible to pool staff experience in this way as it builds up. The larger the staff involved at a particular service point, the more this makes sense. Nipp and Shamy (1992) outline the seven basic steps in writing a CD-ROM trouble shooting manual for librarians. The authors claim that, while the original intention of the document was as a reference manual for dealing with equipment problems, an added benefit has been an increased level of skill in managing the equipment.

Documentation

Despite the last comment, documentation in itself is not the most effective training method for any skill, particularly a practical one like interactive searching. It does play an important support role, both to hands-on self instruction and to supplement formal training sessions. The quality of documentation provided with CD-ROMs is improving, but making the full manual available to novice end-users is useless. Expert users may wish to know that one exists for occasional reference use. Some suppliers provide a prompt card of basic functions, but making these easily available at the workstation when they use different formats and physical layout can cause more confusion. Many libraries produce their own prompt sheets in a standard layout, so that users become familiar with where to find what they need. Typically they include:

- database coverage – what type of information it contains, scope, limitations, reference to alternative sources;
- steps involved in carrying out a simple search;
- viewing / printing / downloading results;
- 'troubleshooting' – common problems encountered;
- how to get further help.

Two sides of A4 should be adequate; even for more complex databases, headings and layout can remain standard. If it exceeds four sides, you are rewriting the manual, or the system is too complex for this approach. Prompt sheets can be produced cheaply, updated easily using word-processing or desk-top publishing, and handed out at training sessions or provided in multiple copies in the library. This is particularly useful where users may access CDs via a network in different locations – they can carry their own copy for regularly used databases.

Webber (1987; Day and Webber, 1990) has outlined the main steps involved in preparing documentation:

- analyse user need – who will use it? where? and why?
- formulate clear objectives for the document;
- break down tasks into steps;
- pay careful attention to layout, using clear headings and examples of what to do or how the system responds;
- test with a typical user;
- choose an appropriate production method for the situation;
- gather regular feedback from users and update as required.

Do not use an expensive production method when most CD-ROM software is still being updated regularly, but using different coloured paper for each product is helpful to staff and users.

Burton (1992) gives similar advice on preparing 'cheat sheets', giving particular emphasis to the need to prepare them from the user's point of view, not the librarian's as an experienced searcher. The same steps can be followed in preparing more extensive training materials or manuals.

Point-of-need instruction

As noted earlier, giving help on demand does not necessarily fulfil a training function if treated in an ad hoc fashion. It should be distinguished clearly from 'troubleshooting' to enable the user to continue with a search. Condic (1992) describes the development of guidelines for one-to-one instruction at point-of-need which aim to maximize users' satisfaction – they get a result – while making sure they can learn more if they wish, but limiting staff time which will be wasted going into more complex detail. The guidelines are:

- find out exactly what the user wants;
- answer that question ONLY;
- do not be diverted into more complex explanations, e.g. of the advantages of controlled vocabulary over free-text searching;
- be patient but brief;
- indicate the help aids available;
- direct the now satisfied, still inept but motivated user to a training session.

If user requirements and staff resources permit it, or if it is not feasible to run separate training sessions, one-to-one training should still follow a pre-set pattern to avoid information overload and present users with a structured, clear introduction from which they can master the basics. The same rules apply to advanced training for more experienced users.

Formal training sessions

If it is decided to offer formal training sessions, it is best to focus on groups with similar needs, particularly in terms of frequency of use, and to concentrate on a specific product. This may not be possible when sessions are on a 'drop in' basis, but can be done where CD-ROM use can be integrated into an established user education programme as can happen in academic libraries.

Formal training sessions should rarely last for more than 30–45 minutes, much less if it is not possible to include some practical activity, preferably, though not necessarily, hands on experience.

The particular approach will, therefore, depend on a number of factors:

- the kind of information, knowledge and skills to be learnt: promoting awareness, getting started or improving novice skills;
- the background, prior knowledge and inclination of learners;
- how many people you are trying to reach at one time;
- location of the session;
- under what circumstances people attend: compulsory or optional;
- availability of staff to carry out effective training;
- provision for immediate reinforcement of what is learnt;
- how often the knowledge needs to be updated;
- availability of support materials, if any;
- provision and quality of support documentation.

The answers to these questions, some of which will be outside the library's control, will dictate whether there can be direct training, supervision of practical activities, self instruction or a mix of these.

Again, it is important to write down clear aims and objectives for any training activity, however short, within the overall training strategy. These should begin with a definition of the expected audience level and take into account the likely user objectives, which is why compulsory sessions are less successful than those where participants have some choice. Restrictions imposed by availability of accommodation, hardware and software must be faced. Although claims of demonstration to 120 undergraduates using a liquid crystal display (LCD) screen linked to a CD-ROM workstation have been heard, the overall aim could have been little more than awareness of the existence of a CD-ROM database, and motivation to 'have a go' individually.

Whatever the group size, it is important to plan the structure in advance within specific aims and objectives for the particular session, hold it in a comfortable, non-threatening environment for the user, and relate content and level to the prior experience of participants as much as possible.

Demonstration has been shown to be an essential part of any training session, particularly to the novice or intermittent user. Bostian and Robbins (1990) report on a controlled experiment with four groups of undergraduate students at Plymouth State College who were given different levels of instruction before searching *PsycInfo*. The only level of instruction that produced a significant difference in search strategy was a live demonstration of a few searches. Those given least instruction tried to use more search aids, but this produced a largely negative correlation. The researchers concluded that without a demonstration, 'you can teach computer searching till the cows come home, and the students won't know much more than when they started' (Bostian and Robbins, 1990 p.17).

Sample searches should be planned in advance, but should relate where possible to the interests of the group or individual. Asking for suggestions from the audience is dangerous if you are trying to show steps clearly – they rarely work as you expect, and invariably show up problems or features that you do not wish to include in a beginners' session. However, this approach can work well with more experienced searchers, and a confident trainer.

KEEP IT SIMPLE – stick to basics and avoid over-emphasizing the theoretical at the expense of the functional in initial sessions. Incorporate as much user participation as possible. If group size makes hands-on experience impossible, prepare a handout showing the searches you demonstrate, together with further examples to try out themselves and encourage them to do so as soon as possible. Where theoretical understanding is thought necessary, for instance how to develop a search strategy, users can work in pairs following a worked example using an interactive handout with space to answer questions and tasks to complete. People remember very little of what they hear, more of what they see and hear, but most of what they DO. Always aim to teach transferable skills not just how to use database ABC.

Computer aided instruction (CAI)

The main problem with CAI is getting people to work through instruction programmes voluntarily. Most CD-ROM systems offer context specific help, and some make it possible to work through help screens consecutively as a tutorial. This is not interactive and gives no feedback to the user other than by allowing the procedure to be completed correctly. However, if well designed help screens enable the user to carry out a simple search, then some basic concepts may have been learned, particularly if the designer has explained concepts like Boolean searching rather than merely given an example. Harrington (1990) evaluates the tutorials offered on SilverPlatter CD-ROMs. The more advanced interfaces which, for instance, automatically transfer a search term to an index or thesaurus to guide the user to a choice of terms are excellent for that database but will not teach the user much about the steps involved in interactive searching. This is not a criticism of the more sophisticated systems, but rather another example of the problems posed by the diversity of search software. Eventually we may have interfaces that can adapt to what is learnt about the user during a search session and offer advice on search formulation and results, but this is some decades away (Belkin, 1991).

Software exists to create sophisticated inhouse computer aided instruction packages, and hypertext software is being used increasingly for general user education. However production is time consuming and the investment would have to be weighed against likely user resistance. Most users will prefer to muddle through with the real CD-ROM.

Peer training

Enthusiastic novice users showing their new found skill off to friends may be good publicity, but is a dangerous training method. Enthusiasm can be harnessed by libraries where such users can be identified and persuaded to become trained trainers, either through payment, as with students, or by identifying altruistic gatekeepers in, for instance, academic departments or research laboratories.

Sample training programmes

Most training programmes are based essentially on what librarians think users ought to know, tempered by how much users are prepared to learn.

As well as the case studies in this book, several detailed outlines of CD-ROM training programmes have been published, particularly by academic librarians in North America, where it is possible to offer more structured instruction within broader user education programmes to students taking credit-earning library modules as part of their formal teaching programme. There is a common theme in promoting the dual aim of educating users and saving staff time on one-to-one instruction. Johnson and Rosen (1990) outline a useful planning model, as do Amato and Jackson (1990).

Lowe (1990) stresses the need for an integrated approach to promote the effective and efficient use of retrieval tools, thus avoiding users seeing CD-ROM as a library rather than information seeking tool – i.e. emphasizing transferable information skills. Demonstrations followed by weekly 45 minute workshops are offered throughout the academic year on each database held in Brauch College Library, City University of New York. A common conceptual approach is used to each information source, regardless of idiosyncrasies (Lowe, 1990, p.18):

- what is the nature of the information needed?
- where can it be found?
- how can it be retrieved?
- what are the most appropriate terms or subject headings?
- what kinds of indexes or access points are available?

Maxymuk (1991) offers detailed outlines of instructional programmes for both novice and experienced searchers. A model 'script' has been developed applicable to any database at Temple University Library, allowing standard overhead transparencies to be prepared on common steps, e.g. choosing a database, devising a search strategy. Such materials can be used for both staff and end-user training, with user guides prepared to supplement formal sessions following the same pattern (Maxymuk, 1991, p. 49):

- what databases are available on CD-ROM;
- how to form a search strategy;
- basic search commands;
- how to view results;
- how to print or download results;
- field specific search examples;
- miscellaneous useful search hints.

Sullivan (1992) describes a training programme for end-user research scientists of DIALOG OnDisc Medline at Glaxo UK. Training was optional; a quick guide was prepared and provided at terminals and to take away, but those who requested training had up to one hour in ones or twos at a terminal, so hands-on experience could be included. Aimed at novice level it included (Sullivan, 1992, p. 72–73):

Technical details: loading discs; choosing menu options; function keys; saving and reusing a search strategy; getting help.

Searching: what is *Medline*; author searching; subject searching; broadening and narrowing a search; browsing; printing references.

Boolean logic was not covered as it is implicit in the structure of pre-defined menus – a good example of choice of product affecting training need, or obviating the need for it.

There is probably more written on the use of the *Medline* database on CD-ROM in libraries than any other. It was one of the first databases to become available, the same database is available from a wider range of suppliers using different search interfaces than any other, but most crucial of all, it requires the use of controlled vocabulary – MESH (MEdical Subject Headings) to obtain effective results. At Glaxo they decided to keep things simple and not mention indexing complexity as it could not be done justice in the time available.

Hepworth (1992) summarizes a number of end-user training courses for which published accounts exist, some of which go into great detail on database structure and search facilities. He also identified a common thread of a conceptual approach in areas like use of controlled vocabulary and proximity operators. Only a training needs analysis within your organization can determine what can be offered to a particular user group, in the time available, with the resources at your disposal. It is better to set modest aims and achieve them, and leave the end-user with the confidence to learn by doing. There is then more likelihood of convincing users of the need for more advanced training to produce even better results, should you be able to resource it.

Who should train?

A colleague at UNN, Edna Blackie, carried out an informal survey of staff in library and museum services responsible for developing training programmes and ongoing support for the introduction of inhouse databases. All thought that a good trainer needed:

- good communication skills;
- a thorough understanding of what is being taught;
- Some thought trainers should also:
    be able to share objectives with trainees;
    encourage questions and check comprehension frequently;
    give positive feedback;
    be flexible in adjusting methods to individual user needs;
    aim to be indispensable.

The latter is an interesting point, and another way of emphasizing the need for objectives to be those of the user, not the trainer. What trainers do not need to have is technical wizardry, this is seen as a positive deterrent.

While acknowledging the need for all staff to be able to

'troubleshoot', not everyone is a potential trainer in the more formal sense, including one-to-one instruction. The style needed for dealing with students in an education environment, expecting to learn, will not necessarily work with other adults, who may feel inadequate and threatened by the need to acquire a new, computer based skill. Trainers need to empathize with this. Knowing how little information can be learnt in the time available, particularly when it is a passive experience for the learner is essential. If a user is still asking for help after your detailed lecture and complex demonstration, who must change?

Preparation for training sessions is time consuming, and staff responsible must be given the necessary recognition for this additional workload. As CD-ROM technology is developing so quickly, regular updating of teaching and support materials must also be planned as user needs change.

Evaluation

The growing emphasis on performance indicators and cost effectiveness of library services in all sectors is causing more emphasis to be placed on evaluation generally, and the cost and time involved in supporting CD-ROM is no exception. Dolphin (1990) gives a useful general overview. Formative evaluation is commonly used to measure the success of an individual session for a particular user or group in order to improve on content or delivery. It can be gathered by observation during the session, by questionnaire to participants, or by testing if appropriate, and should lead to changes to structure, content or delivery. However, this type of evaluation does not tell us much about the use of CD-ROM in the wider context.

Ideally, evaluation of training needs to be built in at the outset to measure how effective any training activity has been in relation to the aims and objectives set e.g. have users become more self reliant? This type of summative evaluation is often done informally by, for example, monitoring requests for help at the enquiry desk. Basic troubleshooting queries might be expected to diminish, or be replaced by more sophisticated requests by users who are moving into the regular user category. To use a more thorough and controlled method may appear unnecessary and too time consuming, especially if the primary aim of the training activity is to save staff time, but it can pay dividends.

Allen (1990) surveyed 87 inexperienced users who claimed to want training in developing search procedures including use of Boolean logic, and how to use equipment. One-to-one instruction was the preferred method. However, when Barbuto and Cevallos (1991) reviewed their end-user searching programme for users of CD-ROMs they found a high degree of satisfaction with the end-user services, even though end-users did not differentiate between keyword and descriptor searching despite the emphasis placed on these concepts during the formal training program. Students were not found to use the advanced techniques stressed in the training sessions to any significant degree, and it was realized that 'the emphasis on training on thesaurus use seems out of proportion to its contribution to effective or satisfactory end-user searches, and repeat searchers of end-user services make significantly less use of the thesaurus than do first-time users . . .' (Barbuto and Cevallos, 1991, p.214) Questionnaires were administered to users on issue of a CD-ROM disc. The results led to more emphasis on point-of-use guides and instructional materials rather than expanding the content of courses as originally planned.

Bucknall and Mangrum (1992) describe an electronic survey method designed to assess the success of the University of North Carolina's U-Search service, which gives access to 15 CD-ROM products via a local area network. The survey form appeared on the U-Search screen at log-on, and could be by-passed by searchers, but half were prepared to complete the form on-screen. The survey yielded valuable data on the range and experience of users, showing the need to continue offering training at all levels, the preferred method of seeking help was still asking a librarian, and word of mouth was the most effective publicity channel. The survey also showed that many users were searching inappropriate databases, but as they usually found something through the flexibility of search software, they were unaware of the poor quality of the result. More effort was shown to be necessary in educating users on database scope and content. The survey instrument used is included in the article. Examples have been given earlier of evaluation which includes pre- and post testing of knowledge and search behaviour.

In every case cited in the literature, significant changes in content or emphasis have been made to the CD-ROM training and support service as a result of user feedback. Library school students are always willing to get involved in survey activity where library staff cannot be released to do so.

Conclusion

There is overwhelming evidence of a perceived need for end-user training and support for CD-ROM from both users and librarians. Better product design may make individual products more user friendly, but this does not, in itself, solve the problem.

There is no 'best' approach, but the stress in this chapter on a planned approach, within the training triangle of users – staff – system complexity, should result in more effective and efficient training activity. End-user support is an ongoing commitment, with real costs incurred in staff time and energy, space, preparation of materials, not forgetting the users' time.

Librarians may argue that their situation is different, and that a local solution is best. Yet the common themes found in the literature cited, as well as much anecdotal evidence collected at conferences and workshops, shows the potential for more co-operation by librarians working in similar types of library with similar groups of users. Such an idea from a group of academic librarians led to the production of an instruction manual together with prompt cards, posters, notes for presenters, OHP masters and student note masters and a training disc, for use with the ISI databases via the JANET network in the UK (BIDS 1992).

Rather than proving a threat to the professionalism of librarians as was first thought, end-user searching is offering an expanded role for all staff, but particularly former online intermediaries. They cannot only pass on their skills, but also act as facilitators in ensuring the right sources are available, as gatekeepers in ensuring the correct source is used, and, as we have seen, as troubleshooters on the end-user's behalf through what can become a maze of electronic sources. Not least, they should influence the design of better end-user products (Royan, 1992). More librarians will need effective teaching skills not only to plan and deliver training courses, but to reach a better understanding of the end-user in a learning environment – another CD-ROM training need.

References

Allen, G. (1990) CD-ROM training: what do the patrons want? *RQ*, **30**, 88–93

Amato, K. and Jackson, M. (1990) CD-ROMs: instructing the user. *CD-ROM Librarian*, **5**, (6), 14–21

Barbuto, D.M. and Cevallos, E.E. (1991) End-user searching: program review and future prospects. *RQ*, **31**, 214–227

Belkin, N.J. *et al* (1991) User interfaces for information systems. *Journal of Information Science*, **17**, 327–344

BIDS (Bath Information and Data Services) (1992) *ISI Data Service: instruction pack.* Bath: Bath University Computing Services

Bostian, R. and Robbins, A. (1990) Effective instruction for searching CD-ROM indexes. *Laserdisk professional*, **3**, (1), 14–17

Bucknall, T. and Mangrum, R. (1992) U-Search: a user study of the CD-ROM service at the University of North Carolina at Chapel Hill. *RQ*, **31**, 542–553

Burton, M. (1992) The paper chase: how to manage CD-ROM documentation. *Database*, **15**, 102–104

Condic, K.S. (1992) Reference assistance for CD-ROM users: a little goes a long way. *CD-ROM Professional*, **5**, (1), 56–57

Culbertson, M. (1992) Analysis of searches by end-users of science and engineering CD-ROM databases in an academic library. *CD-ROM professional*, **5**, (2), 76–79

Day, J. and Webber, S. (1990) Training and user documentation. In *CD-ROM: a practical guide for information professionals*, ed. A.A. Gunn and C. Moore, pp. 23–26. London: LITC/UKOLUG

Dolphin, P. (1990) Evaluation of user education programmes. In *User education in academic libraries*, ed. H. Fleming, pp. 73–89. London: Library Association

Harrington, J. (1990) Searching SilverPlatter: a computer-based CD-ROM instruction tool. *CD-ROM Professional*, **3**, (6),12–15

Hepworth, J. (1992) Developing information handling courses for end-users. In *Database 2000: Proceedings of the UKOLUG State-of-the-Art Conference* (Guildford, 1992), ed. C.J. Armstrong and R.J. Hartley, pp. 67–75. Oxford: Learned Information for UKOLUG

Jaros, J. (1990) Training endusers/remote users. *Journal of Library Administration*, **12**, (2), 75–88

Johnson M.E. and Rosen, B.S. (1990) CD-ROM end-user instruction: a planning model. *Laserdisk Professional*, **3**, (2), 35–40

Lowe, J.B. (1990) Integrating CD-ROMs into your bibliographic instruction program. *CD-ROM Professional*, **3**, (6), 16–19

Maxymuk, J. (1991) Considerations for CD-ROM instruction. *CD-ROM Professional*, **4**, (3), 47–49

Nipp, D. and Shamy, S. (1992) CD-ROM troubleshooting manual: support for reference desk librarians. *RQ*, **31**, 339–345

Plutchak, T.S. (1989) On the satisfied and inept end-user. *Medical Reference Services Quarterly*, **8**, (1), 45–48

Royan, B. (1992) A practitioner's view of self-servicce information systems. In *Information systems for end-users: research and development issues*, ed. M. Hancock-Beaulieu, pp. 79–84. London : Taylor Graham

Steele, A. and Tseng, G. (1992) End-user training for CD-ROM Medline: a survey of UK medical school libraries. *Program*, **26**, (1), 55–61

Sullivan, M. (1992) Training for MEDLINE on CD-ROM: a case study in an industrial environment. In *Information systems for end-users: research and development issues*, ed. M. Hancock-Beaulieu, pp. 71–78. London : Taylor Graham.

Webber, S. (1987) Making training materials more effective. In *Online information retrieval in practice: Proceedings of the UKOLUG State-of-the-Art Conference (Bristol, 1986)*, pp. 101–112. London : Taylor Graham

Whitaker, C.S. (1990) Pile-up at the reference desk: teaching users to use CD-ROMs. *Laserdisk Professional*, **3**, (2), 30–34

Case study: Training staff and users at the Cairns Library, John Radcliffe Hospital, Oxford

Carol Lefebvre

The Cairns Library and the John Radcliffe Hospital

The Cairns Library is a multi-disciplinary teaching hospital library serving on the National Health Service (NHS) side the Oxford Regional Health Authority, on the University of Oxford side the Faculty of Clinical Medicine, and the Department of Health Care Studies of the Oxford Brookes University (formally Oxford Polytechnic).

The organizational aims of the John Radcliffe Hospital are patient care as an NHS hospital, together with education and research as a university teaching hospital. The Cairns Library endeavours to support these aims through the provision of an up-to-date user-oriented library and information service.

The Library is unusual, if not unique, in that it is open 24 hours a day, although it is only staffed from 9.00 am until 9.00 pm on Mondays to Fridays. This had implications for the introduction of the CD-ROM service, as the intention was to provide end-user access to databases throughout the 24-hour period if at all possible, without the benefits now more widely available of networking and remote dial-up access. The Library has a staff of 4.5 full-time equivalent (FTE) qualified librarians and 4.5 FTE library assistants. It subscribes to approximately 500 current periodicals and has approximately 12 000 books. There is an annual student intake of about 100 clinical medical students (a three-year course) and about

150 nursing students (a four-year course).

The Cairns has a long tradition of online searching, having been involved in a British Library research project in the 1970s to investigate the feasibility of introducing online searching of *Medline* in the UK. CD-ROM has been available in the Cairns since 1987, firstly for review/evaluation purposes, and then as an end-user service since 1989.

Staff training

When *Medline* on CD-ROM was first made available for end-user searching in the Cairns Library (1989), it was decided that the desk staff should spend about 15 minutes showing each individual briefly how the system worked. This would enable staff to explain to end-users how to find references on a particular topic, how to view them on the screen and how to select and print out the required references. In order to enable the staff to do this, a training programme was devised and implemented. All library staff at the Cairns serve on the library desk at some time, and consequently all staff needed to be trained. The programme consisted firstly of meetings of all staff together, either as special meetings or within the monthly general staff meeting structure, to convey general points, and secondly of small-group sessions to learn how to use the system.

The general sessions covered such elements as what is *Medline*, how does it relate to printed *Index Medicus*, how many years of *Medline* were to be made available, how an individual reader would have the discs issued against their reader ticket to use in the Library and how the appointments system would operate. Also, a leaflet entitled *CD-ROM questions and answers* was prepared and discussed with the staff, in order to help them answer questions from library users about the new service. When the staff had had an opportunity to digest the questions and answers contained in it, the leaflet was then made available as a general hand-out.

For the small-group hands-on sessions, staff were grouped according to their previous knowledge and experience; for example, the qualified staff, all of whom had had some experience of searching the *Medline* database online, were trained separately from the library assistants who had not. These sessions covered mechanical details such as how to turn the microcomputer and CD-ROM drive on and off, how to replace ink cartridges and how to deal with printer jams. With regard to assisting end-users in searching the database, the first element to be covered was how to ensure that the CD-ROM disc was inserted correctly, that is which way up and into which slot. (The first CD-ROM drive purchased by the Library, a Hitachi 1503-S, was not a caddy-based system and consequently the temptation to insert the CD-ROM disc into the 5.25 inch floppy disk drive needed to be addressed and overcome! The temptation still existed with the later introduction of caddy-based drives but to a lesser extent.)

Selection of search terms was the next major area. At the time of introducing *Medline* as an end-user service (1989) the SilverPlatter version did not have the thesaurus available on disc and did not offer the 'EXPLODE' option, that is the facility to include narrower, more specific descriptor terms automatically under a broader descriptor term. The qualified librarians found this to be a major disadvantage in comparison with the online searching features to which they were accustomed. The library assistants' previous training had included the use of printed *Index Medicus* (including the broader/narrower terms principles) followed by a demonstration of an online search, so they were also aware of the problem. It was decided that a set of (US) National Library of Medicine Medical Subject Headings (permuted, annotated and tree structures) would be left by the CD-ROM workstation, to enable staff to assist end-users in selecting all the appropriate terms required for each search concept.

Having selected search terms, staff were then shown how to combine them appropriately using the AND and OR operators. For the online searchers this was a familiar concept; for the library assistants it was not. It was helpful to have not only small groups, but groups of staff with a similar level of previous knowledge. Much stress was placed on the importance of selecting the correct operator, and that the use of operators often did not match the use of 'and' and 'or' in everyday English; for example, someone may express their enquiry as concerning the incidence of caesarean section operations in the United States and Canada. The terms for the United States and Canada would need to be combined using the OR operator, not AND as expressed in everyday English. (Relatively few women would have been unfortunate enough to undergo a caesarean in both the United States and Canada!) Examples of this sort were used to demonstrate the implications of incorrect use of the AND/OR operators. It was also explained that use of the NOT operator was not recommended, as this may inadvertently exclude important references.

Several common examples were given of how to reduce the number of references retrieved, in particular limiting the results to English-language articles, to those where the chosen topic was of major importance in the article and to those dealing specifically with humans.

Although it was recognized that the majority of users would wish to do subject searches as described above, staff were also shown how to search for articles by a particular author (including when the initials were unknown or uncertain) and how to find articles in a particular journal, using the correct abbreviated journal title in the source field.

Displaying articles on the screen, noting those required and printing out the references concluded the major part of the small-group staff training sessions. Downloading to floppy disk was discussed but not covered in detail for two reasons. Firstly, the demand for downloading when the service was first introduced (1989) was not substantial as this option was generally only favoured by those with their own microcomputers who needed little or no advice on how to do it. Secondly, at that time very few of the library staff had any familiarity with or need to use floppy disks. It was decided that if all staff were to attempt to advise readers on such matters as size and density of disks, together with the particular complexity in respect of compatibility with various other computer systems being dependent on the exact model purchased (for example Apple Macintosh and Amstrad) this may lead not only to some inappropriate advice being given but also to undue pressure on library staff to become familiar with a whole new area, even though they might rarely be asked about it. For these two reasons it was decided that staff would advise end-users that it was possible to download from the system, but if they needed any further advice in this area they would need to see the Information Services Librarian or her Assistant.

Finally, staff were shown how to exchange discs (the *Medline* database comprises one disc per year of data) and how to re-run the automatically saved search strategy.

Sample questions were made available for staff to test out what they had learnt in their training session and to gain confidence in using the system. When all the staff had been trained in how to use the system, the CD-ROM workstation was set up in the Library and the service introduced.

Implications of one-to-one end-user training

The method of training and support for end-users on an individual basis as described above continued for about a year. One-to-one training had some obvious advantages. The time at which the training was offered was convenient to the end-user. The session could be geared according to their individual requirements. Help could be given in selecting the particular search terms they wished to use. However, there were several disadvantages. Much time was spent repeating basic facts to one user after another. With approximately 10 new users per day at 15 minutes per person, this meant approximately 12½ hours per week spent on training. Although time was being saved by not offering online searching routinely since the introduction of the CD-ROM end-user service, the savings there amounted to no more than six hours per week.

The additional staff time spent on training in this way was hard to justify on two accounts. Firstly, staffing levels were the same as originally set in 1979 when the hospital first opened, despite the fact that levels of library use had increased dramatically since then. Secondly, with only 15 minutes allowed for each session, this meant there was very little time to go into the detail required to explain how to use the *Medline* thesaurus, which had in the meanwhile been introduced with the latest release of the SilverPlatter software. More importantly, there was inadequate time to explain that use of the thesaurus was fundamental for subject-searching of the database since the indexing of records is hierarchical, and references indexed under a narrower term would be missed if the thesaurus were not used correctly. Consequently, it was felt that the 15 minute period of individual tuition achieved a relatively rudimentary level of competence on behalf of the end-user, while involving library staff in constant repetition of the basic features of the system. Another feature of this ad hoc individual tuition was that as the training was to be conducted by whichever member of staff happened to be serving on the library desk at the time, this meant that all library staff had to be trained and kept up-to-date on how the system worked. The relatively high turnover of library assistant staff posed an added burden on staff time. Moreover, staff needed to be trained in how to convey what they themselves had learnt and understood to a wide range of users with varying ability and previous experience in the use of computers and/or databases. We began to feel that this was probably not only inefficient but also ineffective use of staff time. Consequently, in the summer of 1990 we invited an MSc student, Terranum Abbas from the Department of Information and Library Studies at Loughborough University, to undertake some research into end-user use of *Medline* in the Cairns. Her main findings were that the majority of users were aware of only the most basic features; even those who were aware of the more advanced features like the thesaurus did not know how to use them properly, and most importantly the majority of users wanted more in-depth training in the use of the system.

Group training sessions for end-users

Terranum's research confirmed our view that formal training sessions should be introduced. Furthermore, it was decided that the sessions should be made near-compulsory, that is anyone asking to book an appointment to use the CD-ROM would first be asked, 'have you had a training session?'. In the early days, it was hard to persuade many of those who had been regular users that there would be any benefit in them attending a training course, though a few did and found it useful. However, all those who had never used the system before were told that they had to go on a training course first, as no other staff support would be available.

The training courses were based heavily on a booklet, the first edition of which was produced inhouse by the Assistant Information

Services Librarian (Anne Lusher), entitled *Guide to using MEDLINE on CD-ROM*. The booklet was handed out to people when they made an appointment for a training session, and they were asked to bring it back with them to the session. They were encouraged to write notes in the booklet during the training for future reference, and to bring the booklet with them whenever they used the CD-ROM. The aim was for self-sufficiency after the training programme, partly to reduce pressure on the desk staff, but also to enable end-users to make full use of the system 24 hours a day. If it was felt that any individual would benefit from a second training session they were encouraged to book a second appointment.

The content of the group training sessions for end-users did not differ greatly from the training sessions for library staff. The main difference was that SilverPlatter in the interim had introduced the thesaurus option into the software and this then constituted a major element in the end-user training programme. It was necessary to convey to users of the system that the thesaurus had two major functions. Firstly, it standardized both terminology and spelling within the descriptor terms. Secondly, and in some ways more importantly, it enabled narrower terms to be included under a single broader heading. This concept was often the most difficult to convey and an example was demonstrated to indicate how many references would be missed by using the correct Medical Subject Heading but not 'exploding' it to incorporate the more specific terms underneath it in the hierarchy.

We offered two courses a week, and varied the days of the week and times of day to accommodate our users' work patterns. The groups were invariably mixed, particularly with respect to computing skills and command of the English language. We set a limit of eight people per session to make sure that everyone could see the screen properly, and so that the trainer could judge how members of the group were progressing. If fewer than five people turned up for a session then we would quickly go round the library and invite readers to join us! This could often add one or two to the numbers.

In addition to the general training sessions discussed above, special sessions were offered as part of induction programmes, particularly to nurses on post-registration education courses. These courses had some advantages over the general ones. Firstly, it was more likely that previous experience of computers and databases would be less varied in a group of this sort than in a general group, which may include an 18 year old nursing degree student together with a post-doctoral researcher. Secondly, a particular topic of interest to the whole group could be selected for the demonstration, as opposed to a standard example, which would be understood by a wide variety of people. Thirdly, the training session would be viewed as an integral part of the course, and would be prepared for and followed up by the course tutors as part of the educational process.

Special sessions were also offered to departments in the John Radcliffe and surrounding hospitals, which had chosen to buy their own CD-ROM drives and to have their own subscriptions to *Medline*; (a venture much encouraged by the Library, despite the fact that many departments expected us to wholeheartedly disapprove of such an action!)

Training sessions were carried out by the Information Services Librarian (myself) or the Assistant Information Services Librarian (Anne Lusher, then latterly Sandy Astin).

As no special training suite or even meeting room facilities were available in the library, all general sessions were held in the main library reading area. This had the disadvantage of noise, both that created by the session itself and the noise of other library activity distracting the participants. Also we were restricted to eight people, as the maximum number who could sit round a screen and see clearly enough without the added aid of an overhead projector.

Future plans

We see the following areas providing scope for developing and improving the services presently offered. We need to offer more sessions per week to cope with increasing demand, and to extend the range of times offered to include evening sessions.

The training role should be broadened to cover more of the qualified staff, not just the Information Services section. Special arrangements also need to be made for the student intakes (100 clinical medical students and 150 nursing students every September).

Because of the numbers of students involved in contrast to the number of staff available these may have to take the form of a combination of introductory seminars and demonstrations using overhead projection facilities, followed up by group sessions on worked examples.

Ideally a do-it-yourself training programme should also be made available for those who find it impossible to come in during staff hours, for example those based in the community who are fully committed throughout the normal working day. This could be based on the tutorial package that comes with the SilverPlatter *Medline* software, together with appropriate documentation available at the CD-ROM workstation.

The sessions currently offered cover *Medline* on SilverPlatter but also mention the other SilverPlatter databases to which the library subscribes, *Nursing & Allied Health (CINAHL)-CD* and *HealthPLAN-CD*. Other courses need to be developed to cover non-SilverPlatter databases, for example the *Maxwell Compact Library: AIDS* database. Similarly, training programmes need to be planned for major new releases of software, either as a conversion course for those familiar with the previous version, or as a hand-out.

At the time of writing, plans are well underway for a local area network (LAN) to be installed in the John Radcliffe linking all departments including the Library. One of the main advantages of a network as perceived by staff in the hospital, is the possibility of being able to access *Medline* from their offices. This clearly has implications for future training initiatives. We expect that many more people will use *Medline* once it is networked, partly because of the convenience factor of not having to leave their desks, but also because many more people will be able to use the system at the same time. (The Library currently has two subscriptions to the database, hence there is currently a limit of two users at a time.)

Above all the training sessions being offered need to be evaluated. Are they effective? Is it efficient use of library staff time and end-users time? How could they be made more effective? Should we introduce advanced courses for those who want to make best use of the more sophisticated elements of the system? We hope to follow up Terranum Abbas's[1] work in 1990 with a similar project to throw some light on these issues.

Reference

1 Abbas, T. (1990) *CD-ROM: Use for searching Medline in the Cairns Library, John Radcliffe Hospital, Oxford.* MSC Thesis, Department of Library and Information Studies, Loughborough University of Technology, UK.

CHAPTER THIRTEEN

CD-ROM for inhouse applications

Terry Hanson

CD-ROM, in its first decade, has found its niche as a medium for publishing information. Whether it be bibliographic databases, encyclopedias, statistical compilations, newspapers in full text, or catalogues for publishing companies, it is an ideal medium, with its large storage capacity for this activity, and as indicated in Chapter 2 there are now in excess of 3500 products available. However, the purpose of this section of the book is to look at the idea of inhouse CD-ROM development as a means of solving local storage or database creation problems. John Cox's paper also pointed out that, according to a survey by InfoTech reported in *Byte* (Udell, 1993), there are approximately 5000 titles available when inhouse products are included.

Up until recently the only realistic possibility for most organizations, libraries or otherwise, to use CD-ROM for storage of their own data was to use a specialist CD-ROM production company and pay a lot of money for the end-product. However, in the last couple of years CD recording facilities have come within reach of small companies and organizations with the launch of a range of CD-ROM recorders (or CD-R drives) from Philips, Sony, JVC, etc. With prices below £4000 (in late 1992) it is clear that inhouse CD-ROM production becomes feasible.

Prior to this development, optical storage for local applications has been available using, for example, WORM (Write Once Read Many times) drives. However, CD-ROM has the major advantage of a very large installed base of drives and it is likely that the CD form of optical storage, coupled with the new recordable CD-ROM drives, will dominate in the future.

Typical applications using this new-found enabling technology include:

• Archiving

The traditional archiving technology in libraries has been microfilm or fiche but though it had storage space advantages it has never been a popular medium for access. The great advantage of CD-ROM in archiving is that as well as requiring little storage space, the well designed storage software will be capable of very impressive retrieval performance on all types of information. So the decision to archive using CD-ROM can be taken in order to improve both storage and retrieval problems rather than to improve one at the expense of the other (Bronner and Leek, 1992).

The *Northern Echo* case study by Peter Chapman is a good example of how a company sought to improve the storage and retrieval of its own information and, in the process, produced a marketable product.

Much archiving with CD-ROM can of course be achieved with commercial products such as newspapers. But there are now opportunities to convert local collections of manuscripts, photographs, press cuttings, etc. and to improve access arrangements considerably. Apart from CD-ROM itself, one of the key technologies here is document image processing. This allows graphic images of any kind to be scanned and stored on the CD as a facsimile of the original (Anon, 1992a). However, where the image is of a textual document this is not searchable and indexing has to be provided by a separate index file.

• Creation and distribution of databases

Database distribution has been at the heart of the CD-ROM revolution as an alternative to commercial, network distribution. The same choices are available to organizations wishing to distribute inhouse databases to their scattered users. The most obvious example of this problem is the library catalogue in a multi-site situation or a union catalogue for libraries in a particular region (Townley, 1992). Most libraries use the network model to solve this problem but, as Christopher Marks points out in his case study, the user interface possibilities with CD-ROM are a strong incentive to look at the CD-ROM alternative.

Other examples include the distribution of parts catalogues by aircraft and car manufacturers and even publishers' catalogues. To an extent the CD-ROM alternative offers advantages beyond the attractive interface. In some applications a product can be transformed by the possibilities of CD-ROM with suitable storage and retrieval software and multimedia capabilities. An interesting, early, example of this was the demonstration CD distributed by the Nimbus record company which, as any catalogue would, described the available recorded music. It differed from the norm though by providing not just a textual description of each item but also a picture of the album cover and a sample of the music itself. Current CD multimedia technologies, CD-ROM XA, CD-I and Kodak Photo-CD, present endless possibilities for customized database creation.

Indeed our first two categories overlap at this point. There are interesting possibilities whereby material such as photographs and slides can be stored for archival purposes but incorporated with other material within a database. For example, if a library had a major collection of historical photographs these might be combined in a database with facsimiles of related textual documents; and if the subject matter happened to be music then sound recordings could also be included. Archiving is achieved but in a much more interesting and usable fashion than would usually be the case.

● **Management and distribution of documentation**

This area, often referred to as records management, is not normally seen as in the library domain but it is included here because it shows further the information management potential of CD-ROM coupled with good software (Anon, 1992b; Arps, 1992). It is also included because in many organizations it may well be that the library takes on a role in records and documentation management. This might happen either because the library has a general role encompassing this activity anyway, or because of converging technologies and practices whereby the library is seen as the repository of expertise in computerized information management and retrieval.

The two case studies included here are early examples of library inhouse applications. The literature does not include many others as yet. It is likely however that with CD-ROM recording equipment becoming affordable the library community will generate many more examples in the near future.

References

Anon. (1992a) CD-ROM and document imaging. *Document Imaging Automation Update*, **11**, (3), 1–4

Anon. (1992b) Motives for document image automation. *Document Image Automation Update*, **11**, (10), 1–4

Arps, M. (1992) Using CD-ROM technology to solve information needs at 3M. *Document Image Automation*, **11**, (3), 1–4

Bronner, R.G. and Leek, M.R. (1992) Mining for gold in the information mountains: a comparison of the economics and usefulness of film and CD-ROM for document storage, access and distribution. *International Journal of Micrographics and Optical Technology*, **10**, (4), 195–200

Townley, C. (1992) College libraries and resource sharing: testing a compact disc union catalog. *College and Research Libraries*, **53**, (5), 405–13

Udell, J. (1993) Start the presses. *Byte*, **18**, (2), 116–134

CHAPTER FOURTEEN

Case study: *The Northern Echo* on CD-ROM and the PANDA Project in North East Libraries

Peter Chapman

Introduction

The Northern Echo is the daily morning newspaper serving the North East and North Yorkshire in England. In 1990, the newspaper issued a CD-ROM and, in partnership with Information North, made it accessible to the public through certain libraries within its circulation area.

The case study is in two parts; it first examines the management issues arising from publishing inhouse a CD-ROM, and then considers the issues arising for a CD-ROM publisher in participating in a project such as PANDA (Public Access to a Newspaper Database and Archive). The paper is written from a personal viewpoint as Head Librarian of *The Northern Echo* and may not reflect the views of *The Northern Echo*, Information North, or the individual participants in PANDA.

The Northern Echo on CD-ROM

The germination of the project to publish a CD-ROM was in 1986 when I spoke at the Library Association Information Services Group (ISG) Weekend School on Information and the Media. Peter Gethin of BRS Software Products (BRS) lent me a test CD-ROM which BRS had done for the *Financial Times*. It excited a great deal of interest amongst the delegates and it was clear that CD-ROM could play a part in the archiving of newspaper text.

At this time, *The Northern Echo* was considering ways in which to create a database of the stories which it contained. In due course, BRS/SEARCH from BRS was chosen, partly because of its ability to create CD-ROMs from the database that it ran.

Echo Online, the inhouse database for *The Northern Echo* was up and running from November 1988. Due to financial constraints, the hardware upon which the database ran had limited disk storage space – sufficient for two years of text. It was planned to expand the storage space once the worth of *Echo Online* had been proven.

During the budgeting session for 1990 which took place in the summer of 1989, options for the future of *Echo Online* were discussed. *Echo Online* was successful internally and was to be continued. Therefore, capital had to be found to expand the disk storage space or an alternative way of storing the text had to be arranged. Offline storage of text, though inexpensive if a tape streamer was used, was dismissed as unsuitable because it went against the idea of keeping the text as accessible as possible. WORM (Write-one read-many) storage was considered but the technology was more expensive than the option of additional disk storage and seemed to offer no additional benefits.

Publishing a CD-ROM and removing the text so published from the online system, thus freeing disc space, was attractive. In theory, the cost of publishing a CD-ROM would be recouped through sales which made the future of *Echo Online* assured as no further hardware costs would accrue.

However, no UK newspaper had gone down this road, and the North-East of England seemed virgin territory for CD-ROM at this time. Further, there was the question of the need for a CD-ROM player and the implication that inhouse users would require two searches to obtain a complete overview of the database. In the end, it was decided to expand the disk storage on the online system, and provision was made in the 1990 budget for the necessary capital expenditure.

The change of heart which led *The Northern Echo* to publish a CD-ROM occurred for two reasons. First, in the Autumn of 1989, the UK government announced that funding for projects under the Public Library Development Incentive Scheme (PLDIS) would be offered for the two-year period 1990–1992. Secondly, Information North, the development agency for information services within the Northern Region of England, was prepared to be the facilitator of the PLDIS project. The working of the PLDIS project, which became known as PANDA, is described in the second part of this paper. For the moment, it is sufficient to note that the offer of government funding coupled to a guaranteed placing of the CD-ROM in public institutions meant that *The Northern Echo* could seriously consider producing a CD-ROM instead of purchasing additional hard disk space for its online system.

In planning the publication of the CD-ROM, the objectives were as follows. First, it was to lead to the freeing of hard disk space on the online system, leaving the current configuration to carry a 'rolling' year of the newspaper's text. Secondly, existing inhouse users were not to be discouraged from using it, so the same search interfaces had to be available in both systems. Thirdly, it had to promote *The Northern Echo* as a newspaper through the participation in PANDA. Finally, it had to recoup its direct costs.

The actual production of the CD-ROM was to be done by BRS, but *The Northern Echo* was responsible for the provision of the data to be carried on it, the specification of what was required of the software, and for the publication, marketing, selling, and subsequent support of the CD-ROM. By working closely with BRS, the planning and production of the CD-ROM posed few problems. However, in publishing, marketing and selling the CD-ROM, the staff of *The Northern Echo* were learning by doing.

The work of overseeing the publication of the CD-ROM fell to the library staff at *The Northern Echo*. Two staff were allocated to creating the manual which was to accompany it. The aim in writing the manual was to explain CD-ROM and to guide users in how to get the most out of the text of the newspaper. In this work, they were aided by their knowledge of *Echo Online*. The finished manual was a substantial work and was accompanied by a listing of subject terms used by the indexers of *The Northern Echo*. The same staff were responsible for marketing and selling the CD-ROM. As the cost of the CD-ROM was being absorbed inhouse, the effort to market the disc was limited to the circulation area of the newspaper plus the obvious national outlets such as directories and the professional information press.

A launch of the CD-ROM and the PANDA Project was held in Newcastle in December 1990 (Day, 1990; The Northern Echo . . . 1990), and promotion of the disc was developed in 1991 as circumstances allowed – usually through meetings with prospective CD-ROM users. Once the CD-ROM had been issued, support for the product had to be provided by the library staff in conjunction with BRS. There were bugs in the software of a minor nature but the majority of support calls at this stage resulted from users' inexperience with the new technology of CD-ROM.

The publication of the first CD-ROM met three of the four objectives outlined earlier. Disk space on the online system was freed, and the CD-ROM and online system proved complementary in the eyes of the inhouse users. PANDA raised the profile of the newspaper, although it is impossible to say if this proved to be anything other than an image building exercise. However, the CD-ROM did not recoup its direct costs, for reasons outlined below.

As was noted earlier, the circulation area of *The Northern Echo* was virgin territory for CD-ROM in 1990. Although this was the reason behind PANDA, it did mean that *The Northern Echo* had to sell the concept of CD-ROM as well as its own product. Despite the support of Philips, as suppliers of workstations, the cost of CD-ROM hardware and the lack of understanding of the technology proved great barriers to potential customers. As the cost of the promotion of CD-ROM was being borne inhouse, there was limited scope to develop marketing strategies. Further, as other newspaper CD-ROMs became available, the usefulness of *The Northern Echo* as against national newspaper titles had to be explained. Finally, the pricing structure of the CD-ROM was designed to recoup costs but made little allowance for the number of 'free' discs it became apparent had to be given to prospective dealers and customers. Fortunately, the failure to recoup the direct costs of the CD-ROM did not matter in that the seed money had come from the savings on the no-longer required hard disk for the online system, and also because the CD-ROM had brought a certain amount of kudos to the newspaper. However, it was a warning as to the difficulties which lay ahead for an independent CD-ROM publisher.

During the early part of 1991, the UK Government began to fund a pilot project on the use of CD-ROM in schools and it appeared to be clear that CD-ROM was to be taken up by schools in an enthusiastic way. *The Northern Echo* was committed to publishing a second disc for the PANDA Project, and it appeared likely that schools would wish to purchase the disc. The bugs in the first disc had been cleared by BRS and the opportunity arose to develop further features, namely the holding of graphics to accompany stories and the creation of a small supplementary database of biographical information.

In the expectation of the schools' market for the CD-ROM, the decision was taken to issue three discs for the academic year 1991/92. It was also decided to make the CD-ROM cumulative, as this would make its use easier as a complement to *Echo Online*. The new disc was launched in September 1991 into a developing CD-ROM market nationally, but a limited one within the circulation area of the newspaper. Take-up was satisfactory initially, but failed to develop as schools took longer to get to grips with the technology than had been expected. Ironically, at one stage, the CD-ROM was selling better outside the circulation area than inside it!

Again, the marketing and selling of the disc was being done inhouse in an effort to absorb direct costs. A further economy was made by issuing the disc with a simple manual, as the development of the market had made the original detailed manual unnecessary. As take-up of the CD-ROM increased, the issue of help-desk support needed attention. Two factors increased the workload here beyond what was expected. Firstly, the sheer variety of machines being used and the ways in which they were configured meant that problems were inevitable; secondly, the ignorance of the users both of CD-ROM and of their machines meant that the problems which arose often seemed more complicated than they actually were.

Over the period of the second CD-ROM, it was clear that income would not match the direct costs incurred. The simple reason was that sales did not match the expectations upon which the pricing structure had been set. Behind this reason lay the slow take-up of CD-ROM by education (and lack of take-up by business) and the image problem of *The Northern Echo* when compared to other newspaper CD-ROMs in the market place.

An attempt to examine these issues in detail was made by a business student during a ten-week placement at *The Northern Echo* in the spring of 1992. He talked to dealers in CD-ROM, users of *The Northern Echo*, and to possible users of CD-ROM in business. He found it impossible to quantify the potential market for *The Northern Echo* on CD-ROM. Factors affecting the take-up of the CD-ROM were ignorance of the technology, the cost of the hardware and its lack of availability off-the-shelf, the lack of perceived need of information in this format, and the number of alternative CD-ROMs available for users with only a limited number of CD-ROM players.

Nevertheless, it is likely that *The Northern Echo* will continue to produce a CD-ROM, albeit with a strict control on the costs involved. Partly, this will be because of the internal need for a continued archive for the online system, and partly because it is establishing for itself a niche in the electronic market place which can be built upon.

The PANDA project

Having looked at the management issues to be faced in producing a CD-ROM inhouse, I will consider the issues which arose as a partner in the PANDA Project.

As has been stated, the reason that *The Northern Echo* on CD-ROM was planned in the autumn of 1989 was the prospect of funding through the Public Library Development Incentive Scheme (PLDIS). Under the Scheme, up to 40% of the cost of a project would be met by the government (Northern . . . 1989). Although *The Northern Echo* was not looking for direct funding, money through PLDIS was seen as an opportunity to seed a natural market for the CD-ROM – publicly-funded libraries.

The PLDIS application was to cover two years, 1990–1992, and was made in the name of Information North (IN) in partnership with *The Northern Echo*. IN was responsible for drawing together the libraries who wished to participate in the project, whilst *The Northern Echo* was responsible for the CD-ROM and for the negotiation of the supply of CD-ROM workstations.

The PANDA (Public Access to a Newspaper Database and Archive) project aimed 'to improve access to information carried in a major regional newspaper, and to encourage the public to use CD-ROM technology to access this information directly'. The money from PLDIS was to go to the partner libraries to defray part of the cost of the workstations and to allow an evaluation of the use of CD-ROM by the public to take place.

In the event, the application was turned down for three reasons. First, it was not innovative; second, the proposed CD-ROM would contain only text; and third, it was too similar to the existing *Echo Online* service which could be accessed by libraries if they wished. IN and *The Northern Echo* did not see these reasons as being sufficient to kill off the concept of PANDA, though the loss of the funding was a serious blow to the expected widespread take-up of the project.

Writing the application for PLDIS funding in conjunction with IN was a good discipline in focusing upon the possible uses of the CD-ROM and the possible markets for it. Further it provided the bases for the case being made within *The Northern Echo* for CD-ROM. Most importantly, the exercise highlighted the costs involved, especially in terms of staff time, and the constraints within which all PANDA partners had to work.

The carrot which the PLDIS funding provided was the reduced cost of a CD-ROM workstation for use in partner libraries. Further, as a grant-aided project requiring a low-level of capital input from individual partners, the libraries involved had been able to join by using money already within their budgets. Without the PLDIS funding, several partners had to leave the project because of the increase in cost, whilst some partners had to reduce their commitment to public access by not buying the CD-ROM workstation.

Although the loss of PLDIS funding did not affect *The Northern Echo* financially, it did lessen the value of PANDA for *The Northern Echo*. Firstly, there was the loss of kudos which would have come from involvement with a government-backed scheme. Secondly, the imperative to record and evaluate the project was lost as there was no independent body to receive the information. Thirdly, the authority to enforce the aims of the project which would have come from outside funding was not there. Finally, the loss of many public access CD-ROM workstations lessened the impact that the project had.

Nevertheless, PANDA was launched in December 1990 alongside *The Northern Echo* on CD-ROM. IN was able to provide input from a project officer in the first year who shared the burden of training and help desk support with the library staff of *The Northern Echo* (North . . . 1990). Also, he initiated a monitoring programme for the project. PANDA became an informal project with participating libraries being co-ordinated by IN. Although some libraries were able to develop the concept of public access to the CD-ROM effectively, others finding themselves constrained by financial, staff, or technical circumstances were able to offer only limited access to it (Davies, 1991).

As the project did not develop as had been expected under PLDIS funding, constraints to the involvement of *The Northern Echo* were imposed. Without a high profile project within the circulation area and associated sales, *The Northern Echo* could not afford to put extra resources into the project.

Management issues which arose within *The Northern Echo* concerned the following areas. First, the effective allocation of library staff time in supporting the project set against the other demands upon the library. Second, how to assess the value of such a project if there is not identifiable return in sales of the CD-ROM or sales of the newspaper. Third, how does a company build upon such a project, and identify the market place for a spin-off product from its main operation (PANDA . . . , 1990).

At the end of the two year period of the project, it was likely that the participating libraries would continue to take *The Northern Echo* on CD-ROM. However, there was no indication that further libraries would take the CD-ROM because of the work of the project.

Without PANDA, *The Northern Echo* on CD-ROM would not have been published in 1990, if at all. However, without PLDIS funding, PANDA was unable to deliver further identifiable benefits. Indeed, it is clear that the future of the CD-ROM lies not in the library market place but in that of education.

References

Davies, S.A. (1991) *An evaluation of PANDA (Public Access to A Newspaper Database and Archive), The Northern Echo in full text on CD-ROM and the factors leading to its success in several north eastern libraries*. MA Dissertation, Department of Information and Library Management, Newcastle Polytechnic, UK.
Day, J. (1990) PANDA launch. *UKOLUG Newsletter*, **2**, 24–25

North says Fiat PANDA (1990) *Information North Newsletter*, **9**, 4
The Northern Echo on CD-ROM (1990) *The Northern Echo*, 14 December 1990
Northern Echo proposal (1989) *Information North Newsletter*, **5**, 3
PANDA, an endangered species (1990) *Information Northern Newsletter*, **8**, 1

Case study: The use of CD-ROM for library catalogue production and distribution at Staffordshire University

Christopher Marks*

The background

CD-ROM catalogues have been a long time in coming to the market place and, like many other librarians, I had for years kept an eye on the development of inhouse CD-ROMs in the hope that something suitable would eventually turn up. As early as 1987 I had attended workshops and seminars at which the feasibility of producing a CD-ROM had been discussed. Some speakers had even quoted a price for mastering a disc, then £20 000–£25 000, but apart from the large national libraries, like the British Library and the Library of Congress, no one ventured into this field; certainly not any of the smaller academic libraries.

The obvious reason for our reluctance was the cost, but more important, at least from our point of view, were the difficulties we envisaged in downloading and converting our catalogue database held on a Geac 8000; and even if we succeeded there, we would still have to develop, or perhaps buy, the search software that would allow us to access the data once it had been transferred to the CD-ROM. These are the sort of problems that cause experienced computer users to wrinkle their noses; for how can you maintain a

* I gratefully acknowledge the assistance of Bob Bailey, Head of Library Division, APAK Systems Ltd., for providing information on the development of the SearchMe CD-ROM catalogue. All views expressed in this article are those of the author and do not necessarily represent or imply any views held by Staffordshire University.

reliable, quality, service while you experiment with the latest technology? Throwing money and people at the problem is never an answer; there are just never enough experienced people to go round. So, like many others, we waited for someone to come along with the complete solution – a company that could provide the expertise necessary to download our catalogue, convert it to a standard machine-readable format, master a compact disc, and provide the search software needed to access the database from a microcomputer.

The decision

This was our situation regarding the development of a CD-ROM catalogue when we received a call from the Head of Library Division, APAK Systems Ltd, offering to demonstrate their product 'SearchMe'; a library catalogue on CD-ROM originally developed at Guelph University Library, Ontario, Canada. By coincidence he had previously worked as a software engineer for Geac, and had carried out the bulk of our original catalogue conversion and implementation when we first installed a Geac in 1985. Also, we knew Guelph to be a major and long-established Geac site and, most importantly, there was sufficient money available for just such a project as this. So, the ingredients were in place; we were willing to be convinced. All we needed now were the reasons to justify going ahead, and this is a point of management often overlooked. Experimental projects of this type are rarely based on the reasoned cost-benefit analysis so frequently described in the literature, for the temptation to elaborate justifications after the event is seemingly irresistible. On the contrary, such decisions are more likely to be 'touchy-feely' ones; difficult to articulate, often unacceptable in a conventional, hierarchical, management structure, yet fundamental to the genius of creative management. As many writers have pointed out (e.g. Mumford, 1989), what good managers do, and what theoreticians and organizations think they should be doing, are often entirely different.

Nevertheless, whatever the reason, libraries tend towards a managerial orthodoxy in which justifications are *de rigeur*, wherever they come in the sequence of events. Ours were:

- The CD-ROM catalogue would provide additional functionality to our online catalogue, such as Boolean searching, searching by publication date, or fund code; and the latter would improve our analysis of where and how the bookfund was being spent. It would also allow users to download records, to a printer or text file, in a format of their choice.
- It would help take the load off our increasingly overworked OPAC, for which response times had become a major concern.
- It would allow us to produce lists of periodicals, videos, and other non-book material, something which the Geac 8000 software was incapable of doing.
- It would put our Library on the map. We have done a lot of work in recent years in developing management techniques and introducing information technology; most of this had gone unreported as we are not a 'publishing library'. We saw the CD-ROM as a way of gaining prestige.
- It could act as a back-up to the online catalogue, although this was not as important to us as it seems to be in other libraries. We had abandoned our original microfiche back-up as a matter of policy following the successful introduction of contemporary management techniques, in particular the philosophy of just-in-time developed by Taichi Ohno (Ohno and Mito, 1988) into the cataloguing and acquisitions sections. We had subsequently introduced similar principles into the management of the library system, although with much greater difficulty as I have described elsewhere (Marks, 1990). Removing back-up systems to expose faults and enforce their correction was one of the 'advanced techniques' of just-in-time, and we were anxious not to return to a situation in which it didn't really matter too much if the main system failed for a few hours; 100% availability had to remain our goal.

The product

SearchMe, the CD-ROM public access catalogue, was developed at Guelph University Library, Ontario, Canada, where they use it in place of conventional OPAC terminals. The CD-ROMs are placed on individual workstations; microcomputers with CD-ROM drives and hard disks onto which nightly updates are downloaded. In this way the catalogue is kept up to date while expensive mastering costs are kept to a minimum; a new CD-ROM is produced every six to nine months. To the user the combined search of CD-ROM and hard disk is seamless.

Following widespread interest in this development, the British software company, APAK Systems Ltd, signed a joint development agreement with Guelph and obtained exclusive marketing rights to SearchMe. They introduced the product into the UK in September 1991. Shortly after this the Head of APAK's Library Division paid us a visit to demonstrate the potential of SearchMe.

APAK Systems is a well established company that is well known among librarians in the UK, particularly among Geac users for whom it develops software and hardware peripherals. It has a reputation for cost-effectiveness and reliability among those Geac customers who use its services, although it has been somewhat poorly focused in the past.

Developing and producing a CD-ROM catalogue using SearchMe

At our first demonstration of the Guelph catalogue it was immediately clear that we would require several major changes to the screen layout, indexing, keyboard commands, wording of the help screens, and filing rules. Many of our requirements could be met by the built-in flexibility of the SearchMe software; some, however, would require development work. As we were the first library in the UK to buy this product we agreed that APAK should use our catalogue in future demonstrations. There was therefore an added incentive to include as many adaptations as possible and APAK were flexible and quite generous in this matter.

Such work is very much a partnership requiring each party to have a good understanding of the other's business; something far more difficult to achieve than we had anticipated, as became clear towards the end of the project. The software company needs to appreciate the portfolio of services offered by the library in a not-for-profit environment. The librarian, as customer, needs a good understanding of the limits of the software; of file structures, text editors, and the DOS operating system, and an appreciation of the market-led forces driving a commercial project. Most important of all, both parties need a clear understanding of just what it is they will be selling to the consumer, or rather, what it is that the consumer wants. This is deceptively difficult to achieve and it made our technical difficulties, upon which we spent so much time, seem relatively straightforward. As any perfumer knows: people don't buy scent, they buy hope. In this context we were not creating a shiny plastic disc with a database on it; but what were we in the business of making? This question, which should have been addressed from the outset, was not tackled until the very end of the project.

The downloading of the Catalogue to magnetic tape turned out to be a relatively simple affair. The Geac 8000 software provides a program that enabled us to specify which fields of the MARC database we required to download; though, lacking documentation, we needed to call on APAK's expertise to run it. It took eight hours to download 190 000 records and the work was carried out on a weekend when the Library was closed. The tapes were then sent to APAK for converting to SearchMe format. We specified which fields we wished to appear in the product and which of them should be indexed as either main or added entries; any field could be indexed. This freedom to define the indexes meant that we could include some, such as date of publication and the code number of the fund from which the item was bought, that would greatly improve our stock editing. Unfortunately we had little choice in the presentation of the records though this was not a significant drawback.

The second part of our preparation was to make those amendments that were permitted by the SearchMe software. These included text files such as error messages, help windows, and screen and column headings; screen and text colours, and the position and size of windows. The screen messages are contained in simple text files with extensions such as ERR, and HLP. Editing was simplified by running the test database under Windows 3.1 so that the original message could be displayed in one window while the text file was edited using the Windows text editor, Notepad, in another. The amended files could then be compiled and the new message displayed in its context ready for further editing.

The help screens provided by APAK were based on those used at Guelph, where they use microcomputers with colour-coded keyboards and index a different set of MARC fields to us. We plan to offer our CD-ROM over a network so that users will not necessarily be at library workstations where they would have a copy of the user manual to hand; our help screens would therefore require more detail. This was the most labour intensive part of the project and we soon realized that no matter how much you edit the text, there are always improvements to be made the following day. Eventually, giving in to the law of diminishing returns, we decided to resume editing after we had received comments from users of this first edition.

The default form of the bibliographic display and, to a limited extent, the colour and layout of the screens, are defined in a system file, MAIN.SYS. This again requires a simple text editor. The original 'Guelph' manual supplied by APAK was reasonably clear though lacked details that would be required by someone unfamiliar with the DOS operating system.

There were features that we wanted to improve but were unable to do so. We found that the definitions of many of the function keys were counterintuitive. For example: help windows are invoked by pressing the '+' key when most software now reserves 'F1' for this function; the 'insert' and 'delete' keys are used for shelf browsing from any record at any point, a welcome enough facility, but one that would be expressed more intuitively by the cursor, or 'page up' and 'page down' keys. Above all we felt that better use should have been made of the standard function keys F1 - F12. However, because of the extensive rewriting of software involved in making all the keyboard changes, we agreed to postpone it until after we had seen how users would react to the first edition.

The implementation

The CD-ROM was finally pressed in December 1992 and we received our copies in early January 1993. The original estimate had been Easter 1992, but this had been postponed several times; both sides took longer than anticipated to complete their tasks.

We had no difficulty in loading the CD-ROM onto our PC

workstations; it worked as well as any of the commercially available discs and the response times were good. We have also successfully tested it on the DEC Infoserver 150 which will provide our forthcoming network service.

We are disappointed with some features, and it was only at this late stage that a number of misunderstandings came to light. We did not receive the number of discs we had anticipated. We had expected the access software to have been included on the disc along with the database so that we should not have to supply an installation diskette with the CD-ROM; in the final version the disc could work as a self-contained item but it lacked the introductory screen and installation instructions. The pre-release manual supplied with the discs was unsuitable and would have required such extensive editing that we decided to produce something ourselves. It appeared that all the effort of APAK had gone into maintaining the integrity of our database, something that they had carried out very successfully, but they had devoted less time to the presentation and ease of use of the system – something of equal importance. Which brings me back to the question raised earlier, just what was it we were selling to our customers? Not a shiny plastic disc, nor a database, but something more like a guide to the Library's collection. Like any guide it had to be easy to use and friendly; accuracy and depth of indexing were probably not as important as we had thought them to be. People wanted something they could understand and feel quickly at home with. The history of marketing is littered with products that failed because their real nature, as defined by the customer, was misunderstood. And we failed to realize this until the project was nearing its end. What we were really in the business of making was a patient and knowledgeable friend who would guide our customers around the resources of our Library.

The benefits

The CD-ROM has brought benefits for us and for our customers; some of which we had not anticipated. Even a cursory search shows up inaccuracies in our catalogue, so it has proved to be an excellent aid in database cleaning and stock control. The great uncertainty was how our clients would react to it, or rather, whether they would react at all. We did not have long to wait. Two days after we loaded the disc onto workstations within the Library our automated system went down for 36 hours. Students immediately queued to use the CD-ROM catalogue. Such was the demand that use of any other CD-ROM database was excluded during the time the automated system was down; and these were the same students who had refused to have anything to do with the microfiche catalogue. Any shortcomings in the manual and in the keyboard commands were ignored. We also expect a favourable reaction from lecturing staff once the CD-ROM is mounted on the network and they realize the potential for downloading and printing bibliographies. In time the CD-ROM catalogue should help to relieve pressure on our overloaded OPAC, but it is too early to tell at this stage.

An unexpected use was the historical value of the CD-ROM database for accounting and statistical analysis. Like all catalogues, ours is constantly changing; vigorous stock editing means we are removing more items than we are adding. Keeping track of deleted items has always proved difficult in the past, for although in theory they should be retrievable from back-up tapes produced before any records are purged from the files, the procedure is so long-winded, cumbersome, and uncertain, that we have never attempted it. The CD-ROM database provides snapshots of the Library catalogue as it appears, say, every six months. The speed of mounting and searching makes this a much better alternative; it means that auditing the collection is now feasible – no more fudging.

Statistical analysis is another area which demonstrates the historical value of the CD-ROM catalogue. To monitor the development of the collection at present we must keep printouts of statistics; worse, this involves guessing what information we are likely to need and laying it down for future analysis. With the CD-ROM we can go back at regular intervals and run statistical programs as and when required: for example, to monitor the development of the Literature collection and plot this against the bookfund and number of students. Having readily accessible versions of our catalogue means we no longer have to foresee future requirements for statistics; we simply apply our statistical analysis to the earlier versions of our catalogue.

The future

Early reaction to the CD-ROM has been so favourable that we are planning an updating cycle. Our catalogue requires 70 MB of storage memory, less than 15% of the potential capacity of the CD-ROM. The steady decline in unit cost of storage on a hard disk now means that it may prove more cost-effective, and certainly more efficient, to mount the catalogue on a hard disk attached to a server on our CD-ROM network. This will also provide better response times; though of course, we should lose the portability of the CD-ROM. The historical value can be maintained by copying the disc to magnetic tape.

Producing the CD-ROM was very much a learning experience and we expect most problems to be resolved by the next pressing. In the meantime other vendors have come into the market place, though we have not had the opportunity to review their products.

What would we do differently?

The major confusion over our expectations was a result of not having any substantial agreement in writing. Most of our business was conducted over the telephone and we were left to make a number of changes ourselves. The line between what we were expected to do for ourselves, and what would be done by APAK, was unclear, and should have been more precisely defined. It is quite likely that these matters will be resolved for the second edition. Finally, while the software company concentrated on the technical excellence of its product, and the librarians concerned themselves with its accuracy and indexing features, the customers, who were not involved in the project, wanted a 'friend'. After all, the microfiche had been technically proficient in content, reliability, and speed of searching, but in the end it had proved an absolute disaster; using it came to be regarded as an expression of eccentricity.

The CD-ROM has risen above all our shortcomings and surpassed our expectations. Its usefulness goes beyond providing a guide to our catalogue. It has enhanced our editing of the online catalogue and acts as a store, in an elegant format, of valuable historical and managerial information. We intend to produce an improved version in time for the next academic year.

References

Marks, C. (1990) Managing an automated system. In *Computers in Libraries International 90: Proceedings of the Fourth Annual Conference on Computers in Libraries held in London in February 1990*, ed. John Eyre, pp. 17–19. London: Meckler

Mumford, A. (1989) What managers really do. *Marketing Intelligence and Planning*, **7**, (5,6), 38–40

Ohno, T. and Mito, S. (1988) *Just-in-Time for today and tomorrow*. Cambridge, Ma.: Productivity Press

CHAPTER SIXTEEN

CD-ROM, downloading and related management issues

Terry Hanson

Introduction

Most of this book has looked at the management and deployment of CD-ROM in various areas but the focus of this chapter is on the information which is extracted, or downloaded, from CD-ROM and other databases and how it is used by the end-user. Specifically it is concerned with the role of the library in the process and on the related management issues should the library take an active role.

Downloading is the process whereby information which has been selected or identified in a search or browse of a database, is copied from that source database to a file on either a hard disk or a diskette. This is a facility which is offered on virtually all CD-ROM databases whether they contain bibliographic or other types of information.

Though records may occasionally be downloaded as a convenient method of acquiring a copy of the retrieved references, perhaps where there are no printing facilities, main concern of this paper is downloading for storage and further manipulation in machine-readable form and using appropriate software for the purpose. So, for example, users of company financial information databases such as FAME or *Compact Disclosure* may wish to download data for further processing in a spreadsheet package (Berry, 1991) and users of bibliographic databases will wish to store downloaded references in suitable personal database software. It is the latter scenario which is our main concern.

Scenario

The expression 'information explosion' has long been used to describe the ever-increasing quantities of information that an individual has to confront whether in a professional or private capacity. The reasons for this apparent explosion and the question of the balance between quality and quantity are interesting and important ones but they need not detain us here. The concern here is how a busy researcher can cope with the situation as it is and how information professionals can assist in the process.

It has been suggested by one busy researcher locally that the best management strategy in the face of an information explosion is to ignore it and carry on working. Ignorance may indeed be blissful but only, alas, in the short term. Others might claim that an ideal strategy might be for a subject-expert mediator to filter out all but the most relevant and highest quality publications leaving the researcher with a manageable amount of vital material. Such a situation may indeed have strong and widespread appeal but rarely exists in this extreme sense. The vast majority of researchers will wish to be aware of new material in their specialist areas and will have to perform at least some of the filtering and management tasks themselves though librarian-mediated current awareness services (discussed later) will help considerably.

To manage their personal collections researchers will require access to appropriate information sources in the form of bibliographic databases in their various electronic formats (CD-ROM, online, diskette, OPAC), appropriate tools for the management of personal collections (i.e. bibliographic database software) and a means of transferring references, quickly and easily, from the former to the latter. Downloading only describes the extraction from the source; importing the references into the personal database is the more problematic part of the process and is an example of what is often referred to as post-processing of the downloaded data.

We are concerned here with the process whereby the end-user keeps his or her database well stocked with up-to-date references and the possible role of the library. This might be achieved either by the end-user controlling the whole process by doing the search, downloading and importing him- or herself. Alternatively the library might decide to offer an information service to researchers whereby appropriate databases are searched on a regular basis and the retrieved records downloaded, converted to the appropriate format for the user's database package and dispatched by diskette or electronic mail. In many libraries both of these arrangements prevail and both require careful planning and management. Both are discussed below.

Bibliographic software and importing downloaded records

The specialist bibliographic software packages that have emerged in recent years have their roots in the situation described above. They exist specifically to assist the busy researcher in the bibliographic aspects of the research process. Although there has always been a strong bibliographic element involved in research, it is particularly since the advent of end-user searching, using CD-ROM databases in particular, that the need for a powerful personal management tool has become pressing.

Good quality bibliographic software can be distinguished from other text retrieval database software mainly by its level of specialization and customization. Database Management Systems (DBMS) software, such as dBase and FoxPro, is designed to work with fixed field lengths where the database user (creator) controls the nature of the data to be entered into the fields and records. These packages are not well suited to the management of bibliographic references where the user has no control over the data that is to be stored. Bibliographic references are made up of titles and abstracts etc. which are determined by authors and abstract writers. Thus the software needs to be flexible in its field lengths.

Text retrieval software is designed, as its name suggests, for text-based applications with unpredictable field lengths and typically has a searching model designed for powerful retrieval using Boolean operators, field-specific searching, truncation, proximity and phrase searching, etc. Bibliographic software is a sub-category of text retrieval software and can be distinguished from it by its level of specialization and customization for managing bibliographic references. This is manifested in the three key areas of database creation (where data structures are pre-defined for standard bibliographic document types), printing reference lists (where output formats based on standard bibliographic styles are provided), and importing records downloaded from popular online and CD-ROM databases (where again the routines are pre-defined).

The ability to import downloaded records is, in many ways, the most important feature of bibliographic software packages because without it the process of entering large numbers of records individually from the keyboard would, for most researchers, be unacceptably time-consuming. However, the importing process is not without its difficulties in spite of advertising claims to the contrary.

There are two general approaches to the process of importing downloaded records into a personal database. Either the database from which the records are downloaded can offer the user a file format which is directly compatible with the bibliographic software package in use. For example, the Current Contents on Diskette series and the Citation Indexes on CD-ROM from ISI offer the user a number of file formats for downloading, including four based on specific bibliographic software packages (Pro-Cite, Reference Manager, EndNote and the now-defunct Sci-Mate). Records downloaded in these formats can be imported directly into the target package. The alternative is for the software package to provide the means to reformat the downloaded records from their native form to that required for importing.

The actual import process, in terms of speed of operation or ease of use, may not differ very much according to which of these approaches is used. The important point is to do with whether the software in use and the CD-ROM databases that are available locally are compatible by either route. If there are databases available for which there are no importing arrangements provided, then the obvious question is whether it is possible to create them. Some packages do make this possible, such as Pro-Cite and Papyrus, and some do not, such as EndNote and Reference Manager.

Of the two general approaches the ISI arrangement represents the ideal from the point of view of both the end-user and the librarian. The reformatting route however, is required for 99% of commercial bibliographic databases. The reason why the ISI approach is preferable is because it does not require the bibliographic software package to provide a reformatting arrangement. There is a severe limit to the number of databases that bibliographic software packages can recognize for reformatting purposes. Reference Manager recognizes about 150 mainly biomedical sources and Papyrus more than 70 in various subject areas. EndNote provides a generic arrangement for recognition of tagged output. Pro-Cite's approach to reformatting is by recognizing databases according to online host (DIALOG, BRS, STN, etc.), CD-ROM publisher (SilverPlatter, Wilson) or OPAC producer and thus recognizes a very large number of databases in total.

In the future it is hoped that more commercial bibliographic database producers will offer software-specific download formats for the leading packages, perhaps using a standard file format such as the comma-delimited ASCII format used by ISI and recognized by Pro-Cite and EndNote.

The role of the library

For the library wishing to promote and facilitate the use of bibliographic software several management issues arise. At a general level there is the question of whether the library should recognize a responsibility for getting involved in this area at all. The principal argument in favour of strong involvement lies in the nature of the relationship between the library and bibliographic information, and thus by extension between the library and bibliographic software (Hanson, 1992). It might be argued that the more bibliographic information the library makes available to its users in electronic form, by whichever medium, the greater the library's responsibility for providing the right tools with which to manage it, and training in their use.

If this responsibility is accepted then there is much the library can do to help researchers. Firstly it can bring bibliographic software and its capabilities to the attention of staff in the institution and promote its use. Secondly, it can arrange purchasing deals and perhaps a centrally funded site licence. Thirdly, training can be provided which covers not just the procedures for using the software but also the essentials of bibliographic information management. Fourthly, users should have contact points in the library for troubleshooting when things go wrong. Finally, the library might offer information services to its users whereby references are downloaded by library staff according to individual subject profiles, and supplied on a regular basis in a form compatible with whichever package is in use. Such a service is described in the case study accompanying this chapter.

Whether or not the library wishes to provide an electronic current awareness service the users will still wish on occasion to download references from CD-ROM workstations and import them into their personal databases. If this is the case then there is the question of how this can be managed. If the package in use incorporates importing facilities into the main program as supplied to the user (as is the case with Papyrus) and if the downloaded records are recognized by the import arrangements, then there is no problem. The user controls the situation and librarian mediation is not necessary. However, in the case of the other three leading packages, the import module is an optional extra and may not therefore be available to all users and thus they may come to a librarian asking for assistance. The simplest, though most expensive, solution to this problem is to provide all users with the appropriate import module. If this is not possible then the library will need to consider whether to offer a reformatting/importing service on demand, or to devise methods of automating the reformatting process in such a way that the user could be offered a reformatting service from a simple menu structure on a PC. This might work by a simple dialogue with the user whereby the name of the file (and path) containing the downloaded records is given and, perhaps, a choice is made of output format (based on named bibliographic software packages). The file would then be converted and the user could take it away and import it directly into the personal database.

On the question of database recognition this will depend upon either the adaptability of the import module or the willingness of the supplier to provide additional customizations. Where the import module is flexible and adaptable (Pro-Cite and Papyrus) then it may be possible for experienced library staff to provide recognition for all locally available databases. For the information intermediary this is very attractive, once the methods of customization have been learned, in that potentially all databases can be recognized. Further, both these packages also provide the means of storing individual customizations for named databases such that the end-user will find the import process simple. Thus with Pro-Cite and Papyrus it is possible to contemplate an active library role which offers both a central reformatting service on demand and/or an end-user controlled arrangement based on distribution of the importing module along with appropriate customization files for all locally available databases.

This local control over importing routines is obviously a significant factor when choosing software in an institution which has a multi-disciplinary mission with potentially hundreds of databases to recognize from many sources and in many forms (online, CD-ROM, diskette, OPAC). The objective of library policy may be that, because of the inherent complexity of the import process or because of the additional expense of the import module it is preferable to control this function centrally. However, if the library has decided to give the basic tool, the bibliographic software package, to the user then it follows that the users should, if at all possible, be able to control their own downloading and importing if they so require.

Mediated current awareness services, quality control and the end-user

In the old online model of access to bibliographic databases, mediation by the librarian was necessary for two important reasons: firstly, because time spent online was directly related to cost it was imperative that the search be done as quickly as possible. Many researchers would come to the searcher indicating a maximum amount of money available for the search; clearly the librarian was under some pressure to develop his or her technique so as to be able to provide a speedy result. Thus in turn there had to be a command language that was capable of fast, powerful and sophisticated retrieval. By its very nature such an interface was bound to be 'unfriendly' in that its use would not be obvious to the uninitiated. Librarians were initiated and end-users were not, thus expenditure could be minimized by having the librarian do the search.

A third reason was that of quality control. Not only were librarians trained in the use of esoteric commands, they also understood bibliographic information and would know the best way to find all relevant information. This had the effect of conferring an authority on the search process which, from the user's point of view, was very attractive.

While the CD-ROM era is correctly credited with overcoming the barriers to end-user searching by removing the pressure of time and by providing a simple and attractive user interface, it has at the same time presented librarians with an important management problem. If users can now have direct access to the major bibliographic databases in their areas without the mediation of a librarian, will they be capable of obtaining good results, does this matter and if so what can be done about it? Further, what does the librarian say in response to those researchers who, recognizing the benefits of quality control in the mediated arrangement, request a mediated search on a (free to use) CD-ROM database?

Some might claim that it is unduly arrogant of librarians to suggest that only they are capable of good quality searching and further that if librarians profess such a concern then it is more likely that it arises from a fear of loss of role or status. However, the concern here is not with the question of whether end-users are *capable* of acquiring the best searching techniques; it is only a question of whether they *will* actually acquire them.

Of course in an ideal world information retrieval researchers would overcome the problem by designing search interfaces which are capable, by dialogue with the searcher and interpretation of the search requests, of providing the best results possible and thus providing an alternative, impersonal form of mediation. This may happen in the future but it has not happened yet and in the meantime librarians are justified in their concern about quality in end-user searching.

The enlightened response to these concerns is to look for ways of improving the search results without discouraging end-user direct access. Direct end-user access can be improved by good training and guidance but in circumstances where access is flexible and distributed across an entire campus via a network then the problem is exacerbated.

The situation is further complicated by the fact that while 'end-userism' is a good thing it is not necessarily the ideal as far as information services in academic and research communities are concerned. It should not be assumed that simply because end-user searching is possible that researchers will necessarily rush through newly opened floodgates to avail themselves of it. Convenience of access will help but nevertheless like many other aspects of academic life the job of keeping up to date with the literature will become a chore. Further, there is not necessarily any great virtue, in the view of most researchers, attached to the acquisition of information management and retrieval skills. There appears to be a recognition and acceptance of a division of labour whereby researchers have their domain and librarians have theirs. Information is power whether you get it yourself or somebody gets it for you. It is the possession that counts, not the retrieval skills.

An ideal information service policy has to be defined principally in terms of the consumer of the end product, and in so doing it has to include elements of empowerment (end-userism) and direct service provision through tailored, personalized provision. Researchers have two types of information needs: there will be subject areas in which they have a constant, long-term interest and about which they will require to keep up-to-date and there will be areas in which they have a sudden or short-term interest. A very valuable role for the librarian is to provide a personalized current awareness service taking records from the range of CD-ROM and other databases available locally and making the results available as either a printed list or, more usefully, as a file for importation into a personal database.

Such services overcome the problem of quality control (because the librarian designs the search profile), obviate the need for the researchers to undertake the task of doing a regular update search themselves, raise the profile of the library by providing an attractive consumer orientated service and, importantly, obtain much greater value for money from the expensive CD-ROM and other database subscriptions.

Copyright and licensing issues

The process of downloading records from bibliographic databases raises the thorny question of copyright. It is not proposed to offer a detailed account of the law relating to this activity; for this the reader is referred to two recent articles on the subject (Slee, 1993; Oppenheim, 1993).

Database hosts and producers are understandably disinclined to allow users to download large chunks of their databases and repackage them for commercial gain. Both copyright law and user agreements will be reasonably clear on this point. After this however the situation becomes less clear and the student of the situation has to bear in mind two different legal angles. The first is the more arcane of the two and concerns copyright statute law. In UK law the Copyright, Designs and Patents Act of 1988 is the most recent applicable statute but waiting in the wings is the proposed EC directive on database copyright (Commission of the EC, 1991). Neither is entirely clear on the rights of either end-users or librarians acting on their behalf when it comes to downloading for personal research purposes.

The second approach concerns the law of contract and is for everyday purposes the more applicable and important. The user agreement entered into between the supplier or producer of the database and the user is a legal contract and as such it renders any statute law somewhat irrelevant. The user is bound by the user agreement. Problems arise here however when there is ambiguity in the explanation of what can or cannot be done. The user may then need to resort to even more specific, one-to-one, user agreements in order to be satisfied of the legality of the service that is to be provided.

Case Study: The Electronic Current Awareness Service at the University of Portsmouth

Library policy at Portsmouth in relation to bibliographic software has two components. First it is recognized that the software is designed for the convenience of academic researchers and thus the Library sees an important role in bringing it to their attention. The second objective has been to introduce an electronic current awareness service predicated on the widespread availability of bibliographic software.

Standardizing on Pro-Cite

To implement the policy it was first necessary to standardize on a particular bibliographic software package and devise a support programme for it. Pro-Cite had been discovered in 1987 after Inmagic had been in use for a couple of years. At first, purchases of the software were few in number and resulted mainly from Library recommendations when advice on suitable software was sought by staff in various departments. Later a different and more ambitious strategy was adopted which involved a large centrally funded purchase and free distribution to all departments. This was achieved by a successful bid for capital funds and eventually 130 copies of Pro-Cite were purchased. Distribution to departments was on the basis of staff numbers with a minimum allocation of two. In June 1993 a further major purchase of 100 copies was made with distribution to departments on the same basis as previously.

As well as providing Pro-Cite directly, the Library supports the software in many ways. The most obvious and important service is the provision of training workshops. These are offered every term and are open to either academic or support staff. Each term an average of five workshops are organized with a maximum of 10 participants. Academic staff are the most numerous but increasingly administrative staff are showing interest; encouraged it must be said by their academic colleagues. Other forms of support include the production of local documentation (a pocket guide), seminars and demonstrations, troubleshooting through the eight Subject Librarians, and most importantly the Electronic Current Awareness Service.

The Electronic Current Awareness Service

The idea behind the Electronic Current Awareness Service (ECAS) is to utilize the range of bibliographic databases to which the Library has access, to provide personalized and quality controlled current awareness information to individual academic researchers throughout the institution. The references are provided in electronic form and in a format directly compatible with Pro-Cite so that users can import them directly to their personal databases (Hanson, 1990; Cox and Hanson, 1992).

All academic and research staff are invited to use the service and their first point of contact will be through the appropriate Subject Librarian. A leaflet describing the service is circulated widely and given out on appropriate occasions. This has an 'application form' on the back which the user is encouraged to fill in and send to his or her librarian. The Subject Librarian will discuss the information needs with the user and construct the search profile and decide which database(s) need to be searched.

The main databases used for ECAS updates are the six Current Contents on Diskette products from ISI and the range of CD-ROM databases. Online database SDI services are used occasionally, but for obvious reasons the free databases are preferred. The ECAS service has also been enhanced, since January 1993, by a Tailored Accessions List service which provides updates from additions to the Library's bookstock.

Once the profile has been created, as a database-specific search strategy, it is saved and stored with the appropriate database. Unfortunately, there are many CD-ROM database software interfaces which do not permit the storage and re-use of search profiles. There are even more products which do not permit the identification of the most recently added records on a CD-ROM update disc. These two factors, along with the ease with which records can be downloaded and imported into Pro-Cite, determine the usability of a CD-ROM database for use in the ECAS service.

The Tailored Accessions Lists are produced by downloading all new book records each month from the BLCMP catalogue database and importing them into Pro-Cite. In Pro-Cite search profiles, or 'expressions' can be saved and re-used. Profiles comprise either title keywords, Dewey classification numbers or both. Users can opt for output in either laser-printed form or as a Pro-Cite file.

The task of running the profiles lies with two Library (clerical) Assistants and indeed the whole service depends on all regular updating being reducible to clerical routine. The assistants run the profiles, download the results, convert them to Pro-Cite, by various means, copy the file to a diskette for dispatch to the user, and record what they have done on a record card. The frequency with which updates are supplied is determined mainly by the update frequency of the source database. With Current Contents on Diskette databases however, the user has a choice between weekly, fortnightly, monthly, etc. Most researchers prefer weekly updates. Currently (May 1993) there are about 200 profiles of all types and the time taken by the Library Assistants on this work amounts to approximately one quarter of an average working week each.

When the user receives an update disk and imports the records into Pro-Cite he or she may then wish to acquire some of the items, and to this end the Library has supplied an output format for use with Pro-Cite (a Punctuation File) that will print a document request form for each selected record. Once printed and signed, for copyright purposes, these can be sent to the Library for processing as either inter-library loan or photocopying requests.

Conclusion

As academic researchers become users of bibliographic software packages in ever greater numbers so they will require the facility to transfer downloaded records from end-user databases on CD-ROM etc. In a situation where the process is still far from staightforward it is argued that the library of the institution can and should take on an active role in providing downloading and reformatting services for their users. Further, it argues that the library might also provide customized and quality controlled current awareness services utilizing their stock of CD-ROM, diskette and other databases. This paper and case study has examined some of the issues involved in such services from a library point of view and suggested some ways forward.

References

Berry, D. (1991) Post-processing data from Compact Disclosure using spreadsheets. *Database*, **14**, (2), 58–63
Commission of the European Communities (1992) *Proposal for a Council Directive on the*

legal protection of databases. COM(92)24 Final

Cox, J. and Hanson, T. (1992) Setting up an electronic current awareness service. *Online*, **16**, (4), 36–43

Hanson, T. (1990) The Electronic Current Awareness Service and the use of Pro-Cite at Portsmouth Polytechnic. In *Online Information 90. Proceedings of the 14th International Online Information Meeting* (London, 11–13 December 1990), ed. D.I. Raitt, pp. 277–287. Oxford: Learned Information

Hanson, T. (1992) Libraries, universities and bibliographic software. *British Journal of Academic Librarianship*, **7**, (1), 45–54

Oppenheim, C. (1993) Staying within the law. In *Bibliographic software: introduction and case studies*, T. Hanson. Hatfield: University of Hertfordshire Press. In press.

Slee, D. (1993) Electrocopying from databases. In *Bibliographic software: introduction and case studies*, T. Hanson. Hatfield: University of Hertfordshire Press. In press.

CHAPTER SEVENTEEN

Academic library case study: CD-ROM at the University of Sussex

Mike Lewis

Background

The University of Sussex Library serves a population of over 6700 full time equivalent students, attending courses or undertaking research. The stated policy of the University has been for growth, with student numbers expected to rise by 10% in October 1993. The Library at Sussex has always been in the forefront of service provision; with the loans to students ratio of over 100 per year, the Library is amongst the busiest academic libraries in the UK. As part of the support for research, the Library established a Research Support Group in 1986 with a remit to explore new technologies and their relevance to research. This ensured that the Library could offer specialized information services to the ever important research groups on campus. It was this group that first looked at CD-ROM technology during 1987, with early trial discs in the areas of psychology, biology and a general encyclopedia. By 1988, the Information Services area of the Library was established, providing services for both teaching and research, offering via public PCs *Medline, PsycLIT* and *Books in Print* on CD-ROM. Further details of the early experiences are given by the author (Lewis, 1989). From the start, Library staff recognized CD-ROMs as technology for use by library users directly – menu-driven bright screens, well laid out with help available online, with the capacity to retrieve and output results directly without delay. Our mission was, and still is, to encourage and promote users to find out for themselves what is offered by CD-ROM. This technology, more than any other, has given the keys to the literature back to the users – it is important that one does not lose sight of this basic change.

Selection and acquisition

The first CD-ROMs at Sussex were selected on the basis of heavy online use. CD-ROM databases have, by and large, migrated from online databases, so not unnaturally, the first candidates for selection were those that we would be able to offset against online expenditure. Gradually, a raft of other factors comes into play – can we have a trial disc to test before placing a definite purchase order? What is available, at what charge, and under what arrangement, outright purchase or subscription? Do we keep the discs, or must they be returned when we stop subscribing? What is the user interface like, can we choose between different versions, and if so what are the criteria for choice? There are many technical issues – will the product work sat alongside others, will it network? Is the product full-text, and thus self-contained, or an indicative one containing bibliographic references and abstracts only? If not full-text, the means by which document delivery will be obtained must be considered as part of the selection process. There are licensing issues connected with networking that must not be overlooked. There are political issues on campus to be considered – CD-ROMs are very attractive information resources, usually in specific subject areas. Anything other than a broad spread of titles across the sciences, humanities and social sciences may lead to inter-departmental rivalry and jealousies; a balanced portfolio is required.

At Sussex, we have tried to answer these questions from an informed viewpoint. A committee within Information Services was set up to look at all issues surrounding selection and acquisition, and through a twice-yearly review process, requests from academic faculty, and other subject librarians, as well as within the group, are considered. An up-to-date collection of literature from suppliers supplements more formal directories of CD-ROM products. Although suggestions for purchase can come in from all directions (much like books and periodicals of course), the detailed answers to some of the questions posed above can only be considered by the more select group. In this respect, CD-ROM selection and acquisition is different from other library materials which, generally speaking, do not rely upon sophisticated technology for their delivery.

Budgetary concerns

For the academic library working to an annual budget, CD-ROM purchasing is a set cost that can be allocated funding. If the CD-ROM title is an ongoing subscription, with regular updates, the purchase is akin to a periodical, if the purchase is a one-off (such as a dictionary or an encyclopedia) it is like a monograph. This obviously allows for better planning than is possible with the online searching budget. At Sussex, the purchase of CD-ROMs has led in turn to a saving in the online budget, but not the inter-library loan (or more accurately, document supply) one, which has risen steadily each year since their introduction (almost wholly as a result of them – a third of all undergraduate requests arise from CD-ROM sessions). The content of a CD-ROM is usually the same as its printed or online counterpart; whilst this will save the need for online searches (other than for dates before the CD-ROM starts, or, in cases where updating is very slow, after the last update), it does not necessarily mean you can cancel the hard-copy printed source. The publishers will not make cancelling the hard-copy a financially attractive option and are likely to reduce the price of the CD-ROM for those subscribing to the printed product. (Additionally, they may require the discs be returned to them once a subscription stops, which could leave your library with an annoying gap in holdings of the hard-copy.) If your CD-ROMs are delivered via a network (as they are at Sussex), the licensing charges applied by publishers must also be taken into consideration. After a period of confusion, most publishers now have a policy on networking charges, and their publicity handouts should make it quite clear what is meant by networking, and how much extra it will cost the consumer. Right or wrong, networking license fees are a fact of life and must be paid unless you wish to break the terms of your agreement.

CD-ROM technology is hardware-dependent; without equipment

there is no delivery and a title consisting of several discs, will require more than one drive, if networked. Over half the titles taken at Sussex comprise more than one disc. Unless a 'timeshare' system is employed, each networked disc must have its own drive – currently we have more than 30! This expense cannot be divorced from the acquisition cost, and is non-trivial when compared with the unit cost of adding a book to stock, for example.

CD-ROM acquisition, in whatever form and using whichever delivery method, is thus expensive, with few if any savings to be offset against it. Some academic libraries charge for online searches; few, if any, find it possible or desirable to charge for CD-ROM sessions. In its enormous favour, is its attractivness as a corporate, shared resource which is there for all to use publically over and over again (unlike the online search against which it is often compared). As such, it is a value-added product unlike any other offered within the library building (with the possible exception of the photo-copier!).

Technical and networking issues

Originally CD-ROMs were single-user tools, for use by one person at a time, with a dedicated CD-ROM drive, PC and printer. For over two years at Sussex, from late 1988 to early 1991, we offered our CD-ROMs in this way via two workstations. Since early 1991, the CD-ROMs have been delivered via a local area network (LAN), using OPTI-NET CD-ROM networking software in use with Novell (for further details see Lewis, 1992). In keeping with our mission to let users at the products directly themselves, we have experienced many benefits from the networked approach. Prior to networking, we operated a booking system which was inadequate to cope with the needs of the users. The service was only available for office hours, as security of the discs was a primary concern. Since networking, the users do not handle discs, simultaneous delivery of many products can be made from a growing number of PCs, and performance and reliability is good.

The need for technical 'midwifery' staff should never be underestimated. From the start we ran into problems whenever more than one product was put on to the PCs. Different

CONFIG.SYS files were required by each system, memory shortfalls caused systems to crash, and suppliers could offer only limited help about their own systems, rarely, if ever, advice about the conflicts between different ones. New systems, or even updates of existing ones, could bring yet more technical incompatibilities. These problems can only be solved efficiently by knowledgable, PC-aware, staff, preferably available in the libary at all times (in other words, library staff not busy computing service staff). When products are networked there is even more to go wrong, as the layers of network software, components, leads, cables and connectors make the delivery heavily network-dependent.

CD-ROM networking is not for the timid; the many benefits have only been achieved by hard work by a dedicated team, willing to take their expertise well beyond the original requirement for single-station operation. Add to that the costs for hardware, space, and the network license fees mentioned above, and it is easy to understand why CD-ROM networking is still the exception rather than the rule.

At present our network extends to a few PCs within the Library, although imminently this will be extended to the 25 general purpose ones in the building. Demands for the access to be extended are growing, with academic areas all over campus requesting access from their own offices. For PC networks to talk to each other, a basic requirement for wide-area CD-ROM networking, the full co-operation of network managers across campus is needed. This raises many technical and strategic issues (as well as licensing ones), which at the time of writing only a tiny number of academic sites have answered.

Promotion and publicity

The Information Services division of the Library has adopted a pro-active role within the University, contacting subject groups in all academic areas on a regular basis, advertizing the range of electronic services now available to them to support their teaching and research. CD-ROMs have played a prominent part in this approach – their potential audience appeal ranges from the academic faculty member to the undergraduate. The CD-ROM products (along with networked databases such as BIDS), have an immediate appeal to their target group; to the academic, unlike the online literature search, a CD-ROM session can be carried out without need for intermediary intervention, nor concern about connect costs. The results can be downloaded or printed out there and then. Once a small group of *gatekeepers* know of the existence of a title, the word will spread quickly, and many tutors begin to involve their students, at all levels.

We have also produced publicity leaflets promoting the services to particular subject groups. These mailshots have been followed up by awareness sessions, inviting selected groups of faculty or postgraduates over to the Library to show them what products are of interest to them. These, in turn, lead on to group sessions with undergraduates (where appropriate); as with all user education sessions, the best results coming when working hand in hand with academic colleagues, scheduling in CD-ROM sessions as part of the normal seminar teaching timetable.

Users

For years at Sussex, the printed *Psychological Abstracts* was rarely used by any undergraduate. Postgraduate use was also slight, although there were a steady number of requests for online seaching of the *PsycInfo* database (around 50 per year). Despite the content of the three formats being almost identical, the use of *PsycLIT* CD-ROM has been a phenomenal success – nearly 1000 hours in its first 18 months by over 300 users! (Lewis, 1990). The appeal was not always at a high research level (undergraduates were the largest single group with 45% of total use), reflecting the attractiveness of the medium in providing a few articles on a topic for an extended essay, rather than an exhaustive literature search for everything ever written on the subject. The CD-ROM approach – attractive, well laid out screens, easy to follow menus, the ability to carry out complex information retrieval using Boolean operators, truncation and field searching – not only produces more relevant results, it actually helps focus the enquiry and lead to pathways of discovery previously unknown. A rather vague request can be turned into a finely tuned result after the effective and serendipitous browsing of a CD-ROM session. Although managers have to place a cost on everything, no one should underestimate the value of such a learning aid; the provision of a CD-ROM service is now considered essential in any measure of quality.

The Research Support Group, set up in 1986 with a wholly research-based remit, by 1988 had been subsumed into Information Services, now largely, by dint of numbers, undergraduate-driven. The CD-ROM collection has grown, so that by 1993 the original two titles has swelled to 14, but because of networking without monitoring software, we have not had statistics giving use by category. Monitoring and locking software is now available (using newly installed OPTI-NET 2); as well as providing useful management information about which discs are used, it serves the function of restricting the number of simultaneous users (a feature your network licence may insist upon). Even without the means to quantify accurately over the last two years, it is clear that undergraduates still form the largest single group of CD-ROM users.

Training

The average academic library will have more than one CD-ROM product on open access to its users, and as there is no standard interface in use with CD-ROMs, librarians will have a major headache knowing the best way to teach users how to get the best out of the systems. It is quite likely that users will need to use more than one system as there is overlap between subject disciplines (especially at Sussex where interdisciplinarity is commonplace in the Arts area), so this becomes a problem that librarians are aware of much more so than suppliers, who have no intention of standardizing interfaces! Although suppliers produce manuals and guides to their products, these are rarely pitched at the 'how do I get started' level; one way round this is to produce simple, brief, guides inhouse. Although it is expensive in staff time to produce, a clear, concise leaflet explaining the basics of the system, this will soon repay itself when it comes to dealing with the inevitable request 'Can you show me how I can use this please?'.

To begin with at Sussex, we organized regular, compulsory, training sessions held once or twice each week (depending on demand) at times to suit us, for each system offered. Lasting about an hour, with up to six people crowded around the screen a member of library staff would go through the basic functions of how to search, display, mark and output. When the systems were networked, with the CD-ROMs openly available at all times this system began to break down, and the compulsory element was dropped. The original reasoning behind the compulsory element was to cut down on the number of random enquiries from users; we demanded they attend to save us time. However, training users is best done in a hands-on situation, rather than a listening one; we have now moved over to larger group teaching (linked to the taught seminar programme wherever possible), wherby four or more PCs are pre-booked and the students set an exercise to go through.

However, the resources needed for ideal training are bottomless, and as such, few libraries are likely to perform this function well. A separate training suite, fully equipped with 10 or more PCs, plus overhead LCD display unit for the teacher, fully networked, would seem a working minimum! In an effort to combat the differing interfaces of the systems, we are now producing help guides about the principles of information retrieval techniques (explaining truncation, Boolean operators, field searching, use of thesaurus etc.) and the structure of the bibliographic record output. Other than when taught to seminar groups as mentioned above, the specifics of individual systems are left to brief 'how to' leaflets, plus stressing any on-screen help available (and in the case of *PsycLIT* a video is available).

There is no evidence that our original pattern of teaching was any more successful than the present one; imperfect though that is. The economics of training must be examined very carefully; at a time when small group teaching has all but disappeared from the academic areas, it would seem incautious to commit academic-related library staff to teaching ones and twos, or even fours and fives. In that respect, the present arrangement is more cost-effective; we must hope that the penetration of CD-ROM into school libraries pushes the learning process further down the age spectrum. Just as computing is now on the curriculum at all levels, there is a strong case for information retrieval to join it as a skill for life.

Service issues

Public CD-ROM services have to be managed like any other library service. Based in the Information Services area of the Library, our service is within the broad area that provides the range of specialist information support (though not general enquiries). Staff here include those with backgrounds in reference librarianship, online searching, inter-library loans and user-education, all of which are delivered from this area. There are printed abstracts and indexes, as well as an online search service; an Information Services desk is staffed during office hours by professional staff from within the area. From this one centralized point, staff will advise users which service may be of use to them (printed, online or CD-ROM). The CD-ROMs are offered via six public PCs, networked to include JANET-based information services as well as CD-ROM. Users are encouraged actively to download results to discs (sold within the Library); there was one bookable workstation with a dot-matrix printer, but this has recently been removed. A card-operated laser printer is available on self-service within the building; there are no freely available printing facilities.

Users approach the services via a Windows-based menu. Instructions are given about how to return to this main menu as few users exit systems cleanly. Help sheets and guides may be taken from display racks; an attractive line of wall posters advertizes what is currently available. Announcements about down-times, group training sessions, or other events affecting availability are made via noticeboards at the entrance to the section. The PCs are available throughout opening hours, though staff assistance is limited to office hours. The bank of CD-ROM drives linked to the network via the optical server is situated within a staff office, locked out of hours; users have no call to handle discs.

Conclusion

At a technical level, CD-ROMs are not a perfect medium: too small for really useful bibliographic publishing, most titles spill over to two or more discs. Essentially a single user tool, they are not easily networked without expense and trouble, especially over a wide area. As such, it is unlikely to be the sole technology that academic libraries will depend upon to deliver information services into the 1990s. Yet, at Sussex, CD-ROMs have formed a significant part in the transition from intermediary, to end-user based information services. They have been instrumental in our pro-active approach to the academic areas and as such, have become the piece of information technology, more than any other, which has raised the profile of the Library on campus. The inevitable conclusion is that our users like them – and it is on our users that we ultimately depend.

References

Lewis, M.G. (1989) Experiences with CD-ROM in a University Library. In *SCIL '89 International, the Proceedings of the Third Annual Conference on Small Computers in Libraries*, (London, 1989), pp. 133–136. London: Meckler

Lewis, M.G. (1990) The *PsycLIT* CD-ROM at the University of Sussex: an optical disc for the literature of psychology. *CTISS File*, Number 10, September 1990, 18–20

Lewis, M.G. (1992) Delivering network CD-ROM services at the University of Sussex: the experience of the first year. In *Computers in Libraries International 1992, the Proceedings of the Sixth Annual Conference on Computers in Libraries*, (London, 1992), pp. 50–56. London: Meckler

CHAPTER EIGHTEEN

Public library case study: CD-ROM at Croydon Central Library

Heather G. Kirby

Croydon Library Service

The Reference and Information Service is part of the Central Library in the London Borough of Croydon. It has a staff of 10; a stock of about 50 000 volumes plus collections of official publications, maps, newspapers, periodicals and ephemera; and a modest budget, in common with most other public libraries in Greater London. The Reference Service answered over 80 000 enquiries in 1991. Its online search service has always been used predominantly for business information rather than research, which is hardly surprising in a thriving commercial centre. Very short of space at the moment, the Central Library will move into a large new complex in mid-1993. The opportunities for change which this move offers are being taken to the full, and CD-ROM has an interesting part to play.

Background

Early in 1991 we began to think about introducing CD-ROM, and networking it in the Reference and Information Service. For us, with very little experience of using CD-ROM apart from *Bookbank*, the discovery of newspapers, postcodes, bibliographies and business directories on CD-ROM opened up exciting vistas. The well-rehearsed and commonplace advantages of the format took on new meaning as we became aware of the wealth of general information sources which could be used on CD-ROM and would be popular in any public library. The popularity factor strengthened the case for an efficient multi-user system and the idea of a CD-ROM network became irresistible. At this early stage I was not aware that it would be a first in public libraries in Greater London if not in England. 'When you are "at the cutting edge" you must expect problems' I was told by a software expert, but if this account of our project reads like a cautionary tale, I hope it will also convey something of the excitement and fun we have had from our CD-ROM network.

We were particularly fortunate to have advice on hand from the Borough Libraries and Museum Officer, Chris Batt, who is very knowledgeable in the field of information technology in libraries, and has supported the project throughout. We have also had the benefit of excellent hardware and software support from the Council's Information Technology Department.

Staff

The CD-ROM network project has been managed by two of us, with much technical support, but insufficient time from our other work. It was an extra project, and in an ideal world we should definitely have had more time to devote to it. When enlarged, our network may eventually need some dedicated staff to keep it running smoothly. The stimulation and enjoyment many of our staff have experienced in sharing the network suggest that it is good to involve all staff as far as possible, but this is no substitute for the continuity and consistency of full-time management of the network.

Information strategy: the future with CD-ROM

Emphasis has always been placed on making information available borough wide through all our libraries and discussions about networking have reinforced the principle. At the moment this is achieved through traditional methods of exchanging information, setting standards of reference and information provision, training, and ensuring that staff at all service points are up-to-date with new developments in the central service. The present library management system is online to all branches, and may be the vehicle for wide area networking across the system when we do it, but it could not be considered at this stage. We intended to concentrate on a local area network (LAN) of CD-ROM, investigate how it might fit in with our plans for information provision in the new library, and try to answer some of the questions arising.

- How would its use affect the expansion of business information services? Would it give a higher profile because the public could see and use most of it? Would it stimulate demand for online searching to update and extend what is on CD-ROM? Could we exploit the 'even a child . . .' simplicity to reach the public we were not serving?
- How should we use CD-ROM to respond to the fundamental changes in the UK education system, especially the emphasis on project-based learning in the new national curriculum?
- How do you suddenly manage a completely new system within a busy public service and ensure that it gives back value for money – a load of new databases, software manuals everywhere, the hardware, the network, the maintenance, the budget explosion, staff training, user education, promotion?

Throughout the project we took for granted that the future of the CD-ROM technology was assured and the product would continue to be developed and refined.

The project plan

From an early point in the research and planning it became clear that the main value of the project would be as a pilot scheme for the new library, suggesting future developments, highlighting problems, testing solutions, and giving us a chance to evaluate the benefits of introducing CD-ROM on a network available to the general public.

We had to make decisions on:

- What hardware and networking options to choose
- Which discs to buy
- How to fund the project
- The site, access conditions, installation and maintenance

- Learning to use it, train on it, promote it

How we planned to make the decisions:

- Collect and scan literature, catalogues, blurbs, reviews
- Contact producers for further information
- See several different networks if possible
- Consult at each stage with the Borough Libraries and Museum Officer and the Principal Librarian
- Confer with the Council's Information Technology Network Support Supervisor and staff
- Contact firms which could supply and install a CD-ROM network and obtain suggestions and rough estimates
- Draw up specification and shopping lists
- Order hardware and software
- Plan timetable for installation, staff training, publicity and public launch

The project as it really happened

Brief chronology

Spring 1991   – Research, discussion, visits
Summer 1991 – Planning, estimates, quotations, ordering
Autumn 1991 – Installation, training, demonstrations
Winter 1991/2 – Moving the network, upgrades, demonstrations
Spring 1992   – Hardware problems, considering new discs
Summer 1992 – Sorting out hardware/software problems, planning expansion, further demonstrations and promotion

The following account is focussed on the main decision areas listed in the above plan for the project, and will therefore sometimes cross several datelines to draw together our questions, action and conclusions on a topic without repetition.

What hardware and what network options to choose?

On all the questions of hardware and the local area network we were guided by the Manager of the Council's Network Support Office. He showed us something of his large networks, bridged between buildings, supporting a hundred or more workstations, and all running on Novell Netware. Thus the decision to run on Novell 3.11 was made quite early on his recommendation.

His experience was very helpful when we began discussions with specialist firms outside the Council, but it did not include optical networking and therefore it was also clear very early in the planning stage that the supply and installation would be a joint project: the hardware and Novell network would be acquired and installed inhouse, by the Network Support Office, whilst the optical network and the CD-ROM drives and discs would be installed by an outside firm. This sounds a straightforward approach, making the most of what's in our own backyard, but at first it left us in the middle occasionally, not knowing who or what . . . When one network runs over another is it a good idea for them to be installed independently by different people?

We considered several firms for the personal computer workstations but were persuaded to accept one with which the Council has a favourable contract. The experiment was to start on a small scale, but having only two public workstations was also a question of cost, and space in the Reference Library. These two stations share a Laserjet printer, and the stand-alone PC for staff use shares another Laserjet with the PC used for online searching. A separate CD-ROM drive can be accessed off the network through the staff PC. This facility has been particularly useful for trying new discs, and using others which cannot be networked. All the PCs are 386, the servers and the staff workstation have 60MB hard disk and 4MB memory; the public work stations have 1MB memory.

We visited one firm, after holding several telephone discussions with them, and expecting to see a CD-ROM network in operation. We were shown various hardware components but most of the time was filled with demonstrations of the discs they were selling. We concluded, perhaps unfairly, that they were on the brink of doing what we had in mind, but had not actually done it yet. Our most useful visit was definitely that to the library of South Bank University, to which we were referred by another firm which had supplied the network there, and seemed to be interested in doing one for us. It was particularly helpful at this stage to be able to try an established network and look behind the scenes.

In our later discussions with this second firm and our inhouse network adviser, several important decisions were taken. Everyone agreed that memory size is critical, yet we should have had more, and have just bought an increase for the stand-alone PC in order to run *Extel*.

It was explained that the response time would be faster if the file server and the optical server were separate, though it was technically possible to run the optical network on the file server. We accepted this, bought each of them a PC, and have found that we can access the discs very quickly and simultaneously on three workstations. We have yet to test the system with a higher number of stations.

The CD-ROM tower or jukebox to contain the 10 drives with which we were starting our network seemed a splendid arrangement, obviating the necessity of handling discs and caddies, and putting drives on and off. Ours does not seem to fit together too well, and as it has no intelligence, but simply conceals the daisychaining, how essential is it if the drives are with the servers, not on public view? An expensive dust cover? Those which are constructed as integral CD-Servers (i.e. contain a processor etc. rather than being cabled to a separate PC network server) may be altogether better, particularly when the time comes to enlarge the system.

Final quotations were obtained in late June 1991, and orders were placed with the IT Department for the hardware, network and cabling, and with an outside firm for the CD-ROM items, a 10-drive stack, one separate drive for the staff workstation, OPTI-NET and the interface cards. When the hardware arrived it was set up and the Novell network installed ready for the installation of the optical network and the CD-ROM discs, which was done at the end of August 1991.

Meantime we were building up a list of discs to run on the network, and changing it with every new discovery and contact.

Which discs to choose and why? or why not?

Very few discs we have run have been completely trouble free and without awkward restrictions, although many of them have proved excellent.

Some of the factors which affected our choice:

- Some titles were after all coming soon but not ready yet, so for example we chose *Perinorm* rather than *Standards Infodisk*, but have since changed because the arrangement of the information and the search interface are both superior on the Infonorme London Information (ILI) disc.
- Networking CD-ROM in public libraries? How experimental, wonderful, but how dangerous – someone might download information from a disc.
- The rules and conditions for use were constantly changing, and were of course very different from one producer to another. Some made no networking charge for a single site, only for multi-site wide area networking e.g. Chadwyck-Healey, whilst others demanded 50% extra irrespective of location or number of workstations e.g. Reed International for *Kompass*, which also insisted on a print control device, and copyright guarantees which are unworkable in a public reference library, and would be very difficult even in a library with a restricted membership. *Kompass* did make a concessionary offer but it seemed still too much for our circumstances, especially as it shared out the single print allowance rather than giving extra, so we put the European disc on one workstation, and the UK on another, with references between them. Probably when the network is expanded and much used by the public we will find their multi-user licence more reasonable.
- Sometimes the rules were changed if not made up along the way because there are vestigial fears among some database producers that CD-ROM poses a threat not only to the health of online searching but also to the survival of their hard-copy markets. We naively supposed that some of the new wave of CD-ROM discs were being developed with the aim of supplanting the slow and expensive publication of bound volumes. Thus between one disc and the next HMSO/New Media decided that the public library discount would be offered only to those which had a standing order for bound volume statutory instruments, and no longer

available on standing orders to the original hard-copy edition. (This was changed after some correspondence and the earlier promises were honoured very generously.) Similarly publishers of microfilm editions of newspapers seemed anxious that we might cut our subscriptions, although the CD-ROM of *The Times*, for example, is not a substitute for the microfilm copy of every page, but a superb vehicle for searching the news content of the paper.

- At least one title had to come off the list because its software could not yet be run on a network, although the publishers were considering a new version capable of being networked, e.g. *Harrap Multilingual Dictionary*.
- We decided against buying encyclopedias at this stage because the hard-copy versions are so heavily used that we might have problems whilst there were only two public workstations. Some of the scientific titles would be high on a future wants list, especially if cumulating update discs were available.

The selection we finally put in our 10-drive jukebox was as follows:

- *The Times* 1990 and 1991
- *Guardian* 1990 and 1991
- *Independent* 1990 and 1991
- *British Newspaper Index* (BNI)
- *Statutory Instruments on CD* (SI-CD)
- *United Kingdom Official Publications* (UKOP)
- *Kompass Europe* (EKOD)

There will always be far more likely titles coming on to the market than we can buy but we have acquired some since our first list, including *Standards Infodisk* and the UK service of *Extel*, which completely replaces the labour-intensive card system, and also allows a printout to be sold to the enquirer. One consequence of having a network is receiving offers of more trial discs than we have time to test, and a deluge of publicity. Other titles we are considering for next year are *House of Commons Hansard* and *ICC Keynote Reports* but further expansion will be controlled almost entirely by costs, not content or potential use.

How to fund the project?

This may be the least useful if not the least interesting part of this case study because every library's financial circumstances are different, but I have been asked frequently how we managed to pay the initial costs. During the previous year a selection of unwanted reference works had been sold and the decision taken to re-invest the proceeds in the service, so by great good fortune there happened to be a sum of about the right amount waiting for a worthy cause in the Reference and Information Service. The running costs have been supported by the Libraries' information technology budget, and the discs are purchased from the part of the annual budget which is still called the bookfund, but is used for all library stock.

From the next financial year (1993–1994) we intend to separate the CD-ROM costs within the general fund for accounting purposes. Paying large lump sums at certain times of the year (CD-ROM subscription invoices tend to be gregarious) can upset a budget which is monitored monthly.

One of the discs which we might not have afforded otherwise, the full *Kompass UK*, was paid for from the Council's Economic Programme budget on the grounds that it would improve the quality of the information services provided to the business community in Croydon.

In another instance the purchase of the CD-ROM version was clearly an economy – *EKOD*, or *Kompass Europe* not only offered two updates a year instead of one; it fully replaced the hard-copy, thus truly saving space; made searching far easier by e.g. making it possible to search across all countries in any one of five languages; and cost very little more than the hard-copy total.

The possibilities of obtaining sponsorship for some of the discs have been discussed, but no plans are likely to be made until the network is well established in the new library, and there is something visible to promote. One of the problems may be the continuing commitment as opposed to the single gesture.

Site, access conditions, installation and maintenance

The choice of site was restricted by the present building, its overcrowding, and its age (b.1896); and further complicated by the new building work going on around us. The public workstations would need to be fairly close to the enquiry desk for staff to supervise their use adequately and offer help when required. A position was chosen which entailed only minor rearrangement, and the necessary cabling was done when the hardware had been ordered, although the public workstations were to remain in the workroom with the servers and staff PC during the training period.

From the early research and planning stage we had decided that the conditions for use of the network would need to be quite stringent, at least to begin with, until we could establish safe limits. Only the essential hardware would be placed in the public area i.e. the public workstations. We needed a secure front menu to frustrate the hacker as far as possible. No downloading would be permitted because we could not be sure of upholding copyright, nor could we carry out a virus check on every disc brought in to the library, including those we might have caused users to buy from us initially, had we tried that solution. Drive locks would be placed on the public workstations, and also security devices on each component. The printers would be sited in the workroom with the two servers and the staff workstation, so that a user could press the print button as required during a search, but would then collect the printouts from the desk. This procedure would block the helpful mender and make sure we collected the printout fees, currently 20p for an A4 sheet. Eventually, when the network, greatly enlarged, is being used on three floors of the new building some printers will have to be in the public area, but by then the users will have become accustomed to the system and supervision should be easier.

The hardware and the Novell network were set up and installed by staff from the Council's IT Department; the CD-ROM drives, and the installation of OPTI-NET and the disc software were done by an outside specialist, but thereafter the entire system has been supported by the IT Department. Sometimes it was difficult for us to know and understand what everyone was doing on our behalf, and perhaps it was hard for them also, having the work split. The CD-ROM part of the installation took one person a full day, and did not include any documentation or demonstration.

The day-to-day maintenance is now looked after by one person in the IT Department. He came as a software expert, but is rapidly becoming a CD-ROM expert also. This system works extremely well for us: it eliminates unnecessary explanations and gives continuity to the support of the network.

Learning to use it, train on it, promote it

The intention was to involve all the Reference and Information staff from the beginning so that everyone would take an interest in the developments of the project, and be eager to share in promoting the network by educating and encouraging the users. To keep them informed progress reports were given at the weekly staff meetings, and when items started to arrive, these were shown and explained.

When the training programme began emphasis was placed on the principle of knowing something (in this case the database on each disc) thoroughly in order to teach it or demonstrate it satisfactorily – a tall order to a staff already hard pressed.

Staff were timetabled to try all the discs, working with either the precis manual, if there was one, or the tutorial which most producers included in their manual. Some of them found it helpful to work in pairs. They were all encouraged to play on it as often as possible and real searches were carried out as they occurred, to the surprise and delight of the unsuspecting enquirers who might be presented with a printout of an article from *The Guardian*, or a bibliography of newspaper articles from *British Newspaper Index* for an essay topic. Seeing the quality of our answers to many ordinary enquiries improve so dramatically was one factor which stimulated many of the staff while they were struggling to learn.

We wrote a precis manual or guide of a few pages for all the databases, and tested them on any passing staff. Most producers issue exhaustively thorough manuals without any quick reference guide attached. This problem of manuals, to which those uninitiated or in a hurry need another guide, is caused by another problem, the interface.

More than any technical or mechanical conditions, it will be the interface which will build barriers against rewarding and enjoyable use of CD-ROM, in a public library especially, where searching is usually more random and less frequent than in an academic library.

The difficulties encountered by some staff in mastering very different search methods for our first set of discs highlighted the problems we shall have in user education when we launch the network, especially as we shall by then have far more titles available. One example was the national daily newspapers on CD-ROM – until recently *The Times*, *Guardian* and *Independent*, which would lend themselves to comparative searching for most enquiries, each used very different interfaces.

As opposed to the long slow development of online databases, new CD-ROM discs have been appearing very rapidly, and there seems less excuse for the lack of co-operation on a standard interface. That a few producers are aware that too much variety may be counter-productive rather than good competition, is clear from the recent moves by Chadwyck-Healey to standardize some of their discs.

Early in autumn 1991 the first series of demonstrations was given, beginning with several sessions to staff from other sections and branches of the Libraries, Museum and Arts Department, which created a good deal of interest, sometimes just in the range of information and the flexibility of the search method, but more often in the possibility of networking all this material to their service points. A second series was given to colleagues from Reference Services in all the London Boroughs, none of whom had at that time embarked on a CD-ROM network. They were particularly interested in the functioning of the network, response times etc. so they were quite impressed by our demonstration of identical and simultaneous searches on the three workstations, spoilt only once by conjuring a tartan from the *Guardian* on the third screen. They were of course also interested in the detailed specification and costing.

This programme of demonstrations was to have been extended to other Council departments and outside organizations but it was interrupted by the necessity of moving the network to a clean environment, at a safe distance from the building site (see the following section on problems). Further sessions were held – two of these were interesting in that we combined them with appropriate online demonstrations – and then for a time it became difficult to book any more dates with confidence, due to a series of problems with the CD-ROM drives. The programme was revived in the autumn of 1992, with the aim of promoting the network widely in advance of its public launch in 1993.

Problems encountered

Most of our problems have been caused by the shifting conditions of the new library building programme. We did not know in advance that all the public areas of the Reference Service would have to be closed for several months from January 1992, leaving only the workroom in which to provide a telephone enquiry service for the duration, and even this space was frequently troubled by dust, compressor fumes and vibration. The network was in a particularly unsuitable environment. Early in January 1992 it was moved to a large clean room on the Town Hall side of the present building, where it remains because its previous site is still in a very poor state. Several unfortunate consequences ensued. It may be that the move itself caused dust to sift throughout the system, especially within the drive tower. Whatever the reason there have been recurrent problems with the CD-ROM drives since, so that our programme of demonstrations was interrupted, and then ceased altogether for several months. There seemed to be some difficulty in diagnosing and isolating the faulty parts because one drive can pull another down in the tower, and at one stage interrelated software complications crept in. Finally the hardware and the software experts spent a morning working together on the network, and the system seems to be running in good health again, but we watch it suspiciously.

Having to leave the network at some distance from the Reference Library has prevented our making it available to the public because there is no cabling between the present site and the workroom (which was cabled to the library before installation), and cost aside, it would not be approved as the Town Hall has been redecorated recently. The services are being used by staff on behalf of users, with a very encouraging response, but this situation has nevertheless proved a great disappointment to all the staff, who were enthusiastic to promote and assist its use in the library, and of course we were all eager to launch the network and observe the results closely. To overcome the effects of this delay will require a renewed effort on staff training, in readiness for promoting it when it is made available in the new library.

Among the problems not caused by any physical conditions, software changes and upgrades have caused quite a bit of bother. One producer ran out of answers on the help desk and despatched their software developer to Croydon because we could no longer access *SI-CD* on the network after Context Limited changed the software to *Justis4* in order to make it conform with their other databases. The answer was predictable – the networking aspects of the new programme had not been fully tested – but it was interesting to observe his system of checks, and his despair. The disc works very well now and the search method is much improved.

However, frequent upgrades and changes which all require reinstallation are very time consuming on a network of only 10 discs, so we can look forward to worse when we increase the list next year.

Future developments

Setting up and running this small pilot scheme has been a valuable exercise in many ways, not least in prompting us to think of different routes to expansion. A comprehensive wide area network which will carry any data to anywhere in the system is the ultimate aim, but in the short term, i.e. the next 12 months, the CD-ROM network will remain a local area network to be developed within the new central library complex. Even in this limited field there are a number of possibilities, and questions to answer:

- Should all the databases be accessible on every public and staff terminal throughout the new library? This will be technically possible through a new Ethernet-based data management system, but would all the specialist discs be used everywhere, and what are the staff training requirements to manage such a system in a large public building?
- Should different access levels be used so that basic bibliographic discs such as *Bookbank* could be widely available on public and staff terminals, while the use of subject-specific databases might

be concentrated on small groups of workstations which would be adjacent to the complementary areas of stock?

This arrangement offers immediate advantages of purposeful use and therefore fast access, with knowledgeable staff in the appropriate areas to guide users, or search on their behalf. The data management system would allow any access levels to be changed anywhere in the system in response to new demands.

To begin with, the network as it exists now, in autumn 1992, within the Reference and Information Service will be moved to the new central library with additional public workstations. It will be sited on the third level of the building, the one on which all business information, official publications and backfiles of serials are provided. Even within these areas of information, i.e. leaving aside the bibliographic, literary, and scientific fields for which there are numerous good discs available, we have sufficient databases to require at least double the present number of drives.

Whether the short term expansion is effected through the building of small, discrete subject area networks, or on one large system with a series of front-end menus having different access levels, will depend on the capabilities of the data management system which has yet to be tested in the new complex, and any new developments in optical networking packages. However it is done the conditions for public access will be the same as originally planned, and surveys of staff and public response to the network and to CD-ROM will be a priority during the year following its launch.

CHAPTER NINETEEN

Special library case study: CD-ROM at Bain & Co

Feona Hamilton

Bain & Co is a large strategic management consultancy, with a head office in Boston, USA and 14 other offices scattered around the globe. In Europe, there are six offices, including the London one which is known as Bain UK Inc. This was the company's second office, opened some six years after Boston, and began operations in 1979.

The size of office varies considerably, and only the largest have an Information Services Department (ISD). The largest ISD is, naturally, in the Boston office: other ISDs are in London, Paris, Munich, Milan, San Francisco, and Tokyo. All ISDs work closely together in the provision of information, and all offices are able to request information from any ISD. In practice, the most heavily-used ISDs are in Boston, San Francisco, and London. This is because these are the largest departments, with the widest range of facilities.

The range of materials offered in the London ISD is in both hard-copy and computerized format, The hard-copy consists of:

- Books – directories, textbooks, monographs
- Newspapers – British and American qualities
- Journals – management and trade
- Reports – mainly market research
- Government publications – mainly statistics
- Annual reports – especially FTSE – 100

Computerized services are in online and CD-ROM format. Access is available (via the ISD only, at present) to the online hosts Radio Suisse, DIALOG, Investext Direct, Profile, and PFDS.

The CD-ROM services offered have changed markedly over the last year. In October 1991, there were 13 different discs available for use in the ISD. These were:

- FAME – UK company information
- DIANE – French company information
- DAFNE – German M & A information
- BNB – Belgian and Dutch company information
  (The above five discs are all produced by CD-ROM Publishing)
- *European Kompass on Disc* (EKOD) – the disc-based version of *Kompass* directories, containing abridged company information
- *Compact Disclosure* (Laser-D) – page by page copies of company annual reports, including text and illustrations
- *Dun & Bradstreet : Moody's Company Data* – USA company information, much of it textual and historical
- *Dun & Bradstreet : Million Dollar Directory* – USA company information, listing companies with an annual turnover in excess of $1m
- *Lotus CD/Corporate : UK Private+* – UK company information, covering listed and unlisted companies. Differs from FAME in amount of textual information available on each company
- *Lotus CD/Corporate : UK Public* (now *International Corporate*) – information about companies listed on the stock exchanges of the country in which they are situated. Includes stock exchange announcements where available (e.g. UK)
- *Lotus CD/Corporate : European M & A* – information on mergers and acquisitions activity in Europe. Gives details of successful and unsuccessful bids, bid histories and amounts involved
- *Lotus CD/Corporate : US M & A* – as above, covering US companies
- *Dun & Bradstreet & Lotus : CD/Europa* – a new joint venture, marketed by Dun & Bradstreet, containing information on European companies of all types and sizes.

By July 1992, this had shrunk to seven – and by November 1992 it was reduced further to just four. Those four are:

- EKOD

- *Laser – D*
- *Lotus CD/Corporate – International Public*
- *Lotus CD/Corporate – UK Private+*

What has happened to bring about such a reduction in service levels?

There are three main reasons for the decision to cut CD-ROM services so markedly. Firstly, the size of the office has come down considerably, compared to its size in the 1980s. Then, there were over 300 staff, occupying an entire building. The ISD had 12 staff members. Now (in August 1992) there are just over 70 people, occupying only one floor of the same building. This includes consulting and support staff, only three of whom work full-time for the ISD. The Manager of the department spends half her time on ISD tasks, and half on corporate communications – i.e. marketing.

Secondly, the entire range of information services offered has recently been reviewed, and an effort made to cut out duplication. Thus, the *CD/Europa* disc was tested, but discarded in favour of the existing hard-copy version of the same information. This was the same reasoning behind abandoning the discs for *Moody Company Data* and *Million Dollar Directory*. It will be noted that these are all produced by Dun & Bradstreet : although there was certainly no deliberate intention to cut our expenditure with a specific producer, the fact remains that we have reduced our commitment to them by about 80% because of this decision. Overall, expenditure on CD-ROMs from all sources will drop from £60K pa in 1991–92, to £30K pa in the current year. Thirdly, the chargeback system used in the office means that the decision has been taken to incline towards services operating a pay-as-you-go system (such as is common with online services) rather than up-front subscriptions (which is the usual CD-ROM purchasing system). In this way, when we have received the detailed monthly invoices issued by online hosts, it is an easy matter to allocate costs to case codes, using the information supplied.

This does not mean that CD-ROM services are being abandoned. The nature of information provision needed precludes such a step being taken. Despite the cut in the number of different discs used, the high standard of ISD services has not changed. What it has meant is that the duplication and over-provision of services has been avoided. Instead, a highly focused service is offered, using just those discs which can provide the most relevant information in the most useful format.

Bain, like other management consultancy firms, needs in-depth information about companies and industry sectors, provided quickly and accurately, preferably from a source which will allow the information to be manipulated and analysed from many different viewpoints. Our own network ISDs means that it is no longer necessary – or desirable – for offices to duplicate each others' holdings, or to attempt to respond to all questions from a specific office within that office's own ISD – should there be one. Instead, each ISD tends to select the services which will provide the answers to the majority of enquiries received in that office. This is easily determined by conducting a short survey of the enquiries logged. Thus, since the majority of information required in the London office tends to be about UK industries and companies, and only a minority requires information from other countries, we have concentrated expenditure mostly on the sources – such as *Lotus CD/ Corporate UK Private+* – which will give us the best coverage in our opinion. The fact that the *Lotus Public* (now *International Public*) disc includes international coverage gave us another reason to cancel the very expensive *CD/Europa* disc to which we had subscribed earlier. The decision to concentrate on Lotus, rather than the CD-ROM Publishing 'family' of discs, has proved to be the right one. We now have a selection of discs which require the same research techniques. This cuts down on the time needed to train consulting staff in the use of discs.

Other Bain ISDs will be made aware of our holdings, and any changes which may occur, so that they can plan their own list of services, knowing that they will have access to our discs on request, and vice versa.

The CD-ROMs which have been selected by the London ISD give in-depth provision of company and industry sector information, mainly concerning the UK, but also giving some international coverage. The Lotus products permit a high level of manipulation and analysis enabling the user to produce, for example, competitor intelligence, rankings, geographical information, as well as a straightforward detailed company report. The stock exchange announcements provided on the International Corporate disc are also a source of information not easily available otherwise to the ISD, without using external services. This includes information about personnel changes and company restructuring. The mergers and acquisitions news provided by this section is the reason behind cancelling those discs specifically dealing with M & A information. Thus far, it has proved to be the correct decision, as the level and type of M & A information available from this disc is sufficient to satisfy most enquiries. The decision to stay with Lotus products, rather than FAME and its companion discs was taken mainly because of the extra textual material available on Lotus.

The Laser-D service was retained because of the frequent need for a page-by-page copy of a company's annual report. There is a space problem within the department – a not unusual situation – and it would be impossible for us to store more than the FTSE-100 annual reports listed above. Like many other organizations, Bain uses external providers – mostly ICC for the annual reports of unlisted companies – but to be able to access a complete copy of such a report for a major public company, within minutes of the request being received, makes the Laser-D system indispensable. However reliable the external source, there are still appreciable savings in time and courier charges. The space-saving is considerable, and the system itself, since it includes an increasing number of reports from outside the UK, is becoming more heavily used. Controlling chargebacks is simple, as the Laser-D system already contained the facility. It is impossible to access the service without keying in a case code. Each month, a printout of usage is produced, and charges allocated as appropriate.

The point has already been made that all the company's ISDs work closely together. ISD staff, via the Bain Worldwide Information Network, exchange enquiries and information as a matter of course. The usual methods of contact are by telephone (with a voicemail facility) or by the courier system. There is, as yet, no E-mail service available, although there is no reason why such a service should not be set up. Should E-mail come into use, it would not mean that either of the other means of contact would become irrelevant, as a quick phonecall will always be necessary in some instances, as will the need to post materials between offices.

Who physically uses the facilities available in the ISDs? The answer is emphatically not just the ISD staff. There is a training programme for all consultants as well, to encourage them to have the skills to access information for themselves. This is a very necessary part of training, since there is often a need for information of some kind, outside normal office hours. As the London office is very open-plan, the ISD is available at all times, whether staffed or not.

Training in the use of the ISD is part of the initial induction course for consulting staff. A formal programme exists, and is used for the main (September) intake of Associate Consultants (ACs). It consists of two training packs – the first pack contains an overview of the ISD and the services it provides. It includes a description of each computerized service, and gives details of the charges made for each of these. Other material related to the use of other libraries and information services, and how they are accessed – i.e. which the AC may attend in person (as is the case with the London Business School Library) and which may only be contacted by a member of ISD staff (as is the case with the various information brokers).

The second pack has a series of questions for the ACs to work through during the first weeks of their training. All ACs also have an introductory tour of the ISD, undertaken by a member of ISD staff. This is true of the group intake, and the individual ACs and new consultants (NCs) who may appear at any time during the year. In this way, they quickly become familiar with all the services offered and also get to know a specific member of ISD staff. For the lone newcomer, it can be a daunting experience to join Bain & Company, and any means of breaking down the barriers of shyness and unfamiliarity is welcome.

Some of the answers to the questions in Pack 2 of the AC Training Programme can only be found by using the CD-ROMs. This is the opportunity for them to be shown how to use CD-ROM services. In the time available, it is only possible to show them the most basic techniques. This is usually sufficient for them, in any case, but if a particular interest is shown in the use of such services, the AC will certainly be given more training, so as to enable him or her to find, download, and manipulate the information needed. The level of computer literacy now manifested by newcomers to the company is considerably higher than it used to be, so extra training of this nature is not a problem. The spreadsheet used by consultants is Lotus 1-2-3 and there are further training sessions for all ACs in this, and other software, as well. In a very short while, they are happily conducting complex searches on the CD-ROMs, downloading the results on to a floppy, and taking it to their own PCs to use as they will.

It will be noted, from the last sentence, that the CD-ROMs are all on stand-alone machines at present, rather than being on a network. This is one of the steps under consideration, and it is hoped that it will not be long before it is implemented. The decisions needed will be two: how many stations to have on the licence, and which PCs will be selected as those able to access the service?

The number agreed on will be dependent mainly on the cost. As to those chosen to have access, it would seem to make sense if they were to be the PCs most frequently used for the task of data collection – i.e. those on the desks of the ISS staff and the ACs. This will mean a total of about 12 machines on the network, based on current numbers of ISD staff and ACs in the London office.

One other refinement would make life easier for ISD staff – the installation of a front-end which would force users to enter a case code before they could access the disc required. Lotus is currently testing a commercially produced piece of software on a few 'guinea-pigs'. The alternative, at present, is to try to persuade IT staff inhouse to write the necessary program, while continuing to trust users to enter the required details in a scruffy exercise book tied beside the machine! I understand that many enquiries about such an access system are received by Lotus in the course of a year. Laser-D, on the other hand, came with the facility already installed. Presumably, the difference was because Laser-D comes as a combined hardware/software package, and the PC is used only for that service. Lotus, on the other hand, supplies the CD-ROM player only, which is linked to the user's own PC. No doubt, it will not be long before the software is available.

To summarize, CD-ROMs in a management consultancy context are an indispensable part of the information services. Those which are used in Bain have been chosen because they provide accurate, reliable company and industry sector information, which is regularly updated. They are easy to use, and the basic rules can quickly be learned by a novice. On the other hand, an expert in their use will be able to find, analyse and present the information required, and to manipulate that information in many different ways, to their own and their client's satisfaction. CD-ROMs save a considerable amount of space, and much staff time, since filing is no longer necessary – no more Extel cards!

The only possible disadvantages at the moment are that they might be perceived as expensive. The average price of this type of CD-ROM is about £9000 p.a. but offset against this is the saving in staff time, and it immediately looks more attractive. There is also the problem of chargeback control, but it looks as if that might be solved soon. Finally, it is only possible for one person at a time to access the disc at present – but that was always the problem with books wasn't it, and they are very much still with us.

CHAPTER TWENTY

A future for CD-ROM as a strategic technology?

Terry Hanson

Introduction

In the past the library manager had it easy. There was only one technology available for presenting information and its access tools to the library's users. With the enormous advances in computer and related technologies in recent years the library manager now has an increasingly difficult task in deciding which of a range of technologies to utilize in presenting information to the users. Further, as the technologies develop and proliferate, it becomes not just a question of how best to provide access to traditional bibliographic records. New services become available which challenge the traditional objectives and force the librarian to find new ones.

The purpose of this paper is to consider the current range of technologies available to the library manager for providing access to bibliographic and related information and to look at how the 'information infrastructure' is changing. In particular we are concerned with the place of CD-ROM in the information strategy, now and in the future, and the role and difficulties of the librarian in strategic planning.

As a focus for development it is assumed for the purposes of this paper that the library manager wishes to pursue a strategy which emphasizes the position of the end-user, aims to maximize his or her convenience and seeks to provide the best quality service possible.

In the context of current and future technologies this implies a networking, or virtual library, approach whereby information services are available direct from the user workstation.

CD-ROM in perspective

The perception of CD-ROM as an 'appropriate technology' is conditioned by what it is seen as an alternative to. When seen as an alternative to printed indexes it is correctly judged as a great leap forward. Similarly when compared to the mediated online model its empowerment of end-users represents, to most librarians, substantial progress. But if librarians were to compare CD-ROM as it currently exists to an ideal future information delivery situation they may come to see more readily the former's limitations and assign it a new position in the strategic technology mix. The most important point to make in this Chapter is that the information community is on the verge of a new era of information delivery based on the technology of networking and it is in this context that CD-ROM needs to be seen.

As this scenario develops the library manager has the task of selecting from a range of information delivery options those most appropriate in relation to the strategic objectives of the local institution. And furthermore he or she must remain aware of the constantly changing possibilities and techniques and be prepared to be flexible, adaptable and innovative. Thus it is the intention in this paper to depict CD-ROM as an interim technology that has done an admirable job in bridging the gap between an old mediated and restrictive online access model and the brave new world glimpsed above (more on which later).

However, CD-ROM has not been interim in any deterministic or necessary sense. CD-ROM has not been a necessary prerequisite for the networking revolution that is just beginning. Nevertheless, as a technology it has permitted certain aspects of future network-based service possibilities to be anticipated and experienced and for some lessons to be learned. In particular this is true of end-user searching and the design of user interfaces. Most visions of the future assume the empowerment of the end-user, and librarians have been given the opportunity to explore some of the implications of this through their experiences with CD-ROM.

Before considering future trends and developments we should consider the strengths and weakness of CD-ROM in relation to current alternatives and possibilities.

The main strengths of CD-ROM, from a library point of view, are normally considered to be:

- *Fixed costs* The tyranny of the online 'pay-as-you-go' arrangement can be swept away with a subscription arrangement which allows the library to control and predict its costs.
- *Easy interfaces* The fixed cost allows unlimited searching by end-users, so suitable interfaces are required that present the complexities of Boolean searching in a friendly and attractive manner.
- *Convenience and power* Compared to printed indexes with their annual volumes many CD-ROM databases permit the user to search many years in a single search step and with greater power, flexibility and convenience.
- *Portability* In many ways the most impressive feature of CD-ROM is its ability to store 600 MB of information on a single portable disc. Other mass storage mechanisms, such as magnetic hard disks, are more sensitive and more bulky.

But just as selectivity with the comparisons can show CD-ROM in a favourable light so it can also work in the opposite direction. The most obvious weaknesses are manifested in relation to the more positive aspects of current or potential alternatives:

- *Storage capacity*
  At about 600 MB the storage capacity of a CD-ROM disc is very impressive when the reference point for comparison is the humble floppy disk. But when the storage capacity required to store a sizeable chunk of a major database such as *Medline* is many times this amount the statistic of 1000 diskettes or 200,000+ printed pages per CD is somewhat less impressive. The inconvenience of having to change discs and repeat a search in order to search across several years is correctly seen as a major negative factor for CD-ROM.
  In mitigation it can fairly be claimed that though there is

currently a fixed MB capacity of CD-ROM the database producers have found techniques of improving the situation. The various techniques of data compression have resulted in squeezing more data onto the discs while the inconvenience of disc swapping is addressed in some products by the ability, when all discs that comprise the database are loaded in separate drives, to search across several discs with a single search statement. The question of increasing the basic storage capacity of CD-ROM beyond the 600 MB is raised from time to time but in recent years this seems not to have been an industry priority.

It remains the case though that, in spite of a less friendly interface, online databases have the advantage in this area. The online version of *Medline* or *Chemical Abstracts* will be presented as a single file, unless the user chooses to search in a subset, with no effective limits on the storage capacity.

- *Access times*

At the time of writing the fastest CD-ROM drive on the market has an access time of 200 ms while the average magnetic hard disk inside a PC is between 10 and 15 ms. Further, developing technologies such as flash memory promise access times significantly faster still. More commonly most CD-ROM users will be using an earlier generation of drive with an access time in excess of 300 ms. Clearly magnetic storage has a strong advantage here. Leave aside the hybrid technology of magneto-optical disks that attempt to improve the performance of optical storage media by combining optical with magnetic storage features; our concern is with CD-ROM only.

When large databases are made available, whether on stand-alone machines or networked, the slow response times may become unacceptable especially when it is known that there are alternatives that provide much better performance (see below).

- *Currency of data*

In many ways the strengths of CD-ROM are also its weaknesses. Portability is rightly seen as a strong point for the technology and it is this feature in particular that has allowed the CD-ROM database to supplant the printed index. But when updates to the database are delivered on a monthly basis at best and when this is compared to more frequent updating (normally) of online databases then it is the whole concept of physical delivery of updates that comes into question.

To address this problem some CD-ROM products have an arrangement whereby the online equivalent (if there is one) can be searched seamlessly by a single search statement. The search would take place on the CD-ROM and then in a special update portion of the online file. The workstation for such a service would need to be equipped with a modem and appropriate communications software. Examples of this arrangement include the Wilson databases, DIALOG OnDisc products and the *Celex* (EC law) database through Context Ltd. of London.

- *Not designed for networking*
If the local information strategy is built around the idea of delivering information to the desktop then the key technology must be networking. And though CD-ROM networking is now commonplace it is still true to say that it is not a technology that was designed with multi-user access in mind. Networking has been 'grafted on'. None of the standard networking software, such as Novell Netware of Microsoft LAN Manager, could recognize CD-ROM as standard. Third party software has had to be developed to either operate independently (peer to peer network software such as Lantastic) or, more commonly, to be grafted on to server-based networks such as Novell Netware. (The recently released version 4 of Novell Netware does now recognize CD-ROM as a so-called 'Netware Loadable Module' without having to purchase a separate package such as SCSI Express to achieve this).

Not surprisingly it has taken CD-ROM networking a long time to reach a satisfactory level of performance and reliability. However, just as CD-ROM suffers in comparison to magnetic storage online in the manner described above, so cumulatively it is weak in the strategic networking sense. Thus, where efficient and timely delivery of information to the user's desktop is the primary objective in the organization, so the networking of CD-ROM is relatively uncompetitive when compared to magnetic-based alternatives.

Current alternatives to CD-ROM

The current position of CD-ROM owes much to the absence of effective alternatives. When printed indexes and mediated online are the only possibilities it is not at all surprising that CD-ROM has received the attention it has over the last 10 years. It is a testament in fact to the weaknesses of these two established models of information dissemination. For the majority of librarians CD-ROM has been a much welcomed opportunity to open up, or 'democratize', access to powerful information retrieval facilities which had hitherto been so restricted. However, as the options increase, CD-ROM has to be seen in an increasingly competitive context. Currently the principal alternatives to CD-ROM for bibliographic information delivery are:

- *Online access: Commercial hosts*
  The position of CD-ROM in relation to online access to bibliographic information is assessed above but the situation is not static. CD-ROM's advantages of interface and predictability of costs will not be permanent. The former is largely a matter of technology and will be overcome once the bandwidth of the networks becomes broad enough to transmit graphic images, or once the host service migrates to a client-server model whereby the nature of the interface may be decided locally (see below). In the meantime most of the host services now offer an 'end-user-friendly' alternative to the traditional command line interface. The question of costs is also changing with more online hosts now offering subscription arrangements. An interesting recent example of this convergence with CD-ROM is the FirstSearch service from OCLC which provides access to a range of databases and combines a very simple (some might say too simple) search interface with a charging arrangement based on a standard cost per search. US libraries buy FirstSearch cards pre-charged with multiple search units (10 or 25) which can then be sold (or given) to the users (O'Leary, 1992; Snure, 1991). In May/June 1993 the UK academic community were invited to consider, by way of a free trial, whether to subscribe to FirstSearch via BIDS on JANET (see below).
  Once the commercial online vendors have overcome the two

barriers of interface and cost control there is every reason to think that this method of access will become much more popular, at the probable expense of CD-ROM. The advantages inherent in the online model of speed of access, frequency of updating, convenience of searching an entire database, and also of conducting a search across several different databases simultaneously, make for an attractive option.

- *Online access: Academic hosts*

An alternative online arrangement is available to the UK academic community using the Joint Academic NETwork (JANET). This is a network to which all universities and research institutes have access and which is being seen increasingly as a vehicle for information service provision. In 1989 CHEST (the Combined Higher Education Software Team) negotiated a deal with ISI (Institute for Scientific Information) to mount the latter's databases on JANET and, in return for a fixed annual fee, to provide unlimited searching for each university site. This arrangement has proved to be very popular and CHEST have since negotiated a further deal to mount the EMBASE medical database with a similar access arrangement. At the time of writing (May 1993) CHEST is in the process of consulting the British academic community on which other databases should be considered for access via JANET, with the prospect of most of the major bibliographic databases becoming available in this fashion.

In the meantime, progress is being made on upgrading the JANET network to provide much greater capacity and faster communication speeds. The SuperJANET project began pilot operation during the first half of 1993 and access will soon be available at all sites.

Clearly, for the academic community, this option has much to offer but the weak link remains the user interface. As with the commercial hosts, this problem will eventually be solved, but in the meantime CD-ROM interfaces remain the more attractive to the end-user. There may also be a local problem in some universities with the notion of universal access; students for example are sometimes not permitted to use JANET.

- *Local loading of tapes*

This option has been available for many years to large

organizations where the economics of the situation are such that the high cost of subscribing to the tapes from the database producer are nevertheless somewhat lower than the costs involved in 'normal' online searching. This arrangement is similar to CD-ROM in that updates are delivered and loaded, for a fixed annual fee. There is thus a timeliness problem but there are advantages of access speed and file size once the tapes are loaded on the local mainframe computer. The interface question becomes a local issue. It would normally be possible to import the data from the tapes into a known and preferred database software package such as BRS/SEARCH or BASIS. Another possibility is to integrate the tape files into the same interface as already used for the local OPAC system. Thus H.W. WILSON have worked with OPAC system producers (Unisys and Sirsi) to allow the WILSONTAPE databases to be used with the same interface as the OPAC.

- *Local hard disks*
  With the tape loading arrangement, the tapes themselves are simply a means of physical delivery of the data to the subscribing site whereupon it is loaded onto a magnetic hard disk connected to a mainframe or minicomputer. A similar arrangement is now available, with data delivered by either CD-ROM or DAT (Digital Audio Tape) and loaded onto hard disks connected to a PC network server. Leading CD-ROM database publishers such as SilverPlatter and CD-Plus will now provide this kind of service, though at a significantly higher cost than conventional CD-ROM. However, economics apart, it is a very attractive option in that the interface and fixed cost advantages of the CD-ROM are retained but without the access speed, file size and networking disadvantages. Timeliness is obviously still a problem.

  The costs associated with this option are the main obstacle for most libraries and they relate not only to the subscription to the data but also to the purchase of hardware. For a large database such as *Medline* it may well be necessary to acquire three or four 1.2 GB hard disks. At about £1500 each it means that the cost of the network server will be in the region of £10 000.

Future trends and developments

Thus far we have described the current situation and hinted at possible developments in the future. If we take the best of all the options described and assign equal importance to all features, then it is clear that CD-ROM cannot be the strategic long-term option because of its weaknesses in access speed, limited capacity and updating arrangements. On the other hand, it is also clear that the online model, though it currently suffers from many weaknesses, still has many advantages and is conceptually an attractive model which is capable of meeting most ideal scenarios for the future.

However, there are still two questions that need to be addressed and which affect the viability of the online, or wide area networking, model of access: the notion of a standard or consistent interface to databases from different sources and the question of network bandwidth which determines the speed of transmission of information and in turn the types of information that can be transmitted.

Standard interfaces

When the hard-pressed library manager makes choices among the different delivery methods there may be only three or four technologies involved: (online, CD-ROM, local OPAC), but there may be hundreds of separate databases and possibly a few dozen different interfaces for the user to encounter. Thus it is common to find the notion of a single standard interface to a wide range of databases high on the list of ideals in future information scenarios. But, although in the past there have been attempts to design and promote the notion of a standard interface, such as the Common Command Language, that would be made available on all hosts, the main focus is now on the idea of making the choice of interface entirely a matter for local decision. Thus if the library wished to adopt the interface used in the local OPAC as a standard for use with all other available databases, then this would be possible. The advantages to the user are very clear and attractive.

The technology that makes this possible is the client-server model of networking. Essentially this involves separating the user interface from the database and its retrieval software. The conventional online model, also known as the multi-access model (Addyman, 1992, p.314), has the data, retrieval software and the user interface all running on the host machine. The user can log-on to the machine using either a dumb terminal or a PC with communications software and use the service remotely. The client-server approach allows the interface to reside on the local machine, rather than be downloaded from the host, and requires a communication, or information retrieval, protocol to interact with the 'search engine'.

If the information retrieval protocols between client and server are in the public domain then this implies two very important points:

- the user interface can be variable so long as it complies with the required protocols;
- the database, no matter where it is mounted, can comply with the required protocols and thus be made available to the compliant client.

The implications of this arrangement as far as the library manager is concerned are enormous. It will mean that there can be a single user interface to all available databases. It opens up the possibility of 'designing' the local information service rather than simply providing access to it. For this vision to be realized there needs to be adequate client-server information retrieval protocols and for these to be adopted by database producers and publishers.

Information retrieval protocols

The notion of inter-operability between different database systems is so attractive it has generated many different attempts to achieve standards (Davis, 1992; Heacox, 1991):

- Z39.50. This is the standard developed by the US National Information Standards Organization (NISO). It was originally adopted as a standard in 1988 but has since been revised to comply with international standards (OSI Search & Retrieve). The standard is seen as holding the most promise in networked services and library systems. At the time of writing most library systems suppliers have announced that they are working on Z39.50 compliance in their products. OCLC uses the standard in a recently introduced SiteSearch service which provides a standard interface to the range of FirstSearch databases alongside other local offerings. Other early implementors of the protocols include the library systems supplier NOTIS, the US based Research Libraries Group (RLG), the National Library of Canada and the online host Mead Data Central.

There are several draft standards competing for attention in the CD-ROM area:

- CD-ROM DXS (Data Exchange Standard) is a standard developed by SilverPlatter in 1991 and submitted to NISO for consideration as a standard for CD-ROM inter-operability.
- CD-RDx. This is the CD-ROM Data Exchange Standard produced by the Information Handling Committee of the CIA first issued in 1991. Its brief is to offer inter-operability between CD-ROM databases in US government departments and agencies.
- Structured Full-Text Query Language (SFQL). This is intended as the equivalent of the SQL standard in DBMS applications. It was developed by the US transportation industry.
- CD-ROM Consistent Interface Guidelines produced in 1991 by the CD-ROM Consistent Interface Committee of the Special Interest Group on CD-ROM Applications and Technology. Known as CD-CINC.

The enormous promise of these consistent interface developments is such that the local information infrastructure can be customized to local requirements but there is another aspect of interface design which will be the next major hurdle to clear. In an electronic or virtual library the notion of the empowerment of the end-user is considered paramount. But when access is gained from the user's desktop workstation to the information service there is no librarian on hand to help out with search strategy or other aspects of using the system.

This presents a challenge to the librarian which may be answered partly by distributing general and database specific guidance materials to potential users and by providing a telephone help desk.

But, as also argued in Chapter 16 there is perhaps much still to achieve in providing some 'expert' assistance from within the interface in the choice of database(s) and with the search strategy. The interface may enter into an interpretative dialogue with the user until satisfied about what is required and then undertake the search. The initial input from the user may, in this scenario, include natural language queries.

Network bandwidth

One of the advantages of the client-server model in information networking is that it reduces the amount of traffic on the network to the minimum because all that needs to be transmitted are the search requests and the resulting references. However this does not address the more fundamental question of the types of information that can be transmitted and their speed. Thus the online networks as they currently exist are not designed for transmitting graphic images, sound or video. This presents a problem for full-text article services which invariably contain some graphic images. It also presents a problem for those who wish to develop their information services to include document delivery.

CD-ROM is taking advantage of this situation and carving out a niche for itself with products like *Adonis* and *Business Periodicals Ondisc* but plans are well advanced in the UK and the USA to develop high bandwidth network infrastructures. In the UK the SuperJANET project and the US National Research and Education Network (NREN) are making progress and hold out the promise of high speed transmission of all forms of information. Similarly powerful networks will eventually be available for general purpose commercial services.

Conclusion

With these elements in place the new era of information delivery possibilities mentioned earlier has begun. The only barriers to ideal information scenarios are now organizational and/or concern economics rather than technology. The design of the local information service will be largely a matter of choosing from services offered across wide area networks. Location of the database server will not be a significant factor and the interface will be standardized. All forms of information will be available whether bibliographic references, full-text, graphics, sound or video and speed of transmission will not be a problem.

It is difficult to see a significant role for CD-ROM in this picture. If it figures at all it will be primarily as a physical delivery mechanism for small subsets of data or of software and perhaps in the multimedia consumer products market. It has proved invaluable as an interim technology but for the library manager with an ambitious user-oriented information strategy CD-ROM is unlikely to be the key technology. However, it is also clear that the 'interim' period in which CD-ROM features prominently in local information strategies has a few years yet to run.

References

Addyman, A. (1992) Networking CD-ROMs using Z39.50. In *Online Information 92. Proceedings of the 16th International Online Information Meeting* (London, 8–10 December 1992), ed. D.I. Raitt, pp. 313–322. Oxford: Learned Information

Davis, D. (1992) Evaluation of SIGCAT's CD-ROM Consistent Interface Guidelines, and US standards and draft standards affecting distributed computer applications. In *Online Information 92. Proceedings of the 16th International Online Information Meeting* (London, 8–10 December 1992), ed. D.I. Raitt, pp. 323–329. Oxford: Learned Information

Heacox, S. (1991) CD-ROM standards: can we make them a reality? In *12th National Online Meeting, Proceedings – 1991* (New York, May 7–9, 1991), ed. M.E. Williams, pp. 129–134. Medford, N.J.: Learned Information

O'Leary, M. (1992) FirstSearch takes the lead. *Information Today*, February, 11–14

Snure, K.R. (1991) The FirstSearch experience at the Ohio State University. *Library Hi-Tech*, **9**, (4), 25–36

Select bibliography

This bibliography represents a selection of recent material covering the topics addressed in the book. Many of the references from the individual chapters are included but the intention is to provide a reference source for recent material on managing CD-ROM in libraries. The vast majority of the references are from 1991 and later and include books and conference proceedings as well as journal articles.

General

1. Adkins, S. (1992). *CD-ROM in libraries: a reader*. Westport, CT: Meckler

2. Gunn, A. A., and Moore, C. (1990). *CD-ROM: a practical guide for information professionals*. London: LITC/UKOLUG

Resourcing issues

3. Akeroyd, J. (1990) CD-ROM evaluation. *Library and Information Research News*, **13**(47), 7–12

4. Brandt, J. M. (1991) CD-ROM licenses: what's in the fine or nonexistent print may surprise you. *CD-ROM Professional*, **4**(2), 13–16

5. Clark, K. (1991) A practical commentary on the selection of CD-ROM vs. online databases. *CD-ROM Professional*, **4**(4), 115–116

6. Davis, T. (1993) Acquisition of CD-ROM databases for local area networks. *Journal of Academic Librarianship*, **19**(2), 68–71

7. Erkkila, J. E. (1991) The basic economics of CD-ROM pricing. *CD-ROM Professional*, **4**(1), 85–88

8. Haar, J., Clark, J., Jacobs, S., and Campbell, F. (1990) Choosing CD-ROM products. *College & Research Libraries News*, **51**(9), 839–841

9. Jensen, M. B. (1991) CD-ROM licenses: what's in the fine or nonexistent print may surprise you. *CD-ROM Professional*, **4**(2), 13–16

10. Johnson, D. (1991) CD-ROM selection and acquisition in a network environment. *Computers in Libraries*, **11**(9), 17–22

11. King, A. (1991) Kicking the tires: the fine art of CD-ROM product evaluation. *Online*, **15**(3), 102–104

12. King, A. (1991) To CD-ROM or not to CD-ROM, that is the question! *Online*, **15**(2), 101–102

13. LaGuardia, C. (1992) Virtuous disc selection or, how I learned to stop worrying and love to buy CD-ROMs. *CD-ROM Professional*, **5**(1), 58–60

14. LaGuardia, C., and Bentley, S. (1992) Electronic databases: will old collection development policies still work? *Online*, **16**(4), 60–63

15. Levin, C. S. (1990) CD-ROM pricing: time for some new ideas. A proposal for a radical restructuring of the pricing of library CD-ROM products. *CD-ROM Professional*, **3**(6), 8–9

16. Nahl-Jakobovits, D., and Tenopir, C. (1992) Databases online and on CD-ROM: how do they differ, let us count the ways. *Database*, **15**(1), 42–50

17. Nicholls, P. T. (1993) 15 quick tips for navigating the CD-ROM literature. *CD-ROM Professional*, **6**(1), 93–97

18. Nicholls, P. T. (1990) A buyers guide to CD-ROM selection: CD-ROM product directories and review tools. *CD-ROM Professional*, **3**(3), 13–21

19. Nissley, M. (1990) CD-ROMs, licenses and librarians. In *CD-ROM licensing and copyright issues for libraries*, eds. M. Nissley, and N.M. Nelson, pp. 1–17. Westport, CT: Meckler

20. Pooley, C. (1990) CD-ROM licensing issues. In *CD-ROM licensing and copyright issues for libraries*, eds. M. Nissley, and N.M. Nelson, pp. 31–43. Westport, CT: Meckler

21. Tenopir, C. (1992) Evaluation criteria for online, CD-ROM. *Library Journal*, **117**(4), 66–68

Case studies

22. Abella, G. V., and Kittle, P. W. (1992) The CD-ROM experience at Loma Linda: the issues of training, logistics, and creative financing. *Medical Reference Services Quarterly*, **11**(2), 1–11

23. Bailey, C. W., and Gunning, K. (1990) The intelligent reference information system. *CD-ROM Librarian*, **5**(8), 10–19

24. Bailey, C. W. (1992) The intelligent reference information system project: a merger of CD-ROM LAN and expert system technologies. *Information Technology & Libraries*, **11**(3), 237–244

25. Beckett, G. (1990) Tearing down the walls: providing access to library data bases and services. *Bibliotheca Medica Canadiana*, **12**(2), 82–87

26. Belanger, A. M., and Hoffman, S. D. (1990) Factors related to frequency of use of CD-ROM: a study of ERIC in an academic library. *College & Research Libraries*, **51**(2), 153–162

27. Bucknall, T., and Mangrum, R. (1992) U-search: a user study of the CD-ROM service at the University of North Carolina at Chapel Hill. *RQ*, **31**(4), 542–553

28. Burris, R. A., and Molinek, F. R. (1991) Establishing and managing a successful end-user search service in a large special library. *Online*, **15**(2), 36–9

29. Butcher, K. S., and Scott, S. R. (1990) Effects of CD-ROM in a university library. *Journal of Educational Media & Library Sciences*, **27**(3), 257–269

30. Dalrymple, P. W. (1990) CD-ROM Medline use and users: information transfer in the clinical setting. *Bulletin of the Medical Library Association*, **78**(3), 224–232

31. Deschatelets, G., and Carmel, L. (1990) Optical technologies, CD-ROMs and libraries. 3. A strategy for implementation. *Documentation et Bibliotheques*, **36**(2), 45–68

32. Erkkila, J., June, M., and Neveu, R. (1991) The case study of a small academic library with many CD-ROMs. *CD-ROM Professional*, **4**(5), 133–137

33. Faries, C. (1992) Users' reactions to CD-ROM: the Penn State experience. *College & Research Libraries*, **53**(2), 139–149

34. Goddard, C. (1991) CD-ROM at the Royal Army Medical College: an examination of the 'threat' which it poses to online literature searching and the role of the librarian. *State Librarian*, **39**(3), 32–40

35. Madsen, L. (1992) Introducing CD-ROM in a university library: problems and experiences. *INSPEL. International Journal of Special Libraries*, **26**(1), 42–50

36. Maranda, S., Ludwin, V., and Law, J. (1990) Medline on CD-ROM at Bracken Library, Queen's University. *Bibliotheca Medica Canadiana*, **11**(4), 193–197

37. Maxymuk, J. (1990) Implementing a CD-ROM installation: the Temple program. *Laserdisk Professional*, **3**(1), 24–27

38. Ryan, S. M. (1992) CD-ROMs in the smaller US Depository Library: public service issues. *Government Publications Review*, **19**(3), 269–278

39. Schmidt, D., and Davis, E. (1992) CD-ROM use in a science library. *Science and Technology Libraries*, **12**(2), 29–41

40. Schoch-King, N., Goldstein, S. E., and Williams, L. A. (1990) Medline and PsycLIT on CD-ROM: a survey of users in an academic medical library. *Medical Reference Services Quarterly*, **9**(1), 43–58

41. Schultz, K., and Salomon, K. (1990) End users respond to CD-ROM. *Library Journal*, **115**(2), 56–57

42. Siddiqui, M. A. (1992) CD-ROM searching in an academic library in a developing country. *CD-ROM Librarian*, **7**(5), 23–28

43. Sieburth, J. F., and Barnett, J. B. (1991) CD-ROM in a marine science library. *Science & Technology Libraries*, **12**(1), 55–67

44. van Boven, M. C. A., and Spikman, G. (1991) Introduction to end users of new electronic media in the library of the Wageningen Agricultural University: an evaluation. *Quarterly Bulletin of the International Association of Agricultural Information Specialists*, **36**(1–2), 11–13

45. Wiksten, S. (1990) Learning the hard way: a public library's experience with CD-ROM. *Electronic Library*, **8**(2), 107–109

CD-ROM and full-text

46. Barden, P. (1990) ADONIS: the British Library experience. *Interlending & Document Supply*, **18**(3), 88–91

47. Barden, P. (1991) New technology at the British Library Document Supply Centre: developments and obstacles. *IATUL Quarterly*, **5**(2), 117–121

48. Barnes, J. (1992) Solving the physical access dilemma. *CD-ROM Librarian*, **7**(3), 19–20

49. Browning, M. M. (1991) Is Business Periodicals Ondisc the greatest thing since sliced bread? A cost analysis and user survey. *CD-ROM Professional*, **4**(1), 37–41

50. Butler, M. (1990) Full-text CD-ROM libraries for international development. *Microcomputers for Information Management*, 7(4), 273–291

51. Cornish, G.P. (1992) CD-ROM: a new phase in document supply? *INSPEL. International Journal of Special Libraries*, 26(1), 5–13

52. Ion, B. (1990) Developing document delivery systems using CD-ROM technology: the UMI experience. In *IOLS '90. 5th Integrated Online Library Systems Meeting. Proceedings*, (New York, 2–3 May 1990), ed. D.C. Genaway, pp. 85–90. Medford, NJ: Learned Information

53. King, A. (1991) Full text & CD-ROM: variations on a theme. *Online*, 15(5), 107–108

54. Korwitz, U. (1990) ADONIS: between myth and reality: trial document supply using CD-ROM technology. *IFLA Journal*, 16(2), 215–219

55. Stern, B. T. (1990) ADONIS: a vision of the future. In *Interlending and Document Supply: First International Conference. Proceedings*, (London, November 1988), ed. G.P. Cornish, and A. Gallico, pp. 23–33. British Library

56. Stern, B. T., and Compier, H. C. J. (1990) ADONIS: document delivery in the CD-ROM age. *Interlending & Document Supply*, 18(3), 79–87

CD-ROM and in-house applications

57. Anon (1992a) CD-ROM and document imaging. *Document Imaging Automation Update*, 11(3), 1–4

58. Anon (1992b) Motives for document image automation. *Document Image Automation Update*, 11(10), 1–4

59. Arps, M. (1992) Using CD-ROM technology to solve information needs at 3M. *Document Image Automation*, 12(1), 11–12

60. Ashley, M. (1991) ACCESS: new OPAC interfaces at the Library of Congress put a new face on software development. *CD-ROM Professional*, **4**(6), 83–86

61. Berglund, C. M. (1990) The New England Law Library Consortium: resource sharing with CD-ROM technology. *Microcomputers for Information Management*, **7**(3), 205–216

62. Berkery, M. J. (1992) Optical disk storage is an alternative to paper. *Office*, **115**(6), 64–65

63. Bronner, R. G., and Leek, M. R. (1992) Mining for gold in the information mountains: a comparison of the economics and usefulness of film and CD-ROM for document storage, access and distribution. *International Journal of Micrographics and Optical Technology*, **10**(4), 195–200

64. Hallgren, S. (1990) CD-Kat in Swedish public libraries, or how to make a shared disc act as a local catalogue. In *Bibliographic Access in Europe: First International Conference. Proceedings, (Bath, UK, 14–17 September 1989)*, ed. L. Dempsey, pp.204–211. Aldershot: Gower

65. Hallgren, S. (1991) The CD-Kat story. *Resource Sharing and Information Networks*, **7**(1), 133–145

66. Hallgren, S. (1990) Developing your CD-ROM. *Electronic Library*, **8**(5), 331–335

67. Jordahl, G. (1991) The in-house adventures of CD-ROM. *Inform*, **5**(6), 26–29

68. Kersten, A. (1992) Keys to successful publishing of technical documentation on CD-ROM. *CD-ROM Professional*, **5**(1), 49–54

69. Kosmin, L. J. (1990) Resources for tracking CD-ROM in-house development options. *CD-ROM Professional*, **3**(3), 56–60

70. Meyer, F. (1990) In-house CD-ROM publishing moves toward the desktop. *Laserdisk Professional*, **3**(1), 40–41

71. Meyer, F. P. (1992) Recordable capability keeping compact discs rolling in the '90s. *CD-ROM Professional*, **5**(3), 127–129

72. Mischo, L. (1990) The Alice-B information retrieval (IR) system: a locally developed library system at Tacoma Public Library. *Library Hi-Tech*, **8**(1), 7–20

73. Nixon, P. E. (1990) A university library's OPAC on CD-ROM: various views on the technology. *INSPEL. International Journal of Special Libraries*, **24**(3), 120–127

74. Pozo, L., and O'Connor, M. A. (1992) The army marches forward with CD-ROM. *CD-ROM Professional*, **5**(3), 62–66

75. Pozo, L., and O'Connor, M. A. (1992) U.S. Army conquers paper monster with imaging technology. *Document Image Automation*, **12**(2), 36–38

76. Ralphs, J. (1990) Planning the distribution of technical documentation on CD-ROM. In *OIS International 1990. Seventh Annual Conference on Optical Information Systems. Proceedings*, (London, UK, 17–19 July 1990), pp.107–111. London: Meckler

77. Smorch, T. (1990) CD-ROM public access catalogs: one way to get there. *CD-ROM Librarian*, **5**(4), 30–34

78. Thiel-Thomas J. (1992) Integrated CD-ROM and WORM optical disk systems on the Navy's paperless ship. *CD-ROM Professional*, **5**(3), 17–26

79. Townley, C. (1992) College libraries and resource sharing: testing a compact disc union catalog. *College and Research Libraries*, **53**(5), 405–13

80. Townley, C. T. (1990) A value-added, compact disk union catalog. *College & Research Libraries News*, **51**(9), 835–839

81. Udell J. (1993) Start the presses. *Byte*, **18**(2), 116–134

82. Uricchio, W. (1993) From card catalog to OPAC: using CD-ROM to cross the great divide. *Computers in Libraries*, **13**(1), 16–20

83. Uricchio, W., Duffy, M., and Depp, R. J. (1990) From amoeba to request: a history and case study of Connecticut's CD-ROM-based statewide database. *Library Hi-Tech*, **8**(2), 7–21

84. Williams, B. (1991) CD-ROM at British Airways. *Information Media & Technology*, **24**(1), 22–24

CD-ROM hardware and software

85. Andrews, C. (1990) Understanding CD-ROM software. *CD-ROM Professional*, **3**(4), 59–62

86. Bash, A. (1993) Keeping the CD station rolling: tips to enhance the life of your CD-ROM workstation. *CD-ROM Professional*, **6**(1), 36–41

87. Befeler, M. (1992) Where no drive has gone before: ruggedized CD-ROM drives. *CD-ROM Professional*, **5**(6), 142–143

88. Beheshti, J. (1991) Retrieval interfaces for CD-ROM bibliographic databases. *CD-ROM Professional*, **4**(1), 50–53

89. Beiser, K. (1992) Memory management solutions. *Online*, **16**(3), 103–105

90. Beiser, K. (1993) Real life in the CD-ROM trenches. *Online*, **17**(2), 93–95

91. Belkin, N. J. *et al* (1991) User interfaces for information systems. *Journal of Information Science*, **17**(6), 327–344

92. Bhatt, K. (1991) Optical storage unravelled. *Management Services*, **35**(1), 34–37

93. Bolin, R. L. (1991) Setting up general purpose CD-ROM workstations. *Library Hi-Tech*, **9**(4), 53–62

94. Bouley, R. J. (1992) The life and death of CD-ROM. *CD-ROM Librarian*, **7**(1), 10–17

95. Bowers, F. J., and Shapiro, N. R. (1992) CD-ROM standards: essential for progress. *CD-ROM Librarian*, **7**(8), 33–36

96. Brueggeman, P. (1991) Memory management for CD-ROM workstations. I. *CD-ROM Professional*, **4**(5), 39–43

97. Brueggeman, P. (1991) Memory management for CD-ROM workstations. II. *CD-ROM Professional*, **4**(6), 74–78

98. Brueggeman, P. (1990) The versatile CD-ROM workstation: making information available to both IBM and Macintosh users. *CD-ROM Librarian*, **5**(5), 34–38

99. Brueggeman, P. (1993) 19 tips for enhancing CD-ROM performance. *CD-ROM Professional*, **6**(1), 17–22

100. Charles, S. K., and Clark, K. E. (1990) Enhancing CD-ROM searches with online updates: an examination of end-user needs, strategies and problems. *College & Research Libraries*, **51**(4), 321–328

101. Ciuffetti, P. D. (1992) CD-ROM data exchange standard (DXS) version 1.0 overview. *CD-ROM Librarian*, **7**(8), 26–32

102. Ciuffetti, P. D. (1991) A plea for CD-ROM interchangeability. *CD-ROM Librarian*, **6**(8), 27–28

103. Clark, K. (1992) CD-ROM retrieval software: the year in review. *CD-ROM Professional*, **5**(3), 114–116

104. Corbitt, T. (1993) CD-ROM: the mass storage media. *Management Services*, **37**(1), 22–24

105. Davis, D. (1992) Evaluation of SIGCAT's CD-ROM Consistent Interface Guidelines, and US standards and draft standards affecting distributed computer applications. In *Online Information 92. 16th International Online Information Meeting. Proceedings*, (*London, 8–10 December*), ed. D.I. Raitt, pp.323–329. Oxford: Learned Information

106. Fletcher, L. (1993) Is there a chance for a standardised user interface? *Electronic Library*, **11**(1), 29–32

107. Francis, B. (1993) CD-ROMs drive toward new standards. *Datamation*, **39**(4), 57–60

108. Green, M. (1991) Setting standards. *Aslib Information*, **19**(6), 211–212

109. Grossman, B. L. (1992) Buying your next CD-ROM workstation? some practical tips. *CD-ROM Professional*, **5**(1), 70–71

110. Grossman, B. L. (1992) Budgeting for CD-ROM drives. *CD-ROM Professional*, **5**(6), 139–141

111. Heacox, S.A. (1991) CD-ROM standards: can we make them a reality? In *12th National Online Meeting. Proceedings 1991*, (New York, NY, USA, 7–9 May 1991), ed. M.E. Williams, pp.129–134. Medford, NJ: Learned Information

112. Hughes, A. (1991) Selecting and managing equipment for CD-ROM. *Aslib Information*, **19**(6), 209–210

113. Jackson, K. (1992) Disc technology and long-range planning. *CD-ROM Professional*, **5**(3), 123–125

114. Jackson, K. (1993) Separating the wheat from the chaff: finding out what you really need to know about CD-ROM and related technology. *CD-ROM Professional*, **6**(1), 142–144

115. Jacso, P. (1990) The ideal CD-ROM workstation for the 1990s. In *Online Information 90. 14th International Online Information Meeting. Proceedings*, (*London, UK, 11–13 Dec. 1990*), ed. D.I. Raitt, pp.25–32. Oxford: Learned Information

116. Jacso, P. (1993) Different folks, different strokes: the future of CD-ROM user interfaces. *Information Today*, **10**(2), 25–26

117. Jaffe, L. D., and Watkins, S. G. (1992) CD-ROM hardware configurations: selection and design. *CD-ROM Professional*, **5**(1), 62–68

118. Jones, A. (1991) DOS CD-ROMs: not just for DOS computers. *CD-ROM Professional*, **4**(6), 48–50

119. Ka-Neng, Au (1992) CD-ROM interoperability. *CD-ROM Librarian*, **7**(8), 22–25

120. King, A. (1991) The care and feeding of your CD-ROM disk. *Database*, **14**(6), 105–107

121. Large, A. (1991) The user interface to CD-ROM databases. *Journal of Librarianship and Information Science*, **23**(4), 203–217

122. Lockwood-Grossman, B. (1992) CD-ROM drive buying tips Part 1. *CD-ROM Professional*, **5**(1), 70–71

123. Lockwood-Grossman, B. (1992) CD-ROM drive buying tips Part 2. *CD-ROM Professional*, **5**(3), 68–70

124. Machovec, G. S. (1991) CD-ROM and optical disc longevity. *Online Libraries and Microcomputers*, **9**(5), 1–3

125. Marshall, M. E. (1991) Compact disc's 'indestructibility': myth and maybe. *OCLC Micro*, **7**(1), 20–23

126. Meyer, F. P. (1991) Information management: an overview of CD-ROM technology. *Data Resource Management*, **2**(2), 14–19

127. Nazim-Ali, S. (1990) Retrieval commands of CD-ROM databases: a comparison of selected products. *CD-ROM Professional*, **3**(3), 28–33

128. Nickerson, G. (1991) The CD-ROM workstation: what it is and what to look for. *CD-ROM Professional*, **4**(3), 40–41

129. O'Connor, M. A. (1992) Emerging standards for CD-ROM development. *CD-ROM Professional*, **5**(2), 135–137

130. Rosen, L. (1992) CD-ROM interface activities could bring important changes to the industry. *Information Today*, **9**(5), 26–29

131. Saffady, W. (1992) (ed.) *Optical storage technology 1992: a state of the art review*. Westport, CT: Meckler

132. Steel, A. (1991) Making the right optical storage choice. *ComputerData*, **16**(2), 13–15

133. Storleer, R. (1992) State of the art: technology and products application areas for CD-ROM. *INSPEL. International Journal of Special Libraries*, **26**(1), 14–41

134. The, L. (1992) CD-ROM reaches for critical mass. *Datamation*, **38**(9), 47–50

135. van Brakel, P. A. (March 1991) Problems and pitfalls in using CD-ROM technology. *South African Journal of Library and Information Science*, **59**(1), 19–26

136. van der Walt, H. E. A., and van Brakel, P. A. (1991) Method for the evaluation of the retrieval effectiveness of a CD-ROM bibliographic database. *South African Journal of Library and Information Science*, **59**(1), 32–42

137. Weiman, L. (1992) CD ROM drives: into the mainstream. *Macworld*, **9**(10), 144–149

138. Young, A. (1991) The CD-ROM standards frontier: Rock Ridge. *CD-ROM Professional*, **4**(6), 53–56

139. Young, A. (1992) Standard fuels CD-ROM acceptance. *Computer Technology Review*, **12**(4), 18–21

140. Zink, S. D. (1991) Toward more critical reviewing and analysis of CD-ROM user software interfaces. *CD-ROM Professional*, **4**(1), 16–22

CD-ROM in schools

141. Bankhead, B. (1991) Through the technology maze: putting CD-ROM to work. *School Library Journal*, **37**(10), 44–49

142. Butterworth, M. (1992) Online searching and CD-ROM in British schools. *Education for Information*, **10**(1), 35–48

143 Teger, N. (1991) MultiPlatter goes to school. *CD-ROM Librarian*, **6**(6), 21–28

CD-ROM market

144. Arnold, S. E. (1991) Making CD-ROM product winners. *Online Review*, **15**(5), 275–291

145. Arnold, S. E. (1992) Checking the pulse of developers for the library market. *CD-ROM Professional*, **5**(4), 91–92

146. Arnold, S. E. (1991) Storage technology: a review of options and their implications for electronic publishing. *Online*, **15**(4), 39–51

147. Arps, M. (1991) Hardware and media options for CD-ROM publishing. *CD-ROM Professional*, **4**(4), 66–68

148. Barron, G. (1992) The role of optical technology in megamedia applications. *CD-ROM Professional*, 5(4), 36–40

149. Capers, R. (1991) CD-ROM: the advantages and barriers to market growth. *CD-ROM Professional*, 4(4), 88–89

150. *CD-ROM market place: 1992: an international guide to the CD-ROM, CD-I, CDTV & electronic book industry* (1992). Westport, CT: Meckler.

151. Finlay, M., and Mitchell, J. (1991) (eds) *The CD-ROM directory 1992*. London: TFPL Publishing

152. Finlay, M., and Mitchell, J. (1992) (eds) *The CD-ROM directory 1993*. London: TFPL Publishing

153. Foulds, M. S., and Foulds, L. R. (1991) Librarians' reaction to CD-ROM. *CD-ROM Librarian*, 6(1), 10–14

154. Nicholls, P. T. (1989) Information resources on laserdisk: statistical profile of currently available CD-ROM database products. *Laserdisk Professional*, 2(2), 101–108

155. Nicholls, P. T. (1988) Statistical profile of currently available CD-ROM database products. *Laserdisk Professional*, 1(4), 38–45

156. Nicholls, P. T. (1991) A survey of commercially available CD-ROM database titles. *CD-ROM Professional*, 4(2), 23–28

157. Nicholls, P. T., and Sutherland, T. (1992) CD-ROM databases: a survey of commercial publishing activity. *Database*, 15(1), 36–41

158. Nicholls, P. T., and Van-Den-Elshout, R. (1990) Survey of databases available on CD-ROM: types, availability and content. *Database*, 13(1), 18–23

159. Nicholls, P., and Sutherland, P. (1993) The state of the union: CD-ROM titles in print 1992. *CD-ROM Professional*, 6(1), 60–64

160. O'Connor, M. A. (1992) Market predictions for multimedia/CD-ROM publishing. *Multimedia Review*, 3(2), 60–63

161. Tamule, H., Gaus, K., and Desmarais, N. (1992) A new look at CD-ROM prices. *CD-ROM Librarian*, **7**(9), 22–26

162. Tenopir, C. (1990) CD-ROM in libraries: distribution option or publishing revolution? *CD-ROM EndUser*, **2**(2), 56–59

CD-ROM networking

163. Addyman, A. (1992) Networking CD-ROMs using Z39.50. In *Online Information 92. 16th International Online Information Meeting. Proceedings*, (*London, 8–10 December 1992*), ed. D.I. Raitt, pp.313–322. Oxford: Learned Information

164. Akeroyd, J. (1991) CD-ROM networks. *Electronic Library*, **9**(1), 21–25

165. Akeroyd, J. (1992) CD-ROM networking. *Information Services & Use*, **12**(1), 55–63

166. Akeroyd, J. (1992) CD-ROM networking: an introduction. In *CD-ROM Networking in practice*, eds. C. Moore, and N. Whitsed, pp.1–7. London: UKOLUG/LITC

167. Akeroyd, J. (1991) CD-ROM networks. *Electronic Library*, **9**(1), 21–25

168. Akeroyd, J., Winterman, V., and Royce, C. (1990). *CD-ROM networking*. Boston Spa: British Library.

169. Atkinson, R., and Yokley, J. (1993) Multiplatform CD-ROM networking. *CD-ROM Professional*, **6**(3), 73–81

170. Barbour, B., and Rubinyi, R. (1992) Remote access to CD-ROMs using generic communications software. *CD-ROM Professional*, **5**(2), 62–65

171. Beheshti, J., and Large, A. (1992) Networking CD-ROMs: response time implications. *CD-ROM Professional*, **5**(6), 70–77

172. Bell, S. (1990) Spreading CD-ROM technology beyond the library: applications for remote communications software. *Special Libraries*, **81**(3), 189–195

173. Bell, S. J. (1993) Providing remote access to CD-ROMs: Some practical advice. *CD-ROM Professional*, **6**(1), 43–48

174. Biddiscombe, R. (1991) Networking CD-ROM in an academic library environment. *British Journal of Academic Librarianship*, **6**(3), 175–183

175. Blackwelder, M. B., Wu, E., and Brodie, K. (1990) CD-ROM access via a VAX: one institution's experiment. *CD-ROM Librarian*, **5**(10), 24–29

176. Bonness, E. (1992) The application of CD Net at the University of Bielefeld. In *CD-ROM networking in practice*, eds. C. Moore, and N. Whitsed, pp.47–49. London: UKOLUG/ LITC

177. Bovenlander, J., Binkhorst, R., Bleeker, A., and VanLaar, A. (1993) CD-NET on Ethernet using Novell Netware 3.10: the experiences of Erasmus University Rotterdam. *CD-ROM Professional*, **6**(2), 30–35

178. Breeding, M. (1993) The healthy LAN: tips and advice on the care and maintenance of CD-ROM networks. *CD-ROM Professional*, **6**(1), 75–78

179. Brown, C. L., and Coleman, D. E. (18) Testing and development of an efficient, remote CD-ROM system. *CD-ROM Librarian*, **6**(9), 13–16

180. Butcher, S. (1990) The rewards and trials of networking. *Database*, **13**(4), 103–105

181. Ciuffetti, P. (1991) Networking CD-ROMs: practical applications for today and solutions for the future. *CD-ROM Librarian*, **6**(11), 12–17

182. Donel, J., and Holbo, R. (1993) The CD-ROM network experiment at Oregon State University. *Online*, **17**(1), 104–106

183. Flanders, B. L. (1990) Spinning the hits: CD-ROM networks in libraries. *American Libraries*, **21**(11), 1032–1033

184. Folmsbee, M. A., Manion, R. M., and Murray, J. M. (May 1990) Developing inexpensive multiuser access to CD-ROM: Lasercat at Gonzaga University Law School library. *CD-ROM Professional*, **3**(3), 34–38

185. Francis, E. (1992) Mainframe compact disc networking at Glaxo Inc. *CD-ROM Librarian*, **7**(4), 12–15

186. Harman, T., and Pretty, R. (1991) CD-ROM access across a WAN: the experiences of the Polytechnic of Central London. *VINE*, **85**(December), 16–18

187. Harris, R. J. (1991) Installation of an OPTI-NET CD-ROM LAN at Eastern Virginia Medical School Library. *CD-ROM Professional*, **4**(1), 25–26

188. Hill, C. (1992) Networking CD-ROMs without MSCDEX. *Computer Technology Review*, **12**(4), 12–15

189. Ifshin, S. (1992) Technical aspects of networking CD-ROMs. In *CD-ROM networking in practice*, eds. C. Moore, and N. Whitsed, pp.9–14. London: UKOLUG/LITC

190. Ka-Neng, A. (1992) Hardware options: from LANs to WANs. *CD-ROM Librarian*, **7**(3), 12–18

191. Kittle, P. W. (1992) Networking the light fantastic: CD-ROMs on LANs. *CD-ROM Professional*, **5**(1), 30–37

192. Knowles, J. (1993) A soft system analysis of a CD-ROM network for a multi-site polytechnic. *Journal of Librarianship and Information Science*, **25**(1), 15–21

193. Koch, T. (1992) LANtastic in combination with OPTI-NET. In *CD-ROM networking in practice*, eds. C. Moore, and N. Whitsed, pp.51–53. London: UKOLUG/LITC

194. Koren, J. (1992) Multiuser access to CD-ROM drives without a CD-ROM LAN. I. *CD-ROM Professional*, **5**(4), 59–66

195. Koren, J. (1992) Providing access to CD-ROM databases in a campus setting. II: Networking CD-ROMs via a LAN. *CD-ROM Professional*, **5**(5), 83–94

196. Kratzert, M.Y. (1991) Installation of a CD-ROM local area network: the untold story. In *12th National Online Meeting. Proceedings*, (New York, NY, 7–9 May 1991), ed. M.E. Williams, pp.201–207. Medford, NJ: Learned Information

197. Kriz, H. M., Jain, N., and Armstrong, E. A. (1991) An environmental approach to CD-ROM networking using off-the-shelf components. *CD-ROM Professional*, 4(4), 24–31

198. Lee, R. B., and Balthazar, L. B. (1991) The evolution and installation of an in-house CD-ROM LAN. *Bulletin of the Medical Library Association*, 79(1), 63–65

199. Leman, P. (1992) Journey to SCSI Express. In *CD-ROM networking in practice*, eds. C. Moore, and N. Whitsed, pp.65–67. London: UKOLUG/LITC

200. Lewis, M.G. (1992) Delivering network CD-ROM services at the University of Sussex: the experience of the first year. In *Computers in Libraries International 1992, Sixth Annual Conference on Computers in Libraries. Proceedings*, (London, February 1992), pp.50–56. London: Meckler

201. Lewis, M.G. (1992) Licensing issues. In *CD-ROM networking in practice*, eds. C. Moore, and N. Whitsed, pp.27–30. London: UKOLUG/LITC

202. Malmgren-Scholz, M. (1993) CD-ROM Networks. *Serials*, 6(1), 31–32

203. Mangrum, R. (1990) LANtastic: simple, powerful local area network for PCs. *Electronic Library*, 8(6), 425–427

204. Massey-Burzio, V. (1990) The Multiplatter experience at Brandeis University. *CD-ROM Professional*, 3(3), 22–6

205. McQueen, H. (1992) File server-based CD-ROM networking using SCSI Express. *CD-ROM Professional*, 5(6), 66–68

206. McQueen, H. (1992) Fundamentals of LAN/WAN access to CD-ROM and alternative information technologies. *Quarterly Bulletin of the International Association of Agricultural Librarians and Documentalists. IAALD Symposium on Advances in Information Technology*, 37(1–2), 89–90

207. McQueen, H. (1990) Networking CD-ROMs: implementation considerations. *Laserdisk Professional*, **3**(2), 13–16

208. McQueen, H. (1990) Remote dial-in patron access to CD-ROM LANs. *CD-ROM Professional*, **3**(4), 20–23

209. Metz, R.E. (1991) Mounting CD-ROM products on a campus network: site licenses, training, and evaluation. In *12th National Online Meeting. Proceedings*, (New York, 7–9 May 1991), ed. M.E. Williams, pp.271–3. Medford, NJ: Learned Information

210. Mitchell, L. (1992) OPTI-NET on a campus-wide network. In *CD-ROM networking in practice*, eds. C. Moore, and N. Whitsed, pp.55–60. London: UKOLUG/LITC

211. Moore, C. (1992) Buying CD-ROM network products currently available. In *CD-ROM networking in practice*, eds. C. Moore, and N. Whitsed, pp.15–25. UKOLUG/LITC

212. Moore, C., and Whitsed, N. (1992). *CD-ROM networking in practice*. London: LITC/ UKOLUG

213. Murphy, J. (1993) Building a CD-ROM server (for fun and profit . . .). *Medical Reference Services Quarterly*, **12**(1), 55ff

214. Onsi, P. W., Capodagli, J. A., and Hawkins, D. K. (1992) Dial-in access to CD-ROM databases: beyond the local area network. *Bulletin of the Medical Library Association*, **80**(4), 376–379

215. Pantry, S. (1991) Networking and you. *Libri*, **41**(4), 220–227

216. Paul, D., Latham, J., Mitchell, K., and Nikirk, J. (1991) The over-the-counter CD-ROM network solution. *CD-ROM Librarian*, **6**(9), 19–23

217. Perratore, E. (1991) Networking CD-ROMs: the power of shared access. *PC Magazine (US edition)*, (31 December), 333–363

218. Price, D.J. (1992) CD-ROM networking developments amongst the Oxford libraries. In *Innovation for information: international contributions to librarianship. Festschrift in honour of Dr. Ahmed H. Helal*, ed. J.W. Weiss, pp.183–96. Essen, Germany: Essen University Library

219. Rao, S. N. (1991) The implementation of high-tech reference services in a medium-size academic library. *CD-ROM Librarian*, **6**(11), 18–20

220. Reinitzer, S. (1992) The Logicraft approach to networking CD-ROM. In *CD-ROM networking in practice*, eds. C. Moore, and N. Whitsed, pp.61–63. London: UKOLUG/LITC

221. Rutherford, J. (1990) Improving CD-ROM management through networking. *CD-ROM Professional*, **3**(5), 20–27

222. Ryder, A. (1992) Making compact disc technology work in education: OPTI-NET in a school library. In *CD-ROM networking in practice*, eds. C. Moore, and N. Whitsed, pp.39–41. UKOLUG/LITC

223. Sarig, A. (April 1992) CD-ROMs in local area networks – the supplier's view. *Bulletin of the Israel Society of Special Libraries and Information Centres*, **18**(2), 19–22

224. Sloan, S. (1990) The networked CD-ROM system: gathering information through the user interface. *CD-ROM Professional*, **3**(4), 25–29

225. Sloan, S. (1990) Remote control of a CD-ROM LAN. *Computers in Libraries*, **10**(11), 47–49

226. Starr, K. (1993) The building blocks of a CD-ROM local area network. *CD-ROM Professional*, **6**(1), 65–68

227. Sylvia, M. (1993) Networking your CD-ROMs: a Texas tale. *CD-ROM World*, **8**(7), 34–41

228. Van Dyk, M. T. (1992) ROMOTE: an off-campus dial-up service for CD-ROM databases. *LASIE*, **22**(6), 148–155

229. Volkers, A. C. W., Tijam, I. A. S., vanLaar, A., vanEijk, H. G., and Bleeker, A. (1992) Multiple usage of CD-ROMs using Meridian Data's CD-Net: performance in practice. *CD-ROM Professional*, **5**(6), 91–96

230. Whitsed, N. (1992) Experiences with MultiPlatter in a medical school library. In *CD-ROM networking in practice*, eds. C. Moore, and N. Whitsed, pp.43–46. London: UKOLUG/LITC

231. Winterman, V. (1991) CD-ROM networking: an overview. *Library Micromation News*, (33), 7–10

Downloading and post-processing

232. Berry, D. (1991) Post-processing data from Compact Disclosure using spreadsheets. *Database*, **14**(2), 58–63

233. Cox, J., and Hanson, T. (1992) Setting up an electronic current awareness service. *Online*, **16**(4), 36–43

234. Easingwood, C. (March 1991) CD-ROM for record supply: the BNB experience so far. *Library Micromation News*, (31), 2–4

235. Foulds, M. S., and Foulds, L. R. (1990) Downloading CD-ROM search results into a database management system. *CD-ROM Librarian*, **5**(9), 13–18

236. Hanson, T. (1990) The Electronic Current Awareness Service and the use of Pro-Cite at Portsmouth Polytechnic. In *Online Information 90. 14th International Online Information Meeting. Proceedings*, (*London, 11–13 December 1990*), ed. D.I. Raitt, pp.277–287. Oxford: Learned Information

237. Hanson, T. (1992) Libraries, universities and bibliographic software. *British Journal of Academic Librarianship*, **7**(1), 45–54

238. Heinisch, C. (1992) Integrated CD-ROM-retrieval in networks: how to automate the post-processing of downloaded export files. In *Libraries and Electronic Publishing: Promises and Challenges for the 90's. Festschrift in Honour of Richard M. Dougherty*, (*Essen, Germany, 14–17 Oct. 1991*), eds. A.H. Helal, and J.W. Weiss, pp.73–82. Essen, Germany: Universitatsbibliothek Essen

239. Jacso, P. (1990) Bibliofile for serials cataloging. *Serials Librarian*, **18**(1/2), 47–80

240. Jacso, P. (1991) Data transfer capabilities of CD-ROM software: Part I. *CD-ROM Professional*, **4**(1), 63–66

241. Jacso, P. (1991) Data transfer capabilities of CD-ROM software: Part II. *CD-ROM Professional*, **4**(2), 61–66

242. Keen, E. M. (1990) Transferring records from CD-ROM to an inhouse database; some practical experiences. *Program*, **24**(2), 187–191

243. Lardy, J. P., and Bador, P. (1992) Downloading: using downloaded citations imported into a database manager. *Documentaliste – Sciences de l'Information*, **29**(1), 35–39

244. Oppenheim, C. (1993) Staying within the law. In *Bibliographic software: introduction and case studies*, ed. T. Hanson. Hatfield: University of Hertfordshire Press

245. Sieverts, E.G., and Muller, S.H. (1991) The use of Hypercard to store downloaded bibliographic information. In *Online Information 91. 15th International Online Information Meeting Proceedings*, (*London, UK, 10–12 Dec. 1991*), ed. D.I. Raitt, pp.269–281. Oxford: Learned Information

246. Slee, D. (1993) Electrocopying from databases. In *Bibliographic software: introduction and case studies*, ed. T. Hanson. Hatfield: University of Hertfordshire Press

247. Tonsing, R. E. (1991) Downloading and reformatting external records for researchers' personal databases. *Program*, **25**(4), 303–317

248. VonVille, H. M., and Weaver, B. A. (1992) Downloading from CD-ROM: a preliminary survey. *CD-ROM Professional*, **5**(2), 48–49

Future of CD-ROM

249. Baycroft, M. (1990) Public access CD-ROM workstations: design and management. In *Computers in Libraries '90. 5th Annual Computers in Libraries Conference. Proceedings*, (*Washington, DC, USA, 5–7 March 1990*), ed. N.M. Nelson, pp.3–5. Westport, CT: Meckler

250. Black, G. (1991) Will CD-ROM conquer the online world? *Advanced Information Report*, (January), 11–13

251. Brooks, M. (1991) Multimedia and the future of CD-ROM. *CD-ROM Professional*, **4**(5), 8–10

252. Cardinali, R. (1991) Desktop information retrieval: why CD-ROM is not the answer! *PC Business Software*, **16**(3), 6–8

253. Chester, S., Pennington, C., and (1992) The compact disk breakthrough? not yet, but soon. *Law Practice Management*, **18**(4), 22–31

254. Dreiss, L. J., and Bashir, S. (1990) CD-ROM: potential and pitfalls. *CD-ROM Professional*, **3**(5), 70–73

255. Griffith, C. (1992) What's wrong with CD-ROM? *Information Today*, **9**(7), 16–18

256. Halbert, M. (1990) Multimedia: the agony and the ecstacy for information professionals. *CD-ROM Professional*, **3**(5), 6–9

257. Herther, N. K. (1992) The past, present and future of the compact disc, multimedia and the industry: an interview with Dr. Toshi Doi. *CD-ROM Professional*, **5**(4), 17–21

258. Kesselman, M. (1991) CD-ROM trends. *Wilson Library Bulletin*, **65**(5), 84–86

259. Law, D. G. (1990) CD-ROM: a young technology with a great future behind it? *Serials*, **3**(3), 34–35

260. Law, D. G. (1991) The impact of CD-ROM on the end-user. *International Cataloguing & Bibliographic Control*, **20**(1), 7–9

261. Lynch, M. J. (1992) Access technology in academic libraries. *College & Research Libraries News*, **53**(4), 243–244

McSean, T. (1993) This CD-ROM thing. *New Library World*, **94**(1107), 23–25

263. McSean, T., and Law, D. (1990) Is CD-ROM a transient technology? *Library Association Record*, **92**(11), 837–838

264. McSean, T. (1992) CD-ROMs and beyond: buying databases sensibly? *Aslib Proceedings*, **44**(6), 243–244

265. Piety, J. (1992) The anatomy of a decision: tape vs. CD-ROM: which product and why? *Online*, **16**(5), 62–65

266. Porter, G. M. (1991) What does electronic access to bibliographic information cost? *College & Research Libraries News*, **52**(2), 90–92

267. Siddiqui, M. A. (1991) Can CD-ROM replace online? *International Information, Communication and Education*, **10**(1), 40–48

268. Tenopir, C., and Neufang, R. (1992) Electronic reference options: how they stack up in research libraries. *Online*, **16**(2), 22–28

Geographic case studies

269. Addo, D. B. (1992) CD-ROM as appropriate technology in meeting information needs of medical scientists in developing countries. *CD-ROM Librarian*, **7**(5), 20–22

270. Ali, S. N. (1990) Databases on optical discs and their potential in developing countries. *Journal of the American Society for Information Science*, **41**(4), 238–244

271. Attaullah (1990) CD-ROM technology and its application for library use in developing countries. *Pakistan Library Bulletin*, **21**(3–4), 28–34

272. Awogbami, P. A. (1992) The diffusion of CD-ROM into Nigerian libraries. *CD-ROM Librarian*, **7**(5), 30–33

273. Compton, A. (1992) Opportunities for CD-ROM information services in Africa. *Information Services and Use*, **12**(3), 283–290

274. Deschatelets, G. (1993) An inventory of CD-ROM in developing countries. *New Library World*, **94**(1105), 25–26

275. Dmitriev, S. (1992) CD-ROM in the new Commonwealth of Independent States? *CD-ROM Professional*, **5**(4), 50–52

276. Ephraim, P. E. (1991) The development of CD-ROM and its potential for African researchers. *Journal of Information Science*, **17**(5), 299–306

277. Gayas-ud-din, and Buxton, A. (1993) The potential of CD-ROM for biomedical information in developing countries. *INSPEL*, **27**(1), 13–26

278. Heinisch, C. (1991) Networking CD-ROM in German libraries. *CD-ROM Librarian*, **6**(11), 21ff

279. Johnston, C. S. (1992) The development of CD-ROM provision at the Sultan Qaboos University in the Sultanate of Oman. *Program*, **26**(2), 177–182

280. Keylard, M. (1993) CD-ROM implementation in developing countries: impacts and pitfalls. *IFLA Journal*, **19**(1), 35–49

281. Langerman, S. (1990) CD-ROM in Israel: usage problems, prospects. *Bulletin Israel Society of Special Libraries and Information Centres*, **17**(2), 24–30

282. Lenoir, M. (1990) The use of CD-ROM in American libraries. *Health Information and Libraries*, **1**(1), 17–30

283. Meyers, J. K. (1991) The contribution of CD-ROM in overcoming information isolation: insights from an African experience. *CD-ROM Librarian*, **6**(7), 11–21

284. Moore, N. L. (1990) Problems of online database access in rural and isolated areas with particular attention to developing countries: applications of CD-ROM as appropriate information technology. In *1st East–West Online Information Meeting. Proceedings*, (*Moscow, USSR, 11–13 October 1989*), ed. D.I. Raitt, pp.58–71. Oxford: Learned Information

285. Nwali, L. O. (1991) The potential value of CD-ROM in Nigerian libraries and information centres. *Journal of Librarianship and Information Science*, **23**(3), 153–157

286. Oxbrow, N. (1992) CD-ROMs in the City. A report of TFPL's survey of CD-ROM use in London. *CD-ROM Professional*, **5**(1), 26–29

287. van Hartevelt, J. H. W. (1991) Introduction of CD-ROM technology in ACP countries: report of a CTA project. *Quarterly Bulletin of the International Association of Agricultural Information Specialists*, **36**(1–2), 101–104

288. Wright, S. (1990) Application of CD-ROM technology to libraries in developing countries. *Program*, **24**(2), 129–140

289. Yan, J., and Lin, S. C. (1990) CD-ROM and its applications in China. *Reference Services Review*, **18**(2), 93–96

Management issues

290. Beaubien, D. M. (1991) The changing roles of 'online coordinators'. *Online*, **15**(5), 48–53

291. Bernal, N. E., and Renner, I. A. (1990) CD-ROM Medline's impact on mediated online searches when patron cost is not a variable. *Laserdisk Professional*, **3**(2), 25–27

292. Bernal, N. E. (1991) Local holdings availability messages on CD+MEDLINE: impact on users and interlibrary loan patterns. *CD-ROM Professional*, **4**(3), 26–28

293. Bonta, B. D. (1990) Library staffing and arrangements for CD-ROM service. *INSPEL. International Journal of Special Libraries*, **24**(1), 5–13

294. Brahmi, F. A., and Tyler, J. K. (1990) The effect of CD-ROM Medline on online end-user and mediated searching: a follow-up study. *Medical Reference Services Quarterly*, **9**(3), 15–20

295. Brown, C. S. (1991) A day in the life of a CD-ROM librarian. *CD-ROM Librarian*, **6**(4), 10–13

296. Bucknall, T., and Mangrum, R. (1992) Using Saber Meter and Saber Menu to manage access in a CD-ROM network. *Library Software Review*, **11**(3), 2–7

297. Burke, D. L. (1991) CD-ROM Master: a complete CD-ROM statistics gathering program. *CD-ROM Professional*, (6), 58–65

298. Burton, M. (1992) The paper chase: how to manage CD-ROM documentation. *Database*, **15**(2), 102–104

299. Cardinali, R. (1993) The emerging technology: an overview of the impact of CD-ROM on offline services. *Journal of Educational Media and Library Sciences*, **30**(2), 122ff

300. Clark, K. (1992) To cancel or not to cancel. *CD-ROM Professional*, **5**(4), 126–128

301. Cornish, G. P. (1991) CD-ROM: impact on the interlending area. *ABI-Technik*, **11**(1), 11–14

302. Cox, J. (1991) Making your electronic information products promote and pay for each other. In *Online information 91. 15th International Online Information Meeting. Proceedings, (London, 10–12 December 1991)*, ed. D.I. Raitt, pp.421–428. Oxford: Learned Information

303. Crawford, G. A. (1992) The effects of instruction in the use of PsycLIT on interlibrary loan. *RQ*, **31**(3), 370–376

304. Crea, K., Glover, J., and Helenius, M. (1992) The impact of in-house and end-user databases on mediated searching. *Online*, **16**(4), 49–53

305. Crellin, J. (1992) Implications of CD-ROMs for reference services in university libraries. *Library Management*, **13**(3), 20–28

306. Culbertson, M. (1992) Analysis of searches by end-users of science and engineering CD-ROM databases in an academic library. *CD-ROM Professional*, **5**(2), 76–79

307. Cutright, P., and Girrard, K. M. (1991) Remote access to CD-ROM for the distant learner. *CD-ROM Professional*, **4**(6), 80–82

308. Davidoff, D. J., and Gadikian, R. (1991) 'If it's not here, I can't be bothered . . .': limiting searches to in-house journals. *Online*, **15**(4), 58–60

309. Ensor, P. (1990) Controlling CD-ROM growth in academic libraries. *CD-ROM Librarian*, **5**(8), 20–25

310. Erkkila, J. E. (1990) CD-ROM vs. online: implications for management from the cost side. *Canadian Library Journal*, **47**(6), 421–428

311. Flanders, B. (1992) Protecting the vulnerable CD-ROM workstation: safe computing in an age of computer viruses. *CD-ROM Librarian*, **7**(1), 26–29

312. Foulds, M. S., and Foulds, L. R. (1991) CD-ROM planning and managerial issues. *Canadian Library Journal,* **48**(2), 111–114

313. Froehlich, T.J. (1991) Ethical considerations in end-user searching and training end users to be self searchers of CD-ROM and online databases. In *National Online Meeting 1991: 12th National Online Meeting. Proceedings, (New York, 7–9 May 1991),* ed. M.E. Williams, pp.93–98. Medford, NJ: Learned Information

314. Giesbrecht, W., and McCarthy, R. (1991) Staff resistance to library CD-ROM services. *CD-ROM Professional,* **4**(3), 34–38

315. Goldfinch, R. (1990) The impact of end-user searching of CD-ROM on online use. In *Online Information Retrieval Today and Tomorrow. UKOLUG Conference 1990, (Ripon, UK, April 1990),* eds. C.J. Armstrong, and R.J. Hartley, pp.75–83. Oxford: Learned Information

316. Grant, M.A., and Weinschenk, A. (1990) The Multiplatter statistical module: determining optimum staffing and training needs. In *Computers in Libraries '90. 5th Annual Computers in Libraries Conference, Proceedings, (Washington DC, 5–7 March 1990),* ed. N.M. Nelson, pp.68–71. Westport, CT: Meckler

317. Hughes, A. (1991) Managing a CD-ROM based service. In *Computers in Libraries International 91. 5th Annual Conference on Computers in Libraries. Proceedings, (London, February 1991),* pp.164–167. London: Meckler

318. Jones, D. (1991) Establishing an end user searching service utilizing CD-ROM and low cost on-line systems: the changing role of the intermediaries in providing access to information. *Quarterly Bulletin of the International Association of Agricultural Librarians and Documentalists. VIIIth World Congress of the International Association of Agricultural Librarians and Documentalists: Information and the End User,* **36**(1–2), 146–149

319. Kaltenborn, K. F. (1991) End user searching in the CD-ROM database Medline. *Nachrichten fur Dokumentation*, **42**(2), 107–114

320. Kaltenborn, K. F. (1991) End user searching in the CD-ROM database Medline. 2. evaluation and user research on search quality and human–computer interaction. *Nachrichten fur Dokumentation*, **42**(3), 177–190

321. Kinder, J., and Preston, L. (1993) CD-ROM management: planning for success. *CD-ROM Professional*, **6**(1), 24–25

322. Kistner, J.C. (1992) Integrating CD-ROM into networked information services. In *Online Information 92. 16th International Online Information Meeting. Proceedings*, (*London, 8–10 December 1992*), ed. D.I. Raitt, pp.301–312. Oxford: Learned Information

323. Marks, C. (1990) Managing an automated system. In *Computers in Libraries International 90. Fourth Annual Conference on Computers in Libraries. Proceedings*, (*London, February 1990*), ed. J. Eyre, pp.17–19. London: Meckler

324. Moore, M. M. (1990) The effects of compact disk indexes on interlibrary loan services at a university library. *Journal of Interlibrary Loan & Information Supply*, **1**(1), 25–42

325. Nazim-Ali, S., and Young, H. C. (1992) Information access through CD-ROM and its impact upon faculty research output: a case of a university in a third world country. *Microcomputers for Information Management*, **9**(3), 177–189

326. Nicholls, P. T. (1991) Sex, lies and CD-ROM: the seven deadly sins of CD-ROM revisited. *CD-ROM Professional*, **4**(6), 126–129

327. Nipp, D., and Shamy, S. (1992) CD-ROM troubleshooting manual: support for reference desk librarians. *RQ*, **31**(3), 339–345

328. Priore, C., and Miller, R. (1992) Local holdings searching in CD-ROM databases. *Information Technology and Libraries*, **11**(3), 307–309

329. Seago, B., and Campbell, F. (1993) A comparison of Medline CD-ROM and librarian-mediated search service users. *Bulletin of the Medical Library Association*, **81**(1), 63–66

330. Shear, V. (1992) CD-ROM and metering – an overview. *CD-ROM Professional*, **5**(2), 85–87

331. Silver, H., and Dennis, S. (1990) Monitoring patron use of CD-ROM databases using SignIn-Stat. *Bulletin of the Medical Library Association*, **78**(3), 252–257

332. Sylvia, M., and Kilman, L. (1991) Searching on CD-ROM in an academic environment. *Computers in Libraries*, **11**(10), 44–46

333. Thornburg, B. J. (1992) CD-ROM and the academic reference librarian: a review of the literature. *Electronic Library*, **10**(4), 219–221

334. Vasi, J., and LaGuardia, C. (1992) Setting up CD-ROM work areas. 2. integrating CD-ROM functions into library services. *CD-ROM Professional*, **5**(3), 38–43

335. Vasi, J., and LaGuardia, C. (1992) Work areas. I. ergonomic considerations, user furniture, location. *CD-ROM Professional*, **5**(2), 44–46

336. Wilkinson, D. (1992) Multiple database operation on the stand-alone public CD-ROM system: considerations for system management. *CD-ROM Librarian*, **7**(7), 22–28

337. Wilkinson, D. W. (1992) Public CD-ROM workstation security: contexts of risk and appropriate responses. *CD-ROM Librarian*, **7**(1), 20–25

Training and documentation

338. Aarvold, J., and Walton, G. (1992) CD-ROM: towards a strategy for teaching and learning. *Nurse Education Today*, **12**(6), 458–463

339. Allen, G. (1990) CD-ROM training: what do the patrons want? *RQ*, **30**(1), 88–93

340. Amato, K., and Jackson, M. (1990) CD-ROMs: instructing the user. *CD-ROM Librarian*, **5**(6), 14–21

341. Barbuto, D. M., and Cevallos, E. E. (1991) End-user searching: program review and future prospects. *RQ*, **31**(2), 214–227

342. Blumenthal, C., Howard, M., and Kinyon, W. (1993) The impact of CD-ROM technology on a bibliographic instruction program. *College and Research Libraries*, **54**(1), 11–16

343. Bostian, R., and Robbins, A. (1990) Effective instruction for searching CD-ROM indexes. *Laserdisk Professional*, **3**(1), 14–17

344. Broughton, N., Herrling, P., and McClements, N. (1991) CD-ROM instruction: a generic approach. *CD-ROM Librarian*, **6**(10), 16–19

345. Condic, K. S. (1992) Reference assistance for CD-ROM users: a little goes a long way. *CD-ROM Professional*, **5**(1), 56–57

346. Day, J., and Webber, S. (1990) Training and user documentation. *CD-ROM: a practical guide for information professionals*, eds. A.A. Gunn, and C. Moore, pp.23–26. London: LITC/UKOLUG

347. Dolphin, P. (1990) Evaluation of user education programmes. In *User education in academic libraries*, ed. H. Fleming, pp.73–79. London: Library Association

348. Earl, M. F., and Hamberg, C. J. (1991) Medical students as CD-ROM end-user trainers. *Bulletin of the Medical Library Association*, **79**(1), 65–67

349. Froehlich, T., and Ruhig DuMont, R. (1990) Educating librarians to be trainers of end-users on online or on disk databases. In *IOLS '90. 5th Integrated Online Library Systems Meeting. Proceedings*, (*New York, 2–3 May 1990*), ed. D.C. Genaway, pp.55–63. Medford, NJ: Learned Information

350. Hepworth, J. (1992) Developing information handling courses for end-users. In *Database 2000: UKOLUG State-of-the-Art Conference. Proceedings*, (*Guildford, April 1992*), eds. C.J. Armstrong, and R.J. Hartley, pp.67–75. Oxford: Learned Information

286   CD-ROM in libraries

351. Jaros, J. (1990) Training endusers/remote users. *Journal of Library Administration*, **12**(2), 75–88

352. Johnson, M. E., and Rosen, B. S. (1990) CD-ROM end-user instruction: a planning model. *Laserdisk Professional*, **3**(2), 35–40

353. Kanter, J. (1992) User guides for CD-ROM: the essentials of good print documentation. *CD-ROM Professional*, **5**(5), 31–4

354. Maxymuk, J. (1991) Considerations for CD-ROM instruction. *CD-ROM Professional*, **4**(3), 47–9

355. Morton, M. L. (1991) Training for a changing environment: the challenges in a decentralized system. *Quarterly Bulletin of the International Association of Agricultural Information Specialists*, **36**(1–2), 133–135

356. Nickerson, G. (1991) Bibliographic instruction for CD-ROM: developing in-house tutorials. *CD-ROM Professional*, **4**(5), 45–7

357. Piele, L. J. (1991) Reference services and staff training for patron-use software. *Library Trends*, **40**(1), 97–119

358. Plutchak, T. S. (1989) On the satisfied and inept end-user. *Medical Reference Services Quarterly*, **8**(1), 45–48

359. Richwine, P. W., and Switzer, J. H. (1990) CD-ROM medline training: a survey of medical school libraries. *Medical Reference Services Quarterly*, **9**(3), 21–29

360. Rigglesford, D. (1992) CD-ROM – the answer for end-users? In *Information systems for end-users: research and development issues*, ed. M. Hancock-Beaulieu, pp.35–44. London: Taylor Graham

361. Royan, B. (1992) A practitioner's view of self-service information systems. In *Information systems for end-users: research and development issues*, ed. M. Hancock-Beaulieu, pp.79–84. London: Taylor Graham

362. Stabler, K. (1991) A model for training academic librarians on CD-ROM. In *12th National Online Meeting 1991. Proceedings, (New York, 7–9 May 1991)*, ed. M.E. Williams, pp.361–365. Medford, NJ: Learned Information

363. Steele, A., and Tseng, G. (1992) End user training for CD-ROM Medline: a survey of UK medical school libraries. *Program*, **26**(1), 55–61

364. Sullivan, M. (1992) Training for MEDLINE on CD-ROM: a case study in an industrial environment. In *Information systems for end-users: research and development issues*, ed. M. Hancock-Beaulieu, pp.71–78. London: Taylor Graham.

365. Whitaker, C. S. (1990) Pile-up at the reference desk: teaching users to use CD-ROMs. *Laserdisk Professional*, **3**(2), 30–34

Index